"It is level ground that when the state robs Peter to pay Paul it can count on Paul's enthusiastic support. As Matthew Sinclair reveals in LET THEM EAT CARBON, nowhere is this more true than with the modern fashion of climatically meaningless, environmentally harmful and economically ruinous 'green' statism.

Sinclair explains not only how this scheming is so disastrous, but how it all must end (hint: badly). Deliciously, while also giving co-promoters Big Green a well-deserved outing, Sinclair also exposes an ugly truth: quite often, the entire enterprise was Paul's idea to begin with."

Chris Horner, Senior Fellow at the Competitive Enterprise Institute and author of the *New York Times* bestseller *The Politically Incorrect Guide to Global Warming (and Environmentalism)*

"Combines real rigour in analysis of the costs and benefits of various proposals to address the problem of climate change with an accessible and jargon-free presentation."
Jim Manzi

"Putting aside the scientific doubts about the theory that dangerous global warming is driven by man-made carbon dioxide emissions, it is absolutely vital that the people of this country are aware of the huge costs that are being incurred, and will be incurred, in pursuing Britain's ambitious plans for decarbonising the economy. Plans, one might add, that will not be followed by much of the rest of the world. The switch to costly low-carbon, renewable sources of energy is already costing households and businesses dear. And it will get much dearer – further damaging people's living standards and undermining competitiveness.

Matthew Sinclair's LET THEM EAT CARBON is a terrifically well-researched, well-argued and persuasive exposition of the huge economic and personal costs of our current energy policy. Read it. And heed it."
Ruth Lea, Economic Adviser, Arbuth
former Head of the Policy Unit, Instit

D0257535

LET THEM EAT
CARBON

THE PRICE OF FAILING CLIMATE CHANGE POLICIES, AND HOW
GOVERNMENTS AND BIG BUSINESS PROFIT FROM THEM

MATTHEW SINCLAIR

Biteback Publishing

First published in Great Britain in 2011 by
Biteback Publishing Ltd
Westminster Tower
3 Albert Embankment
London
SE1 7SP

Copyright © Matthew Sinclair 2011

Matthew Sinclair has asserted his rights under the Copyright, Designs and Patents Act 1988 to be identified as the author of this work.

All rights reserved. No part of this publication may be reproduced, stored in a retrieval system or transmitted, in any form or by any means, without the publisher's prior permission in writing.

This book is sold subject to the condition that it shall not, by way of trade or otherwise, be lent, resold, hired out or otherwise circulated without the publisher's prior consent in any form of binding or cover other than that in which it is published and without a similar condition, including this condition, being imposed on the subsequent purchaser.

Every reasonable effort has been made to trace copyright holders of material reproduced in this book, but if any have been inadvertently overlooked the publishers would be glad to hear from them.

ISBN 978-1-84954-116-9

10 9 8 7 6 5 4 3 2 1

A CIP catalogue record for this book is available from the British Library.

Set in Bookman Old Style and Helvetica by Namkwan Cho
Cover design by Namkwan Cho

Printed and bound in Great Britain by
CPI Group (UK) Ltd, Croydon, CR0 4YY

CONTENTS

ABOUT THE AUTHOR

Matthew Sinclair is the Director of the TaxPayers' Alliance (TPA) in London. He has produced a range of pioneering and influential economic policy research, particularly on climate change policy. That work has had a global impact. It has received prominent coverage on the front pages of newspapers from the *Daily Express* and *Metro* in the United Kingdom to *The Australian*. It has also been widely cited in leader columns from the *The Sun* and the *Daily Mail* to the *Wall Street Journal* the day before the vote on Waxman-Markey. It has been cited in evidence to the United States Senate Committee on Environment and Public Works and in the debate in the House of Commons over the Climate Change Act.

He has also represented the TPA frequently on radio, television – with appearances on the BBC News Channel, Sky News, Bloomberg, Fox News, CNBC, the Daily Politics and Newsnight – and in person at a range of events both in the UK and abroad – in Rome, Washington DC, Brussels, Strasbourg and New York.

ACKNOWLEDGEMENTS

Writing this book while working at the TPA – too often ten minutes at a time on the London Underground – wouldn't have been possible without being able to rely on the insights of others and the support of colleagues, friends and family.

Reading Nigel Lawson's speech to the Centre for Policy Studies was what first really convinced me there was a deep dysfunction in the way we are trying to cut greenhouse gas emissions. I've been grateful for his support ever since. Jim Manzi's 2007 essay 'Game Plan – What conservatives should do about global warming' for the *National Review* set out a three-pronged alternative that is still at the backbone of the recommendations in this book. Ruth Lea has been as tenacious on climate change as she has on the euro; hopefully it won't be too long before everyone acknowledges she is right on this issue as well. Chris Horner has been essential to the fight against faulty policies like cap and trade in the United States, and his books like *Red Hot Lies* and *Power Grab* are essential reading for anyone interested in what is going wrong in this area. They were all incredibly kind to give up their valuable time and read drafts of this book.

Experts at the Competitive Enterprise Institute, particularly Iain Murray and Myron Ebell, have been great allies in this cause over the years. They – along with the inimitable Fred Smith – deserve immense credit for working so effectively in the States, as do countless others too numerous to mention here who did their part to stop the drive for cap and trade and are working for a more free-market energy policy.

Colleagues past and present have made the TPA the most effective campaign group in British politics through their commitment and incredible talents. It has been a pleasure working with all of them. Matthew Elliott gave me the most incredible opportunity, starting my career at an organisation that reflects his ideological commitment and work ethic, and deserves all the praise he gets for the entrepreneurial vision to establish the TPA.

Other friends – including Tom Packer, Peter Cuthbertson and Chris Pope – were incredibly helpful, providing their thoughts on drafts of the book, and corresponding with them over the years has been critical to developing my thinking in this and so many other areas. I came up with the title in a conversation with Ross Allan. Arianna Capuani provided an Italian phrase that captures self-interested corporate donations to green campaigns perfectly. My mother was both incredibly supportive and provided the most thorough proof-read I could hope for.

Without all of them, and the staff at Biteback whose hard work has turned this from a private labour of love to an actual book, *Let Them Eat Carbon* wouldn't be what it is. Any errors are of course my own. I am very grateful to everyone who made this possible.

INTRODUCTION

Ordinary families are paying a heavy price for the attempts politicians are making to control greenhouse gas emissions. Climate change policies push up electricity bills, make it more expensive to drive to work or fly away on holiday, put manufacturing workers out of a job; they sometimes even make your food more expensive. They hit some people particularly hard: the industrial worker already struggling to compete with rivals in China; the poor and elderly, who feel rising energy costs particularly keenly; and anyone with a big family who needs to drive their kids around because they don't live in a city centre. At the other end of the scale, politicians who don't drive because they live in city centres and are on above average incomes won't feel the pinch in the same way and could easily underestimate the extent of the pressure on household budgets.

Much of the money goes straight into the pockets of a bewildering range of special interests. Climate change has become big business. Across the world, companies are making billions out of the schemes politicians have put in place to try and stop global warming: from windfall profits for electricity generators under cap and trade schemes like the EU Emissions Trading Scheme in Europe, to huge profits for dodgy projects in the developing world under the Clean Development Mechanism. Climate change has justified entire new organisations in the public sector with hundreds of staff and big grants to fund them. Environmentalist campaigns enjoy big budgets, often including generous taxpayer funding.

At least in the short term there is a lot of money to be made out of the unprecedented interventions in the economy being justified with the threat of climate change. When the backlash comes, companies doing well out of climate change policy now could pay quite a price. But right now there are innumerable opportunities to make money from cap and trade and other climate change policies.

Of course, a policy isn't necessarily a bad one because people can make a profit out of it. There's nothing wrong with that if it is a reward for providing a valuable service. And the impact on consumers could be a price that we have to pay to avoid climate change. Unfortunately, there is precious little evidence that the various schemes and targets that make up climate change policy are actually an efficient way of cutting emissions. They don't represent good value and the public are right to be sceptical of them.

Figure 1.1: CO_2 emissions, Mt, UK

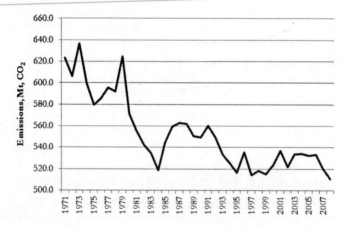

Look at the long term pattern of emissions. You'll struggle to spot the advent of big climate change policies. Figure 1.1 uses International Energy Agency data to show UK carbon dioxide emissions between 1970 and 2008 in millions of tonnes.[1]

1   International Energy Agency, 'CO_2 Emissions from Fuel Combustion' (2010 Edition), http://www.iea.org/co2highlights/co2highlights.xls

In Britain we were being sold higher prices on petrol all the way back in 1993. Then Chancellor of the Exchequer Ken Clarke told the Commons that tax hikes on motor fuel were part of completing 'Britain's strategy for meeting our Rio commitment', referring to the Rio Earth Summit in 1992 where we first pledged to take action to curb greenhouse gas emissions. When you look at the pattern below, can you see any change in the pattern of emissions after the Rio Summit? Or at the introduction of other climate change policies like the Renewables Obligation – which provides big subsidies to renewable energy – around the beginning of the last decade?

Figure 1.2: Emissions intensity, kg CO_2/US dollar (2000 prices)

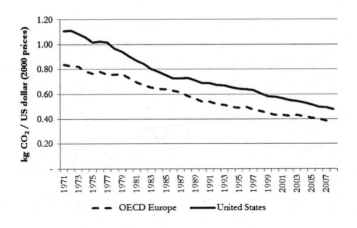

To look at it another way, let's compare the record of the United States – which did not ratify the Kyoto Protocol – and the developed European economies – which did. Figure 1.2 shows emissions intensity, the amount emitted per dollar of GDP over the period.[2] That is a good guide to how efficient an

2   Ibid.

economy is at keeping emissions down without hurting the economy – if a country cuts emissions without lower emissions intensity they are just making themselves poorer.

Again, it's hard to see the achievements of the current approach at the moment. Looking at the numbers like this has led one prominent set of academics to talk about the 'abject failure of existing policy'.[3]

That is why, in some areas, I share important common ground with environmentalists such as George Monbiot. When critiquing current climate change policies, Monbiot is more likely to condemn them for doing little to reduce emissions instead of focusing on their enormous cost. But it is important to understand that there is no contradiction in saying that current environmental policies in many countries will do huge harm to the economy while having little or no impact on carbon emissions. Like a man facing a mid-life crisis who blows all his savings on Porsches and Harleys without becoming any more attractive to younger women, we risk wrecking our economies without achieving significant environmental improvements.

Politicians start out supporting these policies for all sorts of reasons. Some really mean it, are thoroughly convinced that something needs to be done and see the current approach as the best way forward. Others also find it useful as a way of trying to change their image: Prime Minister David Cameron, when he was in opposition and the leader of the British Conservative Party, told voters they could 'vote blue, go green' as part of an attempt to position the party away from the hard-headed legacy of Margaret Thatcher.

There are politicians who find the threat of climate change a convenient excuse for policies they have always wanted. Bureaucrats in the European Union have been looking for an excuse for a new European tax for decades, to free them from the constraints of appealing to member states for revenue,

---

3   Prins, G. et al., *How to get climate policy back on course*, 6 July 2009

and a European green tax is one way of achieving that long-standing objective. For many politicians the opportunity to jack up green taxes makes climate change helpful in paying for their wasteful spending.

It is now mostly about momentum, though. Too much political capital has been sunk into the current set of policies, particularly in those countries where all the mainstream parties have supported them, for a reversal to be possible without a lot of embarrassment. There is a sense that questioning the current approach undermines the entire effort to do anything; that whatever their merits the current measures are what we'll have to work with. That thinking was exposed when a spokesman for the EU Environment Commissioner Barbara Helfferich rejected changes to biofuel policies as disastrous for the environment and the world's poor. She said: 'There is no question for now of suspending the target fixed for biofuels... You can't change a political objective without risking a debate on all the other objectives.' The problem that creates is obvious. Not only are the current policies ineffective and fiercely costly, they were designed to work as part of an international negotiating process that broke down spectacularly in Copenhagen and showed no sign of a serious renaissance at Cancun. Whether or not the politicians and activists like it, the current set of policies can't be sustained and need to change.

So why haven't the vast majority of voters who pay for these policies stopped them?

The basic answer is that they have – when they've been given a chance. When a mainstream party opposes it, climate change legislation rarely progresses. In Europe that hasn't happened, as in most countries the parties have stitched things up without the voters' involvement. But in Australia, Canada, the United States and Japan the push for emissions trading in particular has stalled. In Australia it was remarkable how the inexorable political drive to get an emissions trading scheme in place fell to pieces as soon as the opposition Liberals got rid of their leader and got back into the business of opposing. Since then, the Prime Minister, Kevin Rudd, has put the plans on ice and been deposed by his own party. In the United States the politicians have found a way around inconvenient democracy: if the public don't want greenhouse gas rationing pushing up energy prices, then the Environmental Protection Agency, which doesn't have to appeal to pesky voters for support, can push the regulations instead.

It is understandable that many people prefer to ignore climate change policy as they consider other issues a higher priority, but that allows those committed to the expensive environmentalist agenda to push it forward without real opposition. Whether or not you think climate change is important, no one can afford to ignore climate change policy. In many European countries they don't even need to put new measures in place; the cost will ramp up without any further legislation. For example, Britain's climate change targets are set to make energy bills rise rapidly over the next decade, as they require massive investment in expensive offshore wind power, and the mechanisms to make that happen – like the Renewables Obligation – are already in place.

All sorts of other objectives will be undone if we don't change climate change policies. The fight to reduce poverty and welfare dependency is hard enough without making essential goods like electricity that are a significant part of the budgets of poorer households more expensive. For all the ridiculous hype about green jobs, they'll be more than offset by job losses elsewhere in the economy; manufacturing firms already struggling to keep their edge against competitors in developing countries will find life a lot harder with higher energy costs.

Many developed countries are facing crises in their public finances as irresponsible governments have jacked up public spending and put in place expensive new entitlements. Following the financial crisis bumper tax receipts from the financial sector have evaporated. They now have to borrow

huge and unsustainable amounts of money. Curbing spending to address a fiscal crisis will be a lot harder with climate
change policies pushing up prices. Both attempts to reduce
emissions and spending cuts will put pressure on household
budgets and the combined effect may be simply intolerable.

So much is being staked on the current set of failing policies; we need to ensure politicians reconsider before they up
the ante yet again. Investors need to realise that any business
built on government policies that impoverish ordinary people
will never be secure and sustainable. The danger to our prosperity and freedom, to the competitive and free markets that
have produced unparalleled gains in our standard of living,
and to our nations' place in the world is just too great.

Fortunately, a series of knocks have recently dented the
confidence of the politicians, activists and lobbyists promoting draconian attempts to limit emissions. First, cap and
trade legislation ran into trouble in the US Senate. Then
the climategate leak revealed a culture of secrecy among
key climate change scientists and undermined public confidence in what they were being told about global warming.
Finally, the international negotiating process collapsed at a
Copenhagen conference that had been hyped beyond belief
and could only proceed at Cancun by fudging all the most
critical and controversial issues. After all the shocks recently,
more people are open to the idea that the current direction
might not be the right one.

The time to stop the unfolding disaster of failing climate
change policies is now. This book provides the broadest and
most complete picture yet of what is going wrong.

The first thing to understand is the challenge of cutting
emissions, the problem that climate change policies are
supposed to address, which is the subject of Chapter 2. This
isn't a book about the science of global warming but it is worth
understanding a little about what we know, and what is still
deeply uncertain. The chapter then looks at why cutting emissions is hard and why radical plans to cut emissions probably

don't represent good value for money. It closes by looking at how politicians are setting ambitious targets that are either unserious or potentially disastrous.

After that, we turn to the individual policies that are being put in place by governments around the world. For each of those policies we'll look at how they are designed, whether they are effective and where the money goes – who profits and who pays.

The centrepiece is known as 'emissions trading' in Europe and Australia and 'cap and trade' in the United States. The European Union Emissions Trading System (ETS) is the biggest such scheme in the world, covering more than 11,000 installations across Europe. Its record shows what the rest of the developed world has coming if it follows the EU's example. This is investigated in Chapter 3.

Alongside cap and trade, operators of wind turbines, solar plants and other sources of renewable energy get massive support in many countries; families and manufacturing businesses pay the price in higher electricity prices. Support for renewable energy is covered in Chapter 4.

Green taxes and transport are the focus of Chapter 5. Increasingly, the threat of climate change is used to justify higher taxes on everything from driving to work to flying for a well-earned holiday. The case for these taxes is shaky at best, and they are really an unfair burden on motorists in particular.

Chapter 6 looks at green jobs. They are a myth. Draconian regulations curbing emissions will cost more jobs than they create. There is work to be had, at taxpayers' expense, in the bureaucracy.

For Chapter 7 the story moves on to those backing expensive climate change policies. Firstly, how the rich pickings in climate change policy have increasingly become a target for corporate lobbying. The massive scale of the economic interventions aimed at curbing climate change means that the success or failure of a firm or industry is increasingly more to do with how successful they are in the grubby world of politics than their ability to provide a valuable service to consumers.

Then the green campaign groups, which are now big organisations and increasingly receive generous support from governments and international organisations at taxpayers' expense. Environmentalists aren't just unwashed tree huggers on the political fringe anymore, if they ever were. Their hostility to economic growth is responsible for a lot of the problems with climate change policy today and threatens our standard of living.

Under the Clean Development Mechanism (CDM) companies in the developing world are paid a huge amount for often dodgy emissions reductions. The idea is to buy their support for climate change policies but, once again, consumers in the developed world pay a heavy price. It doesn't work either, as developing countries aren't going to sacrifice economic growth to limit emissions. Developing countries are the subject of Chapter 8.

Chapter 9 looks at politics and how the current direction of climate change policy has never won popular support. Attempts to curb emissions have advanced in spite of voters, and invariably by the least democratic route possible. A new approach is needed that focuses on investing in technology, adapting to a changing climate and building societies free and prosperous enough to respond effectively to whatever the natural world throws at them – a realist climate change policy.

Finally, Chapter 10 sets out my conclusions. Incredibly expensive and inefficient, at times even corrupt, schemes have been put in place to try and cut greenhouse gas emissions. They haven't received the scrutiny they should have. We need, and can get, much better climate change policy.

THE CHALLENGE OF
CUTTING EMISSIONS

Before we get on to the main subject of this book – the actions that politicians are taking and why they are a disastrous rip-off – it is important to think about the problem they are trying to deal with.

People have all sorts of opinions about how big a problem climate change is. Many see a potential catastrophe; others think it is overblown hype or a hoax. The debate over the science of global warming is unlikely to be settled any time soon.

At the same time, there is no real precedent for the task of making cuts in emissions of the sort politicians are planning. Carbon dioxide in particular isn't just one more by-product, which, if we do things slightly differently, can easily be taken out of fuels before they are burned or scrubbed out prior to emissions leave a factory. The modern world is powered by fossil fuels – and burning coal, oil and gas means greenhouse gas emissions.

So what do we know about the science of global warming? And what do we need to know? And what should we make of politicians' claims that they are going to radically cut the size of our nations' carbon footprints?

The science
In this book I'm going to avoid the science of global warming as much as possible. The scientific debate is important but it doesn't settle the issue as many people claim. It is distorted by politicians expecting too clear an answer from a neces-sarily uncertain science. There is a more productive and engaging debate to be had over the policy. We don't need a

definitive answer from the scientists to be able to talk about the economics and politics of climate change.

But we can't avoid the science entirely. We do need some kind of estimate of the potential harms of climate change. Then we can start testing the benefits of attempts to cut emissions – in terms of avoiding climate change – against the economic costs.

Our understanding of the problem of climate change starts from a well-established finding, coming not out of computer models but good old-fashioned experiments by physicists: greenhouse gas emissions in the atmosphere can increase temperatures. The radiation reaching the Earth has more energy, and a shorter wavelength, than that reflected out again. Carbon dioxide and other greenhouse gases in the atmosphere stop the longer wavelength radiation leaving and send it back to Earth again, warming the planet. That finding isn't really in dispute. The vast majority of those labelled climate change 'deniers' don't disagree on that point. But the amount of warming that we can expect from that direct greenhouse effect alone isn't enough to get excited about. If that was the end of the story, then you would expect around 1°C of warming for a doubling of emissions;[4] we could all relax and there wouldn't be many gatherings of world leaders to talk about climate change.

But that isn't the end of the story. That initial increase in carbon dioxide and warming sets in motion a complicated chain of other events. Ice melting might reduce the amount of radiation from the sun reflected straight back into space and mean even more warming. On the other hand, more carbon dioxide is likely to mean increased plant growth, which will take some of that carbon dioxide out of the atmosphere and reduce warming. The factors that amplify the warming are

----

4   MITnews, 'Explained: climate sensitivity', 19 March 2010, http://web.mit. edu/newsoffice/2010/explained-climate-sensitivity.html

called positive feedbacks; the ones that reduce the warming are negative feedbacks.

The debate over the science of global warming that is discussed in the media is mostly about how those positive and negative feedbacks balance out. Establishing the balance is extremely difficult as the climate is a complicated beast and there are a lot of different factors that affect it. Computer models are employed to disentangle the effect of greenhouse gases from other factors. They are then used to try and work out how temperatures are likely to change in the future with a rise in greenhouse gas concentrations. The current estimate from the Intergovernmental Panel on Climate Change (IPCC) is that a doubling of greenhouse gas concentrations is likely to lead to a 2°C to 4.5°C warming, with a central estimate of 3°C.[5]

Some scientists argue that there will be more warming for a given increase in greenhouse gas concentrations. They argue that the IPCC is necessarily cautious, and that more recent research than that summarised in their reports suggests warming will be worse. Others, often referred to as the 'sceptics' or 'deniers' depending on who you read, think that the IPCC's 3°C estimate overstates the likely amount of warming.

Some of the sceptics think that the historical temperature record is unreliable. For the last century or so we have a record from instruments like weather stations, but the network of stations wasn't intended to track global temperature, rather to keep track of immediate developments in the weather, so there are question marks over how faithfully it recreates the global average. In particular, temperatures tend to be higher in denser urban areas – the urban heat island effect. Weather stations are often sited near towns or cities, and as those cities grow they will record warmer temperatures thanks to an enhanced urban heat island effect rather than

---

5 IPCC, 'Climate Change 2007: Synthesis Report 2.3 Climate sensitivity and feedbacks', p.38

because of genuine global warming. The models should take that into account and correct for growing urban heat islands, but statistical studies by Ross McKitrick, Pat Michaels and Nicholas Nierenberg suggest that they haven't done the job completely, and between a third and half of the recorded warming over land could be explained by that.[6]

Looking further back we have to rely on proxy records of the temperature, things like looking at tree rings. The famous 'hockey stick', reported in an IPCC report, showed temperatures steady for a long time over the historical record, then rising sharply in recent decades. This was different to earlier graphs, which had shown a medieval warm period. It was based on a combination of proxies and used some adventurous maths to turn them into a temperature record. There was an extensive debate between Stephen McIntyre and Ross McKitrick and a number of authors attempting to defend the original 'hockey stick' graph produced by Michael Mann. But after official investigations in the United States the 'hockey stick' was dropped by the IPCC for their most recent report.

So there are people making a credible case that we will get more or less warming than the IPCC expect for a given increase in the concentration of greenhouse gas emissions in the atmosphere. That isn't the end of the controversy though. We then need to work out what such a rise in temperature would mean for humanity and the world. What will the effect of global warming be on things like sea levels, natural disasters and the prevalence of infectious disease? Are we looking at a minor change in circumstances that people will deal with easily enough or a catastrophe threatening every part of our way of life?

....

6   McKitrick, R. R. & Michaels, P. J., 'Quantifying the influence of anthropogenic surface processes and inhomogeneities on gridded global climate data', *Journal of Geophysical Research*, p.112, 2007; the study's findings were then defended in McKitrick, R. R. and Nierenberg, N., *Correlations between Surface Temperature Trends and Socioeconomic Activity: Toward a Causal Interpretation*, 2009

The controversy over Al Gore's film, *An Inconvenient Truth*, was mostly over the way it described the impacts of global warming. The film made a big impact by showing dramatic potential consequences. David Miliband, the UK Environment Secretary when it was launched, said: 'I was struck by the visual evidence the film provides, making clear that the changing climate is already having an impact on our world today, from Mount Kilimanjaro to the Himalayan mountains.'[7] He planned to send it to every British school but those plans were challenged in the courts. After looking at the evidence, a High Court judge said that the film exhibited 'alarmism and exaggeration'. The judge found that it overstated sea level rise and the effect on low-lying Pacific atolls; made unsupportable claims about thermohaline circulation shutting down; claimed a more precise link between temperature and carbon dioxide than actually exists; was wrong to claim definitively that melting on Mount Kilimanjaro, the drying up of Lake Chad and the disaster of Hurricane Katrina are the result of global warming; had no credible evidence for its claims about dying polar bears; and suggested that the decline of coral reefs was due to climate change without proper evidence.[8] Take all that stuff away and all the film is left with is a statement of the basic science of global warming, which as I mentioned earlier isn't really what is in dispute.

The inaccuracies in Al Gore's film show just what a minefield the debate over the impacts of global warming is. Many genuine issues, like the drying up of Lake Chad, are being tied into the global warming debate when more mundane and old-fashioned factors like overgrazing may be as much to blame. The same

....

7   The press release that contained this statement has since been taken down from the DEFRA website.

8   Mr Justice Burton, Stuart Dimmock vs. Secretary of State for Education and Skills (now Secretary of State for Children, Schools and Families), in the High Court of Justice, Queen's Bench Division, Administrative Court, Case No: CO/3615/2007

image that so impressed David Miliband, of the retreat of ice on Mount Kilimanjaro, was actually quite spurious.

It is, however, reasonable to expect that changes in global temperature will have consequences.

Prosperous societies flourish in an extremely varied range of climates around the world. Former British Chancellor of the Exchequer Nigel Lawson has pointed out in his book *An Appeal to Reason* that Helsinki, Finland and Singapore are both seen as 'economic success stories', at average annual temperatures of 5°C (41°F) and 27°C (81°F) respectively, a gap of more than 22°C.[9] But we have built our towns and cities to cope with certain temperatures; people run businesses and plant crops suited to a certain climate; we have built our homes by coastlines that can move if too much ice melts at the poles. If greenhouse gas concentrations increase and temperatures change, this will cause a range of unwelcome disruptions (along with a few welcome ones like increased plant growth) that will bring costs in the short term at least. And the more warming, the more rapid and severe those costs are likely to be.

So, at least in the short term, changes in global temperature are likely to be disruptive and therefore bad news. In the long term the picture is more complex. NASA administrator Michael Griffin made a point back in May 2007 that hasn't been taken nearly seriously enough:[10]

I guess I would ask which human beings – where and when – are to be accorded the privilege of deciding that this particular climate that we have right here today, right now, is the best climate for all other human beings. I think that's a rather arrogant position for people to take.

In other words, the temperatures we face today may not be the ideal conditions for humanity to live and flourish. Right

9   Lawson, N., *An appeal to reason: a cool look at global warming*, Duckworth Overlook, 2008, p.27

10 NPR, 'NASA Chief Questions Urgency of Global Warming', 31 May 2007, http://www.npr.org/templates/story/story.php?storyId=10571499

now our patterns of living and working are set up for the kind of temperature that the planet has provided over the last few hundred years. Getting used to new temperatures will mean a costly transition, but over time those costs are likely to subside, at least to some extent.

There is no particular reason to think that the particular balance of the ecosystem right now is necessarily the best for us. Peter Huber also made that point in his 1999 book *Hard Green:*[11]

Most fundamentally, the Hard Green refuses to view the whole of natural creation in the same light as the dairy cow. Cows have been bred to wish us well, but nature as a whole has not. Nature does not wish man good or evil, it does not wish him anything. It wholly lacks an attitude.

We know that on the authority of Charles Darwin. The gazelle's genes have no interest at all in the ultimate survival of the cheetah's, and the same goes for the cheetah's vis-à-vis the gazelle's. The tapeworm evolves to reside in our intestines; our bodies evolve to expel it. Humans have no scientific reason to believe that 'the balance of nature' is generally good for them; indeed, they have no reason to believe in ecological 'balance' at all. The whole notion of ecological 'balance' is anti-Darwinian. Evolution does not progress towards balance; evolution is the flight from it, the consequence of imbalance.

There is, in short, not the slightest reason to believe that, at this precise point in evolutionary history, man happily finds himself situated in the best of all possible ecological worlds.

So we can be pretty confident about the basic science of global warming. After that things get a lot less certain. The climate is intensely complicated and it is hard to know what the impact of adding large amounts of greenhouse gas to that system will be. That doesn't mean we can't decide what to do about potential climate change, though.

....

11　Huber, P., *Hard Green: saving the environment from the environmentalists, a conservative manifesto*, Basic Books, 1999, p.79

When a central bank like the Bank of England or the Federal Reserve hikes or cuts interest rates there is rarely a consensus view on what that will do to the economy, or what state the economy will end up in if they don't act. Economists disagree radically over the right course of action but central bankers still, for better or for worse, come to a decision. When statesmen make mistakes that cost thousands of lives – because they fought when they should have tried harder to find a peaceful resolution, or compromised when it was necessary to fight and not appease a tyrant – that is a testament to the uncertainty involved in decisions about war and peace. If we could really base our decisions on some kind of impeccable scientific consensus then politics would be much simpler, if rather dull. We can't.

The scientific debate over global warming has been corrupted by attempts to get too much out of the science. After a major leak of emails at the key Climatic Research Unit at the University of East Anglia, the climategate scandal hit the newspapers in late 2009. Leading climate scientists were found to be doing some very dodgy things like deleting information to avoid answering Freedom of Information (FOI) requests. If British FOI law didn't have a bizarrely short time frame for prosecution (shorter than the amount of time it normally takes to process a case) there might have been charges brought over the breaches that took place.[12]

Politicians haven't been able to convince the public that the various schemes covered in this book are a good idea. It is hard to escape the conclusion that the scientists caught up in the climategate scandal felt a certain pressure to deliver a scientific message with a clarity and severity that might aid the political project to cut emissions. That pressure is the best explanation of why they started trying to frustrate the criticism essential to good science but unwelcome for anyone

---

12 Randerson, J., 'University in hacked climate change emails row broke FOI rules', *The Guardian*, 27 January 2010

trying to get quick and definitive results. If we want to avoid new scientific scandals, and over time build a more complete and genuine understanding of how greenhouse gas emissions affect the climate, then we should stop expecting too much from a scientific process that isn't supposed to work to a political timetable.

In order to form policy, we need an idea of what we're dealing with; then, in order to be responsible, we need to arrange things so that if we're wrong we won't regret it too much. The IPCC estimate that we'll get warming between 2°C and 4.5°C for a doubling of greenhouse gas concentration, with a central projection of 3°C, is consistent with a long line of similar assessments over the decades. All of the IPCC reports and others as far back as the US Charney Commission in 1979, have produced roughly the same estimate of around 3°C in warming for a doubling of greenhouse gas concentrations.[13] We should also try to ensure that if the actual degree of warming for a doubling of greenhouse gases is between 0°C and 1°C we won't have squandered our prosperity on a red herring. And we should take some precaution so that if that value is more than 4.5°C we won't be kicking ourselves too hard either.

That will do for the purposes of this book. Let's leave the scientists in peace.

Costs and benefits of cutting emissions

So the next question is what kind of action to cut emissions is worth the money. We need to balance the costs of taking action to reduce emissions against the benefit of reducing the likely extent of global warming. There are a

---

13 'Carbon Dioxide and Climate: A Scientific Assessment', Report of an Ad Hoc Study Group on Carbon Dioxide and Climate, Woods Hole, Massachusetts, 23–27 July 1979, to the Climate Research Board, Assembly of Mathematical and Physical Sciences, National Research Council, p.2

number of studies that attempt such a comparison of costs and benefits.

Many politicians cite The Stern Review produced for the British government by then Sir Nicholas Stern, now Lord Stern, in 2005 as a justification for ambitious climate change regulations. The review estimated that the cost of cutting emissions to 'avoid the worst impacts of climate change' could be limited to a permanent 1 per cent of world income, while the harms of climate change would be between 5 and 20 per cent of world income 'now and forever'.[14] If that is credible, it certainly suggests that radical action to cut emissions could be worthwhile, but there are quite a few problems with the review's analysis.

First, it is important to note that the headline figures cited above, and endlessly used as part of the attempt to promote the review in the media, do not quite compare the costs and benefits of cutting emissions. As is acknowledged in the report, the emissions cuts that the review expects can be bought with 1 per cent of world GDP won't stop global warming altogether, and will only allow us to avoid some of the impacts. So the benefits of cutting emissions are only a portion of the 5–20 per cent of GDP total harms from climate change that the review claims to identify. And Stern has already doubled his estimate of the cost of cutting emissions to a permanent two per cent of world income.[15] It seems that the Review's results aren't exactly set in stone.

But, beyond that, there is good reason to think that the review overstates the likely degree of warming and the consequences. Most importantly, many commentators argue that it doesn't properly account for people adapting to a changing climate and therefore overestimates the likely effect of warming on future living standards.

....

14 'Stern Review: The Economics of Climate Change', 30 October 2006, p.vi
15 Jowit, J. & Wintour, P., 'Cost of tackling global climate change has doubled, warns Stern', *The Guardian*, 26 June 2008

A number of key criticisms were made by a range of prominent scientists and economists, who contributed to a study in the academic journal *World Economics*. For example, they pointed out that projections for emissions, and therefore for warming, in the review are based on an estimate of the world population in 2100 that is 50 per cent above the UN's medium population scenario, and 7 per cent above its high scenario.[16] As we will see when we look at the Kaya Identity in the next section, if there are fewer people that is likely to mean lower emissions and therefore less warming.

They also argue that the review doesn't properly allow for agriculture adapting to rising temperatures, that the method used by the study that the review sources is 'tantamount to estimating today's level of hunger (and agricultural production) based on the technology of fifty years ago'. That means yields are unlikely to fall by as much as the review expects given 'appropriate breeding, crop switching and other adaptations'.[17] We can also be more optimistic about the prospects for agriculture because greater concentrations of carbon dioxide will increase plant growth, which could help agriculture and make up for the negative effects of global warming. This isn't taken into account by the review.

Richard Tol, a leading climate economist cited frequently in the review, has also criticised it. He has called the report 'alarmist and incompetent' and made a series of specific criticisms.[18] For example, the review simultaneously expects African economies to grow strongly – rapid economic growth in developed economies underlies its projections for emissions and warming – and to suffer from more famines and deaths from diseases like malaria and diarrhoea. Obviously middle-

---

16 Carter, R. et al., 'The Stern Review: a dual critique', *World Economics*, Vol. 7, No 4, October–December 2006, p.181

17 Ibid., p.182

18 Tol, R. S. J., 'The Stern Review of the economics of climate change: a comment', 2 November 2006, p.4. The method for currency conversions is set out in the Appendix.

income countries would import food rather than starve. And they would also take the relatively simple steps that better-off countries have taken to deal with malaria and diarrhoea. Research has found that malaria is functionally eliminated in a society once annual per capita income reaches around $3,100 (£1,750).[19]

Beyond that, Tol argues that the review consistently chooses the most pessimistic account it can find of a wide variety of climate change impacts, from water shortages to agricultural productivity to human health. Tol even points to a study he produced himself on the likely effects of rising sea levels if global warming causes glaciers to melt. The review cites the study's finding that millions are at risk but, as Tol says, that figure ignores adaptation, which 'is very effective against sea level rise', and was used instead of another measure from the same study that did account for adaptation.[20]

The biggest controversy has been over the discount rate that the review has used. Discount rates might sound like a bit of an arcane issue, but the choice of rate is absolutely critical as it determines how seriously we take consequences of global warming that could manifest themselves not just decades but centuries from now. The review uses a very low discount rate, nearly zero.

That is a very strong assumption. William Nordhaus, Sterling Professor of Economics at Yale and the 'father of climate change economics' according to *The Economist*,[21] has looked at the issue and explained the consequences of the low discount rate. He points out that it means more than half the review's estimated damages 'now and forever' occur after the year 2800; the 'large damages from global warm-

19 Carter, R. et al., 'The Stern Review: a dual critique', *World Economics*, Vol. 7, No. 4, October–December 2006, p.187

20 Tol, R. S. J., 'The Stern Review of the economics of climate change: a comment', 2 November 2006, p.2–3

21 'Dismal calculations: The economics of living with climate change – or mitigating it', *The Economist*, 7 September 2006

ing reflect large and speculative damages in the far-distant future magnified into a large current value by a near-zero time discount rate'.[22]

There are serious questions over whether a near-zero discount rate is the right moral choice. A hypothetical example Nordhaus gives is that under that discount rate it would be right to reduce consumption for a year now from $10,000 to $4,400 to prevent a permanent reduction in consumption from $130,000 to $129,870 starting in two centuries.[23] Those worried about looking after the poor should be concerned that the review essentially justifies massive sacrifices on the part of people today who are relatively poor to help people tomorrow who, according to the economic projections used to support climate change estimates, will be much, much better off.

But an even bigger problem with the near-zero interest rates that the review uses is that we just don't know with any certainty what people in hundreds of years will want. Will they be glad if we take radical action to cut emissions or will they rather we had focused our resources elsewhere, gone for faster growth so they could enjoy greater prosperity?

There is just no way of knowing right now. There are a host of reasons why our descendants might prefer that we maximise growth instead of making efforts to cut climate change. For example, what if, in around fifty to a hundred years' time, we perfect the process of generating power through nuclear fusion? That would allow for massive cuts in carbon dioxide emissions at very low cost. A host of other technological changes could do the same job. That might cause our descendants to wish we had not taken action to curb emissions now, when it is so expensive as we don't have efficient

---

22 Nordhaus, W., 'The Stern Review on the Economics of Climate Change', 3 May 2007, p.25
23 Ibid., p.26

alternatives to fossil fuels ready, and that we had waited and invested the resources elsewhere.

There are a host of other known unknowns and unknown unknowns that surround whether our descendants will value any cuts in carbon emissions we make. To illustrate the potential for surprises, let's pose a bizarre counterfactual. Suppose a Stern-like decision had been made during the Industrial Revolution: 'We're using coal at a dangerous and increasing rate and if it runs out we will lose a vital economic and strategic asset. To ensure that all generations take equal utility from limited stocks we have to impose taxes or rations on coal usage. Otherwise by the twenty-first century the UK will be utterly impoverished.' We would probably have a lot more coal right now but would be significantly poorer, and history would hopefully not have looked kindly on those who made the decision. Coal was vital in the Industrial Revolution, we would be a lot poorer if they hadn't used it, and thanks to the development of other fuels, from oil to uranium, there is no shortage today.

Uncertainty over the value of decisions we make now to future generations is probably reason enough to be sceptical of near-zero discount rates. But, beyond that, there is good reason to think that many of the effects of climate change on human well-being are likely to be temporary.

As I mentioned earlier, NASA administrator Michael Griffin has made a really important point. Why should we assume that our current temperature is the best?

It clearly depends upon the timescale you're talking about. Within a certain range, the long-term effects of higher temperatures and greater greenhouse gas concentrations will probably be mixed. Equatorial regions might suffer, but it is entirely possible that this will be balanced out by areas like Greenland, which might become green again, and Siberia where people will be better able to exploit its huge natural resources. However, in the short term our society is built around a particular temperature. We have cities built in flood plains without proper protection and railways in Siberia that will break up if the permafrost melts. That is to be expected. Our society has been built within the context of a particular temperature range and there will be costs if we ask it to adjust too much, too quickly.

That balance of short- and long-term harms shows that there is every reason to think that the challenge of climate change is primarily a transient one. This has to be crucially important to any discussion of Stern's discount rate. If we have no reason to assume that a higher temperature will be much better or much worse for humans apart from the transitional costs that come with societies adapting, then the expected future harms from climate change should tend to zero over time. Working out just how long it should take before the change in climate has been adjusted to is a matter for some study, and will clearly depend on the extent of warming, but it seems unlikely it would take more than a couple of generations for the kind of warming expected by the IPCC. Certainly, many of the harms that Stern includes more than a few hundred years away have to be written off as quite likely to be utterly irrelevant to humans, who will have learned to live with, or take advantage of, warmer climates.

In the end, the kind of approach that Stern recommends isn't used in other areas of policy because it just isn't practical. If we applied his thinking to foreign policy, taking aggressive action to pre-empt threats decades or centuries away, it could justify almost anything – invading countries in case they invent nuclear weapons and become belligerent in a few hundred years' time. Using a more realistic discount rate you get a much less radical estimate of the likely costs of climate change, which is more in line with that of the established climate change economics literature.

One of the more robust attempts to perform a cost benefit analysis comes from William Nordhaus, who as I mentioned earlier is one of the most respected climate change economists. He has been refining the Dynamic Integrated Model of Climate and the Economy (DICE), the economic model he uses to understand the economic effects of climate change over decades. Using it, he has looked at various proposed responses to climate change. Table 2.1 summarises some of the key results:[24]

Table 2.1: Nordhaus estimates of climate change policy costs and benefits, $ trillion, 2005 prices

	Present-Value Climate Damages, $ trillion, 2005 prices	Present-Value Abatement Costs, $ trillion, 2005 prices
No controls (250-year delay)	22.55	0.04
Optimal	17.31	2.20
Kyoto Protocol with United States	21.38	0.58
Stern Review	9.02	27.74
Gore proposal	10.05	33.90

Under his estimate the total harms we can expect from climate change, without any policy to control it – at least for 250 years – is just over $22 trillion. If we can avoid that at a reasonable cost then it is definitely worth it.

But cutting emissions is expensive. Is it worth it?

He finds that radical, aggressive attempts to cut emissions don't pass the cost benefit test. The kind of plan advocated in the *Stern Review* would see us only facing $9.02 trillion worth of climate change damages, which is a substantial $13.53 trillion reduction from what we expect without action. But that is bought at a cost of $27.74 trillion, so the cure is worse than the disease and we wind up over $14 trillion worse off (more than the annual GDP of the United States). Another radical plan recommended by Al Gore, though not his more recent and even more dramatic proposal to completely decarbonise the US power supply, would be even worse value,

24 Nordhaus, W., *A Question of Balance: Weighing the Options on Global Warming Policies*, Yale University Press, 2008, Table 5-1

as we would avoid less of the potential harm from climate change but pay an even greater price. The expected results of the Kyoto Protocol – the major treaty currently in force that was agreed between a large number of countries in the late nineties but was not ratified in the United States and does not limit developed country emissions – are just underwhelming. It makes only a very marginal difference to expected harms from global warming.

Nordhaus finds that under the optimal result, which he thinks you get with a global carbon tax set at the social cost of carbon (I'll discuss what that means later in Chapter 5), the world would be better off. We would cut climate change harms by $5 trillion at a cost of around $2 trillion, leaving us around $3 trillion better off.

How realistic is that? Well, the story of the rest of this book is that the messy world of politics has produced a final result a long way from the kind of optimal policy that economists draw up on blackboards or in elegant computer models. In the grand scheme of things, with a global GDP of nearly $75 trillion in 2010,[25] $3 trillion (and not in a single year, that's the discounted value over a very long time) if we get things exactly right isn't that big a potential win. And it is easy to imagine, looking at the results from the DICE model, that if politicians don't get things just right then we will wind up worse off than we would have been if they had just left the whole situation well alone. After all, politicians are a lot more interested in the radical plans that Nordhaus expects to make us worse off than the careful approach he has recommended.

A few principle objections to this logic have been raised by those advocating radical attempts to cut emissions.

First, Nobel Laureate and *New York Times* columnist Paul Krugman has argued that the cost of climate policy is likely to be less than expected, and those who respect the capacity

25 CIA, 'The World Factbook', 21 June 2011, https://www.cia.gov/library/publications/the-world-factbook/geos/xx.html

of free markets should expect them to adapt to new climate change regulations at a reasonable cost:[26]

[W]hat the models do not and cannot take into account is creativity; surely, faced with an economy in which there are big monetary payoffs for reducing greenhouse gas emissions, the private sector will come up with ways to limit emissions that are not yet in any model.

He goes on to attack conservative opponents of cap and trade for abandoning their traditional confidence in the capacity of free markets to adapt to the circumstances thrown at them. There are two obvious problems with that analysis.

The capacity of markets to adapt to new circumstances will not just limit the cost of climate change policy but also reduce the value of cutting emissions. Those optimistic about the adaptive capacity of markets must also extend that optimism to the ability of free markets to adapt to a warmer climate. Erring on the side of confidence in how markets will respond to a change in circumstances doesn't necessarily alter the balance between the costs and benefits of cutting emissions.

While markets may respond well to changes in circumstances, that doesn't mean the costs of government programmes will generally come out lower than expected. There is a long history of interventions in the economy producing huge and unwelcome unintended consequences.

The next section of this chapter will talk about how fossil fuels have been critical to modern economic growth. Krugman, later in the same article, holds up the regulation of sulphur dioxide, which causes acid rain, as a relatively cheap success to emulate, I'll discuss the problems with that comparison later in Chapter 3, but for now the key point is that greenhouse gas emissions aren't just another by-product. Emissions are an unavoidable part of the combustion process that currently drives every modern economy. The potential for unintended consequences when trying to effectively

---

26 Krugman, P., 'Building a Green Economy', *New York Times*, 7 April 2010

ration greenhouse gas emissions – as politicians do with cap and trade schemes in particular – is clearly massive. There is no reason to assume that costs will be lower than expected.

Another, more important, objection to the kind of cost benefit analysis that Nordhaus presents is that traditional cost benefit analysis just can't work when we are faced with a potential planetary disaster; that even a small risk of a complete catastrophe makes aggressive action worthwhile. The most respectable form of this argument is in a paper from Harvard economist Martin Weitzman.[27] He argues, to put quite a formal mathematical argument about 'fat-tailed' risks in very simple terms, that we don't know enough to discount the possibility of a catastrophe, and the potential cost if we get a complete disaster is enough to justify taking precautionary action, even if it is expensive.

Jim Manzi, a senior fellow at the Manhattan Institute and Executive Chairman of Applied Predictive Technologies, has pointed out some of the flaws in that argument.[28] First, he notes that Weitzman is very hazy about a lot of the numbers in his paper, calling them 'extremely crude ballpark numerical estimates', 'simplistically aggregated' and 'wildly uncertain, unbelievably crude ballpark estimates'. All this implies that 'Weitzman can't even convince himself about the relevant numerical analysis'. While uncertainty can favour Weitzman's argument, he needs to make a more credible case for there being a good reason to expect that there really is a 1 per cent chance, as Weitzman argues there is, that we are heading for an average, global, year-round temperature of around the 38°C (100°F) that Death Valley, California manages in the

27 Weitzman, M. L., 'On Modeling and Interpreting the Economics of Catastrophic Climate Change', 8 February 2008
28 Manzi, J., 'Weitzman: formalism run amok', *The American Scene*, 1 March 2008

summer. Otherwise 'all we have is a general statement ("the tails might be fat") that is in concept true for any risk'.

As Manzi sets out, the reason why Weitzman is so unsure of his ground is that he is effectively having to conduct his own 'armchair climate science' to try and establish that there is a significant chance we will get much higher warming than expected. He has put some very sketchy work of his own above the conclusions of major inquiries like the IPCC to suggest that there is a 1 per cent chance of massive warming, something that just isn't supported in the well-established scientific literature. And he is assuming that he can combine his numbers, which he admits are ballpark estimates at best, with statistical functions to build up a picture of the risks we are facing from climate change. Putting that above the expectations of those working closer to experimental science is not a good idea.

In the end, we can't accept Weitzman's argument that a long-odds, hard to quantify risk of catastrophe justifies aggressive action to curb emissions, unless we have concrete and robust empirical evidence. The same logic could be applied to too many other risks.

In a recent book, *Global Catastropic Risks*, academics looked at a range of potential disasters that could be sufficiently alarming to warrant invoking the precautionary principle.[29]

After the eruption of a super volcano in Toba, Indonesia the effects were similar to those predicted for a nuclear winter. Land temperatures dropped globally by 5–15°C and the human population fell as low as around 500 reproducing females in a total of 4,000 people. Our numbers were somewhere between those of the giant panda and the blue whale today: an endangered species. If a big enough comet or asteroid – a 10km 'impactor' – hit the Earth, it would have a good chance of causing the extinction of the human race. Other

---

29 Bostrom, N. & Cirkovic, M. (eds), *Global Catastrophic Risks*, Oxford University Press, 2008

hazards could emerge from space like fluxes from supernova explosions and gamma ray bursts. Pandemics have killed tens of millions in the past and we are, in some ways, more vulnerable now. While intelligent computers could help us avoid some risks, they could become dangerous themselves. If scientists have the theory spectacularly wrong, some kind of physics experiment could go awry on a grand scale; one report looked at remote possibilities like a 'phase transition of the vacuum state', which could destroy 'not only our planet but the entire accessible part of the universe'. There are still plenty of nuclear weapons and a nuclear war could happen by mistake. It has been reported that in January 1995:[30]

Russian military officials mistook a Norwegian weather rocket for a US submarine-launched ballistic missile. Boris Yelstin became the first Russian president to ever have the 'nuclear suitcase' open in front of him. He had just a few minutes to decide if he should push the button that would launch a barrage of nuclear missiles. Thankfully, he concluded that his radars were in error. The suitcase was closed.

Nuclear weapons could also fall into the hands of terrorists, who might feel more willing to use them. New diseases could also be not an accident of nature but the creation of humans, whether intentionally or unintentionally. The nanotechnology of today isn't likely to do anything too dramatic, but things could get riskier as the science of molecular manufacturing advances. Finally, it is just possible that a totalitarian dictator could rise to power and do the kind of harm that Hitler, Stalin and Mao did in the last century, or more.

It is a scary world.

As the editors of *Global Catastrophic Risks* set out, climate has become 'the poster child of global threats' but it is far from the only potential source of an exceptional disaster.[31] And some of the other potential catastrophes could appear

---

30 Ibid., p.21
31 Ibid., p.15

out of the blue, far more suddenly. The small but potentially significant possibility of truly catastrophic climate change is something we should keep in mind, but it is much more like the threats above. There are many potential catastrophic risks and we don't have the resources to head them all off; there is a certain amount of risk that we have to accept is a part of life in an uncertain world.

No one would suggest we should fundamentally rework the global economy to protect against comets. We might want to spend a reasonable amount keeping an eye on the situation and put a bit of money into researching potential options if things go wrong. But we have to form policy on the basis of what we can reasonably expect. If we are going to worry about long-odds catastrophic risks, then the premium on any insurance policy has to be reasonable.

A final potential problem that people have raised with the kind of aggregate cost benefit analysis that we've looked at in this section is that it might not take sufficient account of the impact on the poorest. It might be that most of us can live comfortably with the expected effects of climate change, but that many millions who are particularly vulnerable will suffer disproportionately and it is not moral for us to let that happen. Bangladesh, which is highly vulnerable to flooding, is often given as an example of a country whose fate we should be particularly concerned for if the planet warms.

The problem with that argument is that, as we discussed earlier, all of the economic scenarios that underpin projections of significant warming expect incomes in poorer countries to rise rapidly. Without that growth, emissions and therefore warming will not be nearly as high. As Indur Goklany put it in a policy analysis paper for the Cato Institute:[32]

Analysis using both the Stern Review and the fast-track assessment reveals that, notwithstanding climate change, for

32 Goklany, I. M., 'What to Do about Climate Change', Policy Analysis No. 609, Cato Institute, 5 February 2008

*the foreseeable future, human and environmental well-being
will be highest under the 'richest-but-warmest' scenario and
lower for the poorer (lower-carbon) scenarios. The developing world's future well-being should exceed present levels
by several-fold under each scenario, even exceeding present
well-being in today's developed world under all but the poorest scenario. Accordingly, equity-based arguments, which hold
that present generations should divert scarce resources from
today's urgent problems to solve potential problems of tomorrow's wealthier generations, are unpersuasive.*

If we really want to help the poor then our efforts should
be focused on helping people now, rather than their descendants, who are expected to be much better off and will be the
main beneficiaries of attempts to cut emissions and limit
global warming. With strong economic growth countries like
Bangladesh will have the income they need to address specific
vulnerabilities, and we will be able to help.

Looking at the climate change economics literature, there
is no robust case for radical action to curb emissions. There
may be a theoretical economic case that an ideal climate
change policy could make us a bit better off. But, as we shall
see, it is asking too much to expect that gain to make it from
the blackboard into real political action. What politicians
have done instead, across the developed world, is embrace
targets for radical cuts in emissions. The next section looks
at how those targets might be achieved and the price we
might pay.

Meeting climate change targets

To understand just how economically important fossil fuels
are we need to go all the way back to the beginning of modern
economic growth and the foundation of modern industrial
economies in the Industrial Revolution.

As the economic historian Edward Wrigley wrote back in
1988, economists like Adam Smith working shortly before
the Industrial Revolution did not see economic growth as in

any way inevitable: '[For] reasons cogently argued by [Adam] Smith himself and his successors, the momentum of growth was to be expected to peter out after a time... Moreover, the classical economists were unanimous in doubting whether even the then prevailing level of real wages could be sustained indefinitely. Future falls were more probable than future rises.' The 'steady and substantial improvement in real wages for the mass of the population' that we have come to expect was a 'utopian pipe-dream'.[33]

They would definitely not have seen the doubling of incomes each generation that we have now managed for decade after decade coming. Let alone the much faster growth currently being experienced in developing countries like China, which take less than ten years to double their incomes. Abundant energy from fossil fuels has been absolutely critical to making that possible.

Wrigley looked at the importance of fossil fuels in breaking major constraints on economic production. First, in agriculture, farmers can now make use of a range of innovations, from modern fertilisers and pesticides to machines like tractors and combine harvesters, which take energy from outside the farm, ultimately from fossil fuels, and put it to use increasing production. Before that, agriculture had to rely on the limited strength of men and horses – who would eat a significant part of the farm's output – and output could only be increased by using more land or making marginal improvements in the efficiency with which crops and livestock harvested energy from the sun. Farms used to produce about ten times as much energy as they used. With an external source of energy from fossil fuels, they have been able to use about three times as much energy as they produce. That has made possible incredible increases in productivity, to such an extent that one fiftieth of the workforce now produces

---

33 Wrigley, E. A., *Continuity, chance & change: the character of the industrial revolution in England*, Cambridge University Press, 1988, p.3

our food, as opposed to a norm of four fifths in many pre-industrial economies.[34]

In manufacturing fossil fuels have been even more important. Machinery powered at first by steam has allowed huge improvements in the amount that each worker can produce. Physical production is no longer limited by the available strength of horses and men. The French economist and demographer Emile Levasseur described how, if one steam horsepower was taken as equivalent to twenty-one men, in 1840 French industry had 1 million new workers as a result of steam power. By 1885–87 that number had risen to 98 million, or 'deux esclaves et demi par habitant de la France' (2.5 'slaves' for each inhabitant of France).[35]

We can update Levasseur's calculation a little. In 1919 manufacturing in the United States used nearly 30 million horsepower.[36] Working on the same ratio as he did, that is worth nearly 617 million workers. As the US population was just over 100 million in 1919,[37] each American enjoyed the services of around six mechanical workers. Now, particularly if you add the power of engines in cars, trains and planes, and the energy we use at home, the total will be much higher. Britain's final energy consumption in 2009 was just over 150 million tonnes of oil equivalent. Convert that to horsepower running twenty-four hours a day, 365 days a year, and it is equivalent to the labour of 97 men working tirelessly to serve each Briton. And as they are fed with coal, gas or oil the machines don't put pressure on agricultural land as more people or horses would.

....

34 Ibid., p.73

35 Ibid., p.76

36 Fenichel, A. H., 'Growth and Diffusion of Power in Manufacturing, 1838-1919' in Brady D. S. et al., *Output, Employment, and Productivity in the United States after 1800*, NBER, 1966

37 US Census Bureau, 'Historical National Population Estimates: July 1, 1900 to July 1 1999', Population Estimates Program, Population Division, 28 June 2000

Wrigley's work makes clear how the incredible rises in living standards we have seen since the mid-nineteenth century have been driven by abundant fossil fuel energy making possible vast increases in the amount each worker can produce. Economic growth is still associated with greater use of fossil fuels, and therefore greater emissions of greenhouse gases. As we get better off we tend to make more, consume more, go further and trade more. All that activity produces greenhouse gas emissions, either directly, when we burn petrol or aviation fuel for example, or indirectly, because fuel has to be burned in power plants generating electricity. Eating more meat is another thing people tend to do as they get richer and that means more emissions, particularly of methane.

We do use fossil fuels more efficiently over time. The 'emissions intensity' of our economies – the quantity of emissions produced per dollar of national income – tends to fall. That is partly because we do different things, more low emission services and less heavy manufacturing for example, but mostly because we get a lot more efficient over time. Fossil fuels cost money, and engineers and designers are constantly trying to make everything from cars to power plants use less. For example, the average American mid-sized car emitted 13.6 tonnes of CO_2 every 15,000 miles in 1975; by 2008 that figure had more than halved to 5.9 tonnes of CO_2. That is a fall of 2.5 per cent a year on average.[38] An IPCC special report found that in forty years aircraft fuel efficiency had increased 'by 70 per cent through improvements in airframe design, engine technology and rising load factors'.[39]

Generally, the reduction in emissions intensity doesn't keep pace with the increase in consumption. You can

....

38 US Department of Energy, *Transportation Energy Data Book*, Edition 28, 2009, Table 11.8

39 IPCC, 'Aviation and the Global Atmosphere', 1999, Aircraft Technology and Its Relation to Emissions

see this in Figure 2.1: around the world emissions intensity has been falling but emissions rising over a number
of years.[40]

**Figure 2.1: World emissions and emissions intensity,
1971–2007, Mt CO$_2$ and kg CO$_2$/US dollar (2000 prices)**

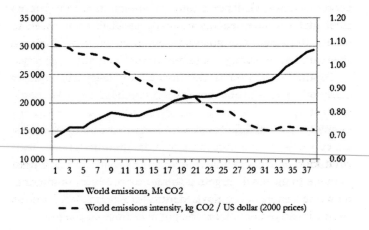

As fossil fuels are of such central importance to modern economies, making the cuts will be a lot harder than making the
promises. If emissions intensity doesn't decline fast enough
then cutting emissions will require drastic falls in income.
Just how much poorer we might need to get depends on how
fast we can improve efficiency and how tough the emissions
target is.

The scale of the challenge can be seen using the Kaya
Identity – named after the Japanese economist Yoichi Kaya
– which provides a simple framework for understanding the
different factors that drive emissions.

---

40 International Energy Agency, 'CO$_2$ Emissions from Fuel Combustion' (2009
Edition), http://www.iea.org/co2highlights/co2highlights.xls

Equation 2.1: Kaya Identity

Emissions = Population x GDP per capita x Energy intensity of GDP x Carbon intensity of energy

In other words, in order to reduce emissions there either needs to be fewer of us – a lower population; we need to be poorer – a lower GDP per capita; we need to use energy more efficiently – a lower energy intensity of GDP; or we need to reduce the amount of greenhouse gas we emit producing a given amount of energy – a lower carbon intensity of energy.

Population control is very much part of the agenda for many of the most radical green activists and there are some interesting insights to be had from separating out energy intensity and carbon intensity. But the key question is how we can expect emissions to rise or fall going forward, and what kind of sacrifice in our national income we might need to make to meet the targets politicians have been promoting. So we can express the Kaya Identity in a simplified form, as shown in Equation 2.2, for the purposes of this book.

Equation 2.2: Simplified Kaya Identity

Emissions = GDP x Emissions intensity of GDP

So to emit less we either need to do less or do more with less.

To put some actual numbers on that equation, let's first look at the global picture. The basic objective agreed by the G8 is to halve emissions by 2050, probably from levels in 1990 or 2005. Let's take the 50 per cent cut in emissions relative to 1990 that was proposed by Sir Nicholas Stern before the Copenhagen conference in his book *A Blueprint for a Safer Planet*.[41] That is probably a decent guide to what the politicians are looking to agree.

....

41   Stern, N., *A blueprint for a safer planet*, The Bodley Head, 2009, p.146

In recent decades, as Figure 2.1 showed, emissions intensity has generally been falling at a pretty steady rate. It has been falling by just over 1 per cent a year and there isn't any sign of acceleration in recent years. But world GDP has been growing by just over 3 per cent a year. If those trends continue to 2050, then emissions will be much higher than they are now, at 68,859 Mt, 328 per cent the level in 1990. To meet the target of cutting emissions in half from 1990 levels – to around 10,490 Mt – without cutting emissions intensity more quickly, you would need to cut world income by 85 per cent, from the expected level of $151 trillion to $23 trillion. Or, in other words, a half century global recession, as world income would need to be lower than the $32 trillion in 2000. British academics have already argued we need a 'planned recession',[42] but the scale of the economic contraction needed to halve emissions from 1990 levels by 2050 would be incredible. With a recession of that scale, we would look back on the aftermath of the current financial crisis fondly.

It is pretty much unthinkable that political leaders around the world, democratic or not, would be able to impose that even if they wanted to. So in order to cut emissions on the kind of scale politicians want, without destroying the world economy, we need to cut emissions intensity faster.

Suppose you double the rate of emissions intensity improvements to over 2 per cent a year. Emissions would still rise to 42,691 Mt by 2050, double the 1990 level. You would still need to cut GDP by 75 per cent to meet the target. So we are still talking about an incredible level of economic sacrifice. We are still talking about initiating a global recession worse than any in living memory.

If emissions intensity improves at an even faster rate of nearly 4.5 per cent, four times as fast as the average in

42 Gray, L., '"Planned recession" could avoid catastrophic climate change', *Daily Telegraph*, 30 September 2009

recent decades, then emissions will start to fall at a fairly rapid pace.

Emissions would fall to 16,145 Mt by 2050, 77 per cent of the level in 1990. That would still require a cut in world income of 35 per cent from the expected level. To get to the international targets without a big cut in income you would need to cut emissions intensity by around 4.9 per cent each year. Few countries have managed that for a sustained period of time. The French managed 5.1 per cent in the eighties as they switched most of their energy supply over to nuclear power.[43] But you can only really do that once and the entire world would need to maintain that kind of performance for four decades. Needless to say, it also doesn't come cheap.

The targets for richer countries are tougher. President Obama pledged an 80 per cent cut in emissions by 2050 at the G8.[44] The final US target if countries sign up to binding emissions targets will almost certainly work from a 2005 baseline, but let's work on 1990 for now just to be consistent. In the US GDP grows by just over 3 per cent a year and emissions intensity falls by just over 2 per cent a year. If that pattern continues, emissions will continue to rise and the US will be headed for 171 per cent of its 1990 emissions by 2050. The US economy would need to shrink by a massive 88 per cent to meet a target of an 80 per cent cut from 1990 levels by 2050. To get an idea of the scale we're talking about, if you took 88 per cent out of the economy today, it would mean cutting US annual national income by around $12 trillion. Ten trillion dollars is enough to wipe out more than half of the US national debt, in a single year, or buy every American a BMW 3 Series sedan, every single year.

---

43 Ibid.
44 America.gov, 'G8 Nations Agree to Cut Carbon Emissions 80 Per Cent By 2050', 9 July 2009, http://www.america.gov/st/peacesec-english/2009/July/20090709153615esnamfuak0.3577082.html

Even if the rate of emissions intensity reductions were doubled to over 4 per cent a year, then the US would still fall well short of its target without cuts in income. Though emissions would fall significantly, they would still be heading for 65 per cent of the 1990 level. You would need a 69 per cent cut in national income to meet the 80 per cent cut target. Again, to get an idea of what that means, if you took 69 per cent out of the US economy today, that would mean cutting annual US GDP by the best part of $10 trillion.

So why did politicians sign up to these targets?

In 2007 Gwyn Prins and Steve Rayner wrote that many of the problems with climate change policy today are the result of the fact that 'Kyoto was constructed by quick borrowing from past practice with other treaty regimes dealing with ozone, sulphur emissions and nuclear bombs'.[45]

Basically, world leaders were in a hurry to do something, anything, on climate change. But they didn't really know how to proceed. So they looked at what had worked to address other problems that seemed similar. Unfortunately, they didn't properly consider the unique place of CO_2 in modern industrial economies and how that would undo their attempts to cut greenhouse gas emissions.

Ambitious targets and timetables agreed around the negotiating table were thought to have worked to cut nuclear weapons. So we had ambitious targets for cuts in emissions. But of course cuts in nuclear stockpiles save governments money, are directly within their power and only need to be agreed and enforced between a far smaller set of countries to be effective. By contrast, the targets for cutting emissions meant enshrining aspirations to remake the economy, in a way no government knew how to achieve, in international

45 Prins, G. & Rayner, S., 'The Wrong Trousers: Radically Rethinking Climate Policy', Joint Discussion Paper of the James Martin Institute for Science and Civilization, University of Oxford and the MacKinder Centre for the Study of Long-Wave Events, London School of Economics, 2007

treaties. That was and is a sure fire recipe for lots of grand-standing and very little consideration of the practicalities.

Regulations agreed between the major halocarbon-producing countries phased out the production of chemicals like CFCs that created a hole in the ozone layer, but CFCs aren't anything like as fundamental to modern industrial economies as CO_2, which is produced by the combustion process and has been instrumental to economic growth and prosperity since the Industrial Revolution, as I set out earlier. Attempting to agree a common set of regulations through the UN and adopting grandiose international treaties (the Montreal Protocol for CFCs, the Kyoto Protocol for CO_2) was always likely to be difficult and often counterproductive.

Now politicians are either hoping that a technological miracle will take place. That if they are sufficiently audacious they will be rewarded with an emissions-free source of energy that is as affordable, available and convenient as fossil fuels. Nothing less will produce the reduction in emissions they have pledged to make without drastic sacrifices in national income. It might not happen, but most of the politicians pushing the targets will be retired or dead by the time the target comes up so why should they care?

Or, they are serious and they actually do think that cutting emissions is so vital that it is worth taking huge chunks out of our economies. That is the really frightening possibility, that they have bought their own rhetoric that there are no other options, and Plan B is to shut down the world's economy and condemn billions at home and abroad to poverty.

Or, they might still not appreciate just how ambitious these targets are.

Regardless of how seriously politicians really take them, and while the targets may not kick in for quite a long time, they are corrupting decision-making now. Everything is assessed not in terms of whether it is a good idea and a productive way of mitigating risks from a changing climate, but whether or not it is needed to meet the targets.

For example, British policymakers have argued that we shouldn't expand our most important airport, London Heathrow, because of the emissions it will create. Never mind that Heathrow is of vital importance to Britain's economy; that making planes circle above the city waiting for a place to land isn't the most fuel-efficient thing to do; that Britons already pay excessive taxes that are supposed to account for the effects of aviation emissions on the climate; that flights are only responsible for a small fraction of global emissions; and that China is currently in the process of building 100 new airports.[46] Despite all that, Members of Parliament have lined up to attack the proposed new runway on the grounds that '[they] came together not so long ago and passed the Climate Change Act 2008'.[47]

Politicians are chasing a target that it might only be possible to meet with an economic disaster; is it any wonder that the policies they are proposing are economically disastrous?

Things are even worse for those countries with short-term targets as well. Most European countries have ambitious targets to cut emissions by 2020, which are being made more onerous all the time. Britain's former Prime Minister, Gordon Brown, wanted to sign us up to a target to cut emissions by 42 per cent from the 1990 level by 2020 at Copenhagen. Research that I produced for the TaxPayers' Alliance suggests that could mean cutting our national income by 30 per cent from expected levels by 2020 if emissions intensity continues to fall at the rate we've managed in recent years.[48]

Given that rate of emissions intensity improvement has been based on one-offs like the switch from coal to gas for power generation, even that will be an achievement. The 2020 deadline is particularly challenging because it doesn't

---

46 A map of the new airports, via Roger Pielke Jr's blog, is available here: http://images.fastcompany.com/magazine/125/chinas-airport-boom.jpg
47 Hansard, 28 Jan 2009, Column 397
48 Sinclair, M., 'The economic cost of a 42 per cent reduction in carbon dioxide emissions by 2020', The TaxPayers' Alliance, December 2009

leave time for a lot of relatively low-cost ways of cutting emissions to be used; it is unlikely to be possible to substantially increase the amount of nuclear capacity by then, for example. As Dieter Helm – Professor of Energy Policy at Oxford University – has said:[49]

There is not much room for nuclear before 2020, or for CCS. Tidal power is not likely to make a significant contribution until post-2020, and the target itself provides no incentive towards the sorts of R&D required. For transport, the focus is on biofuels, since hydrogen and electric based cars are unlikely to be significant pre-2020 technologies.

What is quite clear, looking at the targets politicians have set and how meeting them might require us to limit economic growth, is that even quite efficient policies might struggle to deliver the kind of cuts in emissions that politicians are after without imposing huge costs on ordinary families.

Politicians are banking on a technological revolution but there is little reason to think that one is necessarily coming just because it would be convenient. If our leaders are thinking seriously, they should be trying to work out how to maximise the odds that we get the new options we need.

The problems with non-fossil fuel energy aren't new. Writing about the reasons why fossil fuels were so economically valuable during the Industrial Revolution, Wrigley described some of the shortcomings of the alternatives. Wind power and water power were both unreliable and expanding them would increasingly mean using marginal sites where they would be less productive.[50] As we'll discuss later, some of the same problems, of intermittency and declining productivity as the best sites are used up, are still critical to the inability of renewable energy to offer an economical alternative to coal,

....

49 Helm, D., 'EU climate-change policy – a critique' from Helm, D. & Hepburn, C. (eds), *The Economics and Politics of Climate Change*, Oxford University Press, October 2009, p.7

50 Wrigley, E. A., *Continuity, chance & change: the character of the industrial revolution in England*, Cambridge University Press, 1988, p.75

oil or gas. There is no particular reason to think that, just because it would be convenient, a radical improvement in the performance of non-fossil fuel energy is on the cards. Nuclear power is the only significant and genuinely new option that has been put on the table in recent decades.

So policymakers are wrestling with a very difficult issue. Many of those trying to lead a decarbonisation of the world's energy supply are altogether too sanguine about their chances. Even ignoring the cost, we are talking about an enormous technical challenge. But that technical challenge isn't the hard part. Reducing emissions needs to not just be technically feasible but affordable. If it requires decades of recession in the developed world, or limiting the aspirations of billions in developing countries for a better standard of life, then there is no way that climate change policy will be able to proceed on a democratic basis. The public will rightly reject an unprecedented recession being forced on them by their own governments.

Why everyone needs to pay attention to climate change policy

In many ways the debate over climate change has taken an unfortunate turn. Too often the debate is presented as one in which you either agree with the basic science of climate change and support the actions currently being pushed through to do something about it, or you disagree with the science and therefore disapprove of climate change policy. To the extent that people argue we need to move on from the scientific debate, they too often mean we should simply accept the actions governments are taking to stop climate change as necessary and desirable.

Attempts to pronounce the scientific debate around the science of climate change as over are both unscientific and unnecessary. There is no particular need in this domain of policy for a complete scientific understanding of cause and effect, which has never been established elsewhere. It is hard to think of any domain where governments really know exactly what will happen with and without their interventions.

What is really frightening about climate change policy is that governments are – often in an extremely cavalier fashion – passing climate change targets that command a drastic reduction in our use of the fossil fuels that have been fundamental to prosperity since the Industrial Revolution. If the science of climate change was wrong, but the measures being introduced to address it were cheap, then it wouldn't be that big a deal. Instead, the science that suggests a doubling of emissions leads to around 3°C of warming may well be right, but the measures being taken to reduce emissions and limit warming could mean economic disaster. Governments are taking actions that threaten the material prosperity that underpins our way of life.

EMISSIONS TRADING

If one policy is central to current climate change policy, then it is emissions trading, or cap and trade. Major trading schemes have been proposed by governing parties in every major developed economy. And the European Union has put in place its Emissions Trading System (ETS). Politicians and industry lobbyists don't just want to expand emissions trading to new countries. They also want to apply it to new industries such as international aviation and shipping.

The basic structure of an emissions trading scheme is that firms are required to hold permits in order to do things that emit greenhouse gases; for example, companies in the EU need to present an allowance for every tonne of carbon dioxide they emit at installations covered by the scheme. Those permits are either given to companies for free or governments set up auctions and sell them. But the number of them is fixed and comes down over time. That way, the amount of emissions allowed is cut. Companies are allowed to trade their permits if they have more than they need or need more than they have. A price develops on the markets – say around $20 per tonne of CO_2 – and that means there is a price on emitting. The price exists because for each tonne they emit they either can't sell one of their allowances – losing out on its $20 value as they could otherwise have sold it – or they have to buy an allowance from someone else through the market – paying them $20. That means there is a price on emissions – in that hypothetical case, of $20 – just as there is under a carbon tax.

It wasn't always clear that emissions trading would emerge as the totemic climate change policy, regulating the most important sector, large combustion plants generating electricity. As discussed earlier, academics such as William Nordhaus have tended to work on the basis of a carbon tax instead.

But, while carbon or green taxes are still a major part of climate change policy they have generally been reserved for those areas, like emissions from cars, where a trading scheme was not felt to be practicable.

There are important differences between emissions trading and carbon taxes. The most critical difference is that carbon trading fixes the amount of greenhouse gas emissions allowed and then leaves the carbon price to change in response to supply and demand. A carbon tax, on the other hand, fixes the price on emissions and then leaves the amount emitted to be determined by supply and demand. If the cap on emissions is too high or low in an emissions trading scheme then the price will collapse or shoot up. But then if the carbon tax is too low or too high it might lead to too great, or not enough of, a cut in emissions relative to the targets. An emissions trading scheme therefore fits better with the politicians' approach of setting rigid, inflexible targets, but it doesn't allow the economy the flexibility to emit more or less if it is worth it despite the carbon price.

Gwyn Prins and Steve Rayner have cited sulphur dioxide (SO_2) trading as another supposed success story that inspired the current approach to cutting emissions, along with international treaties to control nuclear weapon stockpiles and CFC emissions earlier discussed.[51] The politicians, bureaucrats and advisors who put in place our current climate change policies thought that the cap and trade scheme for SO_2 in the US had been a low-cost way of cutting emissions of SO_2, and the associated acid rain. Politicians would have been more cautious if they had taken a more careful look at the record of the SO_2 trading programme and the different places of

---

51 Prins, G. & Rayner, S., 'The Wrong Trousers: Radically Rethinking Climate Policy', Joint Discussion Paper of the James Martin Institute for Science and Civilization, University of Oxford and the MacKinder Centre for the Study of Long-Wave Events, London School of Economics, 2007

CO_2 and SO_2 in modern economies. An American Enterprise Institute (AEI) essay in June 2007 made these key points:[52]

First, SO_2 trading was only applied to a single sector: initially, only 110 coal-fired power plants were included in the system, but it subsequently expanded to 445 plants. While coal-fired power plants account for roughly one third of US carbon dioxide (CO_2) emissions and will therefore be central to a GHG cap-and-trade program, a comprehensive GHG emissions-trading program will have to apply across many sectors beyond electric utilities, vastly complicating a trading system.

Second, SO_2 and CO_2 are not comparable targets for emissions reduction. Reducing SO_2 emissions did not require any constraint on end-use energy production or consumption. Coal-fired power plants had many low-cost options to reduce SO_2 emissions without reducing electricity production. Some switched to low-sulfur coal (abetted in large part by railroad deregulation in the 1980s, which made transport of Western low-sulfur coal more economical than previously). The cost of 'scrubbers' – industrial devices which capture SO_2 and sequester it – turned out to be lower than predicted. Other utilities emphasised more use of natural gas. The impact on ratepayers and consumers was modest.

The comparison is stark. The SO_2 scheme covered 110 plants and expanded to 445. The EU ETS covers around 11,000 emitting installations.[53] And a story in the *Wall Street Journal* has provided more evidence that these schemes don't work as well as was thought:[54]

The acid-rain market has struggled for the past two years as utilities, states and investors waited for the Environmental Protection Agency to issue new rules. The rules, released last

---

52 Green, K. P., Hayward, S. F. & Hassett, K. A., 'Climate Change: Caps vs. Taxes', AEI Outlook No 2, June 2007

53 European Commission, 'Emissions Trading System (EU ETS)', downloaded from http://ec.europa.eu/clima/policies/ets/index_en.htm

54 Peters, M., 'Changes Choke Cap-and-Trade Market', *Wall Street Journal*, 12 July 2010

week, put tougher limits on emissions by power plants but rely less on trading. As a result, the allowances that utilities now trade to allow them to emit sulfur dioxide are expected to become worthless.

As the AEI essay notes, the SO_2 emissions price has been extremely volatile since the scheme was created.[55] But now it is expected to fall effectively to zero. Such volatility makes the scheme an incredibly inefficient way of encouraging investment to reduce emissions. It is an unpredictable addition to business costs that makes it harder for them to plan and discourages long-term investments of all kinds.

But it is hard to escape the conclusion that this kind of difference between carbon taxation and emissions trading isn't the main reason that politicians tend to favour one or the other. It seems likely that the main reason emissions trading has been taken up is that politicians don't want to face the fate of Canada's Liberal Party, who lost an election running on a carbon tax that Canadian Conservatives attacked, quite fairly, as a 'tax on everything'.[56] Emissions trading is more complex and less direct. As a result, it is easier to obscure the connection between the emissions trading scheme and higher prices.

But emissions trading does make things more expensive. If it isn't a tax on everything, it is at least a tax on everything it touches, particularly electricity. It also presents some significant opportunities for companies to profit at the expense of their consumers.

The European Union's ETS is the best example we have of an emissions trading scheme in operation. It was introduced on 1 January 2005 and is the largest emissions trading scheme currently in operation anywhere in the world, covering factories, power plants and even large public buildings

55 Green, K. P., Hayward, S. F. & Hassett, K. A., 'Climate Change: Caps vs. Taxes', AEI Outlook No 2, June 2007

56 Delacourt, S., 'Carbon tax plan fuels Liberal unrest', *Toronto Star*, 10 June 2008

like hospitals across Europe.[57] The experience of the ETS makes the problems with cap and trade very clear.

The cost to consumers

Putting in place cap and trade imposes a stiff burden on consumers. For reasons we'll cover later, in the sections on windfall profits and how emissions trading schemes are becoming a massive global tax, consumers wind up paying the price regardless of whether the allowances are given away to industry for free or sold at auction. Cap and trade has the potential to be a tax on almost everything because fossil fuels are so important to modern industrialised economies, as we discussed earlier. But with many other factors, from the price of coal and gas to fluctuations in demand with the weather, affecting energy prices it is hard to get a precise picture of just how much cap and trade costs consumers. You can use some simple maths to get a decent estimate.

The main uncertainty is the extent to which installations regulated by the ETS pass on the cost to their customers – there is a detailed explanation of the estimates in the Appendix – and why firms might or might not pass the carbon cost on. For this book I've produced two estimates. In the first, all installations pass on 80 per cent of the carbon cost; in the second, only power stations pass on 80 per cent of the carbon cost and other industries can't because of international competition. The results under both those approaches are shown in Table 3.1.

Table 3.1: EU ETS cost to consumers, 2010

Verified emissions	Price, € /t CO_2	Pass-through rate	Cost to consumers, €
1,863,646,242	14.34	80%	21,383,752,539
1,863,646,242	14.34	58%	15,569,987,597

....

57 European Commission, 'Emissions Trading System (EU ETS)', downloaded from http://ec.europa.eu/clima/policies/ets/index_en.htm

As that table shows, a basic estimate of the cost of the scheme to consumers is around €15 (£13, $21) to €21 (£18, $28) billion in 2010. That is around €30–€40 (£27–£35, $42–$56) for every one of the roughly 500 million people living in countries covered by the scheme.

Table 3.2: EU ETS cost to consumers, 2010, by country

Country	Total Emissions, Mt CO_2	Combustion installation emissions, Mt CO_2	Cost to consumers, 80% pass-through, €	Refined pass-through rate	Cost to consumers, refined pass-through rate, €
AT	30,917,187	16,723,474	354,748,375	43%	191,887,613
BE	50,103,916	28,184,330	574,899,741	45%	323,391,170
BG	28,670,760	12,640,461	328,972,539	35%	145,038,519
CY	0	0	0	0%	0
CZ	75,579,461	67,364,628	867,209,911	71%	772,951,702
DE	453,974,993	355,950,714	5,208,976,194	63%	4,084,231,123
DK	25,266,314	22,718,556	289,909,423	72%	260,676,071
EE	14,421,268	14,290,487	165,471,761	79%	163,971,161
ES	121,466,229	73,427,491	1,393,721,472	48%	842,517,889
FI	41,300,705	27,054,275	473,890,396	52%	310,424,752
FR	114,710,601	55,200,252	1,316,206,397	38%	633,375,853
GB	237,427,464	193,638,211	2,724,277,828	65%	2,221,833,464
GR	489,323	-56	5,614,564	0%	-643
HU	22,995,006	18,191,880	263,848,099	63%	208,736,321
IE	17,355,996	15,029,086	199,145,264	69%	172,445,955
IT	190,133,165	121,055,427	2,181,616,048	51%	1,389,007,869
LI	0	0	0	0%	0
LT	6,351,011	3,607,757	72,872,439	45%	41,395,937
LU	2,252,660	1,176,540	25,847,354	42%	13,499,794
LV	3,240,137	2,172,808	37,177,811	54%	24,931,120
MT	0	0	0	0%	0
NL	84,333,021	64,148,925	967,649,552	61%	736,054,251
NO	19,333,288	15,098,855	221,833,005	62%	173,246,495
PL	199,434,316	174,799,433	2,288,338,830	70%	2,005,674,540
PT	24,167,127	14,339,680	277,297,189	47%	164,535,609
RO	47,311,186	34,008,406	542,855,544	58%	390,217,479
SE	22,660,939	10,199,511	260,014,965	36%	117,030,697
SI	8,129,855	6,790,292	93,283,158	67%	77,912,814
SK	21,620,314	9,151,010	248,074,680	34%	105,000,042
Total	1,863,646,242	1,356,962,433	21,383,752,539	58.2%	15,569,987,597

This breaks down by country as shown in Table 3.2. Note that the second estimate varies based upon how much of a country's emissions come from power plants.

The extent to which the carbon price is passed on to the consumer will vary in different countries. Italy, in particular, without a liberalised energy market, appears to have seen low pass-through rates. In others, the UK in particular, pass-through rates are high due to highly liberalised energy markets. But the estimates in that table should be a reasonable guide to the cost of the ETS to consumers, and suggest that the cost in Britain, for example, was equivalent to around €85 (£73, $113) per family in 2010. That is roughly the same amount that the average household spends on fruit juices, and tea, significantly more than they spend on bus and coach fares.[58]

And bear in mind those costs are just the start. That is just the cost of a broken, embryonic ETS. There are a number of reasons why the cost of the ETS is likely to rise over time and why other cap and trade schemes are likely to impose a much greater burden on consumers.

This is the cost of the scheme after emissions have fallen and the price has collapsed with the recession. The scheme isn't really capping emissions at all at the moment, as demand has fallen with reduced activity in the rest of the economy and so many firms have been left with more allowances than they need.

The cap is set to steadily tighten. The plan is for a linear reduction of 1.74 per cent each year.[59] That tightening will increase the burden of the ETS on consumers.

Governments are so upset at the low price right now that they are looking at setting a minimum price through other policies. In Britain, EDF Energy – the company which owns most of Britain's remaining nuclear plants and has the greatest ability to build new ones – has been lobbying for some time to get a guaranteed floor under the carbon price produced by the ETS. That floor was introduced in Budget 2011 with a target price of £30/t CO_2. Needless to say, that would mean a big increase in the cost of the scheme. At a price of £30 a tonne the cost of the ETS would have been equivalent to over

---

58 Office for National Statistics, 'Family Spending 2010'
59 Delbeke, J., 'Environmental policy in times of economic crisis – the example of the EU ETS', speech receiving the Adam Smith Prize 2009, Rotes Rathaus, Berlin, 29 May 2009

£178 per family in 2010 in the UK.[60] It would then be more than the average household spends on household appliances, or the amount they spend on buns, cakes and biscuits.[61] Let them eat carbon indeed – their cake budget is gone.

The potential longer-term costs, when cap and trade really kicks in and/or is introduced in a country with higher emissions per capita, can be seen from estimates of the potential cost of US cap and trade. And with the price expected to rise over the next decade, the Congressional Budget Office expect that if John Kerry's American Power Act were enacted, it would take $120.9 (£68.2, €90.3) billion a year[62] off the hands of American consumers by 2020 in revenues for the regulation to hand out. That is over $1,100 (£600, €800) per family, or a bit less than the national income of New Zealand.

The costs of cap and trade are already a reality in Europe, but they are just a mild taste of what is to come. Over time emissions trading is set to become far more onerous.

Allocating the allowances between countries

The first step in the EU ETS is the allocation of the allowances to countries, because it is a multinational scheme, and then to individual companies with installations covered.

The countries have to submit National Allocation Plans to the European Commission, the EU's central bureaucracy. Those plans determine how many allowances they can grant to their companies. They are based on factors like what is needed to meet the country's commitments under the Kyoto Protocol and what is felt to be technically possible.

Even at that early stage there are problems. The allowances

....

60 Based on the same total emissions and pass-through rate as used for the earlier estimates.

61 Office for National Statistics, 'Family Spending 2010'

62 Congressional Budget Office, Letter to Honorable John F. Kerry, CBO estimate of the budgetary impact of the May 12, 2010, discussion draft of the American Power Act, including subsequent corrections and changes to that draft, 7 July 2010

are quite valuable so most countries, looking to their national interest, want to grant as many of them as possible. In the first phase of the scheme (2005–2007) most countries granted more allowances than they needed. The price collapsed and the UK, which had set a tougher target, wound up making a huge transfer to the other European countries. The think tank Open Europe has reported that the transfer amounted to nearly £1.5 ($2.7) billion over the first phase.[63]

In the second phase, the European Commission tightened up the rules and countries weren't able to allocate permits on anything like the same scale. There were still serious issues, though. Between them, Estonia, Poland and the Czech Republic were allowed 102.9 Mt CO_2 less by the commission than they had provided for in their own National Allocation Plans. That is slightly more than the total 2006 emissions of Nigeria. The Czech Republic was allowed 14.8 per cent less than it had proposed, Poland was allowed 26.7 per cent less and Estonia was allowed a massive 47.8 per cent less.[64]

Feeling that they hadn't been treated fairly and that the commission had overstepped the mark, Estonia and Poland took legal action to dispute its decisions. They won their case at the European Court of First Instance. Other countries have also set out to challenge the commission's decisions and the carbon price on European markets fell sharply on the news.

Playing teacher's pet for the commission, Britain actually intervened on their side in the court case. In response to a Freedom of Information request I submitted, the Government revealed that they spent £12,202 (around $21,000) on the case with Estonia and £30,698 (around $54,000) on the case with Poland. That meant British taxpayers' money was being

---

63 Open Europe, 'The high price of hot air: Why the EU Emissions Trading Scheme is an environmental and economic failure', 2 July 2006

64 European Commission, 'Emissions Trading: Commission adopts decision on Estonia's national allocation plan for 2008–2012, 4 May 2007'; European Commission, 'Emissions trading: Commission decides on Czech and Polish national allocation plans for 2008-2012', 26 March 2007

spent in an attempt to ensure a lower supply of allowances, which would mean a higher price and therefore higher costs for British taxpayers.

This kind of horse trading and confrontation isn't just a result of the EU ETS working at a supranational level, involving a number of countries. There is the distinct possibility that in federal countries different provinces or states will fight their companies' corner.

And those running or trying to set up new cap and trade schemes are planning on linking them together across national borders. Jos Debelke, Deputy Director General of the Environmental Directorate-General in the European Commission, told an audience in Berlin that:[65]

The EU ETS also has clear provisions in the legislation for linking the EU ETS with other mandatory and compatible cap-and-trade systems.

The EU ETS and the future US cap-and-trade system – integrated into a transatlantic carbon market – can be the twin engines driving the OECD-wide carbon market.

In the Waxman-Markey cap and trade bill that has passed the House of Representatives in the United States there is a similar provision. The conditions are set out in Section 728 International Emission Allowances:[66]

The Administrator, in consultation with the Secretary of State, may by rule designate an international climate change program as a qualifying international program if:

(1) the program is run by a national or supranational foreign government, and imposes a mandatory absolute tonnage limit on greenhouse gas emissions from one or more foreign countries, or from one or more economic sectors in such a country or countries; and

---

65 Delbeke, J., 'Environmental policy in times of economic crisis – the example of the EU ETS', speech receiving the Adam Smith Prize 2009, Rotes Rathaus, Berlin, 29 May 2009, p.4

66 H.R. 2454, Part C – Program Rules, Sec. 728 International emission allowances

(2) the program is at least as stringent as the program established by this title, including provisions to ensure at least comparable monitoring, compliance, enforcement, quality of offsets, and restrictions on the use of offsets.

For approved programmes – and the intention is clearly that the EU ETS would qualify – emissions allowances from abroad are interchangeable with those granted in the US. Section 722. Prohibition of Excess Emissions makes that clear:[67]

To demonstrate compliance, a covered entity may hold an international emission allowance in lieu of an emission allowance, except as modified under section 728(d).

The latest attempt to get comprehensive climate change legislation through the US Senate is the American Power Act being promoted by Senators John Kerry and Joseph Lieberman.

It includes very similar provisions for international emission allowances as in the previously quoted Section 728 International Emission Allowances:[68]

And for them to be used in place of other allowances in Section 722 Prohibition of Excess Emissions:[69]

To demonstrate compliance, a covered entity may hold an international emission allowance in lieu of an emission allowance.

These provisions are important to the Europeans. Adam C. T. Matthews, the Secretary General of an organisation called GLOBE International, an environmental policy talking shop for parliamentarians, told me that they are something 'which Europe was desperate for'. They think that their carbon market will be in serious trouble without it.

It isn't widely appreciated just how close we are, and have been for some time, to a direct global ration, at least in the developed world, on carbon dioxide emissions. Americans thought they were being sold a US cap and trade scheme.

67 H.R. 2454, Part C – Program Rules, Sec. 722 Prohibition of excess emissions
68 Discussion draft, American Power Act, 'Part C – Program Rules, Sec. 728 International emission allowances'
69 Discussion draft, American Power Act, 'Part C – Program Rules, Sec. 722 Prohibition of excess emissions'

Ironically, the American Power Act, along with Waxman-Markey, wasn't very American at all. It signed the US up to membership of the European Union's existing ETS.

A supranational cap and trade scheme will inevitably lead to disputes over who is being sufficiently stringent, already seen within the EU. After all, the scheme essentially allows governments to print money for their firms by providing a generous number of allowances, with the price paid by companies and consumers in countries with tougher targets.

If the US were to set up a cap and trade system and link it to that of the EU ETS, it is hard to say who would come off worse – who would suffer the fate of Britain in the first phase of the EU ETS, making a big and unwarranted pay out to emitters in other countries. The US has generally set lower targets for emissions cuts. That would tend to mean that its firms have a more generous helping of allowances. But the way the US is governed, particularly with the courts holding the executive to policy pledges, makes it harder for politicians to make commitments and then ignore them. It is easy to imagine that the US would end up losing out if, for example, the price spiked in the economic recovery and the Europeans treated their industries generously but the US authorities couldn't do so without facing legal action.

The end result could easily be more power taken from the hands of elected national governments and given to unelected supranational bureaucracies. It will be an extended diplomatic nightmare attempting to bring countries with such different economies and emissions targets under one scheme. That will surely mean demands for the targets to become more inflexible or for a bigger role to be played by a supposedly impartial bureaucracy. Someone would need to play the European Commission's role on an international scale, perhaps a United Nations agency like the UNFCCC, which has overseen climate change negotiations. Either way, the voting public would steadily lose their ability to decide how much carbon they are allowed to emit.

At the moment, democracy is the biggest danger to expensive climate change regulations. They threaten to become a huge danger to democracy.

Trading

Companies can trade their allowances if they have more or less than they need. That is the 'trade' in cap and trade.

Lots of big companies, from oil majors like Shell and BP to financial services firms like Goldman Sachs, have carbon trading desks. Unfortunately, it is difficult to assess how much money they are making out of it; there isn't any public data to go on. As we'll discuss later, there is a lot of volatility in the market and that creates plenty of opportunities to make money.

Table 3.3: ECX and Bluenext ETS earnings

	Total volume of trades	Transaction fee (for each side of the transaction)	Total transaction fees	Avg price (€)	Traded Volume (€)
ECX EUA Daily Futures Contract 13/3/2009-30/11/2009	54,147,000	€ 0.004	€ 433,176	13.68	€ 740,990,050
ECX CER Daily Futures Contract 13/3/2009-30/11/2009	4,193,000	€ 0.004	€ 33,544	12.26	€ 51,393,105
ECX CER Options Contract 13/1/2009-27/11/2009	84,530,000	€ 0.002	€ 338,120	11.10	€ 938,211,900
ECX CER Futures Contract 2/1/2009-30/11/2009	709,684,000	€ 0.002	€ 2,838,736	11.89	€ 8,437,432,722
ECX EUA Options Contract 6/1/2009-30/11/2009	390,703,000	€ 0.002	€ 1,562,812	13.35	€ 5,216,795,259
ECX EUA Futures Contract 2/1/2009-30/11/2009	3,505,800,000	€ 0.002	€ 14,023,200	15.75	€ 55,216,290,580
ECX total	3,950,650,000		€ 19,229,588		€ 70,601,113,617
Bluenext EUA spot	1,089,440,000	€ 0.0170	€ 37,040,960	€ 13.12	€ 14,295,668,610
Bluenext CER spot	33,939,000	€ 0.0170	€ 1,153,926	€ 12.00	€ 407,268,000
Bluenext total	1,123,379,000	Total	€ 38,194,886	Total	€ 14,702,936,610
Total volume (tonnes)	5,074,029,000	Total	€ 57,424,474	Total volume (€)	€ 85,304,050,227
Per trading day	21,683,885	Per trading day	€ 245,404	Per trading day	€ 364,547,223

It isn't just an opportunity for traders, though. The companies running the exchanges that the trading takes place on also take a cut. This is another area that the think tank Open Europe has looked at in their research into the ETS. They have found that the two biggest exchanges, Climate Exchange (ECX) in London and Bluenext in Paris, have earned millions in transaction fees. Those two exchanges are responsible for 92 per cent of trades, around 21.7 million trades per trading day. That equates to a traded volume of around €85.3 (£76, $119) billion and transaction fees of €57 (£51, $79) million for the two exchanges in 2009.[70]

As that table shows, those two exchanges are making over €245,000 (£218,000, $341,000) per trading day.

It would be surprising if these trading platform fees are more than a tiny fraction of the earnings of those trading in the market. There is a lot of money in emissions trading for the City. Wall Street will make a fortune if cap and trade is passed in the US. Consumers pay the price.

Selling allowances when you have more than you need

Many companies have more allowances than they need for their own use. That can be because they are managing to operate more efficiently and cut their emissions. There is good reason to think that many firms have enjoyed a significant windfall not driven by improving efficiency though, but thanks to generous initial grants and a fall in demand following the recession.

Table 3.4: EUA surplus values, 2009 and 2010

Company	EUA surplus, 2009	EUA surplus value, 2009	Company	EUA surplus, 2010	EUA surplus value, 2010
ArcelorMittal	43,000,000	€565,369,000	ArcelorMittal	31,000,000	€444,540,000
Corus	13,000,000	€170,926,000	Corus	14,000,000	€200,760,000
ThyssenKrupp	11,000,000	€144,629,000	Lafarge	11,000,000	€157,740,000

....

70 Open Europe, 'EU environmental policy awards millions in windfall profits to oil companies and heavy industry', press release, 14 December 2009

The Carbon Market Data service has recorded the three companies with the biggest surpluses of allowances in 2009 and 2010.[71] Table 3.4 shows the size of those companies' surpluses and the value at the average closing prices in 2009 and 2010, at around €13.15 and €14.34. Incredibly, ArcelorMittal enjoyed a surplus worth more than a billion euros in just those two years.

Apart from Lafarge, all of those firms are major steel producers. Their massive surpluses are the result of steel production falling sharply in the recession. In 2009 EU27 crude steel production was down 30 per cent on 2008, from 197,965 to 138,779 thousand metric tonnes.[72] These three firms, and plenty of others, have enjoyed a substantial windfall profit, not because they are operating more efficiently but because they have cut production (and jobs) in the recession. The price is ultimately paid by ordinary consumers in higher energy bills.

The sharp fall in steel production put a lot of people out of work. The closure of just one plant, the 150-year-old Corus factory in Teeside, led to the loss of 1,700 jobs.[73] It is incredible that government policies reward that kind of decision. The ETS may not be the main culprit for those job losses: a fall in demand led to similar reductions in production in the United States though production in China continued to rise.[74] But it is hard to imagine that global groups like ArcelorMittal or Tata Steel – who own Corus – don't, or won't, factor the rewards available from the ETS for cutting production into decisions about where to scale production back and where to increase it as demand recovers.

71 Carbon Market Data, 'Carbon Market Data publishes the EU ETS Company Rankings 2009', press release, 10 June 2010, p.2; Carbon Market Data, 'Carbon Market Data publishes the EU ETS Company Rankings 2010', press release, 16 May 2011, p.3

72 World Steel Association, *Steel Statistical Yearbook 2010*, July 2010

73 BBC News, '1,700 jobs to go as Corus mothballs plant', 4 December 2009

74 World Steel Association, *Steel Statistical Yearbook 2010*, July 2010

Government job creation schemes have a history of failing but at least they are paying to create jobs. The perverse logic of a ration on carbon dioxide emissions is that our money is used to pay off companies that cut production, and thereby cut jobs. And that is just one way in which climate change policies can put people out of work.

Charging consumers for emission allowances you were given for free

But it isn't just traders, exchanges and companies selling their allowances who can make money under the ETS. The companies that make the most money are those that are given allowances for free, but then charge their customers for having to keep them.

The idea that companies are given allowances for free and then charge their customers for them anyway (even, or particularly, in a competitive market) is a bit counterintuitive. A lot of people look at the windfall profits that energy companies, in particular, are making that way and conclude that the companies must be misbehaving, that they have rigged the market.

But it is widely accepted in the academic literature on the ETS that in a competitive market carbon costs will be passed on to consumers; even that in more competitive markets, more of the carbon cost will be passed on.

Allowances are given to the firms for free but they are scarce and have a value, as can be seen from the price in the carbon market. In 2010 that price was mostly between €13 and €15 a tonne of CO_2.

That means that, whether firms are buying the allowances in the market or using those they have been freely allocated, the need to hold them pushes up the cost of production relative to not producing and selling the allowance or not buying it in the first place. The need to hold allowances adds an opportunity cost to activities that produce greenhouse gas emissions.

Increasing the opportunity costs of production increases the price firms charge consumers. All firms need to hold emission allowances and, therefore, face the same costs and cannot undercut their rivals.

Another description of the process has been provided by Manuel Frondel, Christoph M. Schmidt and Colin Vance. I don't want to labour this point too much but it is counterintuitive and critical to really understanding how the ETS operates and when consumers will bear the carbon cost in a cap and trade scheme:[75]

Electricity markets follow the same economic laws as other markets, but with some important particularities. Two key properties of electricity are that, first, it cannot be stored at low cost in large quantities and, second, its demand is highly price-inelastic in the short term, but subject to substantial temporal fluctuations. These properties imply a high degree of volatility of electricity prices. In the public debate, these substantial fluctuations are frequently misinterpreted as a sign of lacking competition among electricity producers. In a similar vein, public scepticism was also aroused by the ETS induced increase in electricity prices following the largely cost-free allocation of CO_2 emission allowances.

Both phenomena, however, cannot be taken as indicators for the presence of market power. Rather, the electricity-price-raising impact of certificates would also arise under perfect and imperfect competition alike. Regardless of whether certificates are distributed at no cost or have to be purchased, they have a value that can be observed on a daily basis at exchanges such as the Leipzig Power Exchange. Because of the possibility to sell certificates and obtain a profit, a rational electricity supplier will only produce a megawatt hour (MWh) of electricity if the profit from electricity generation is at least as high as

---

75 Frondel, M., Schmidt, C. M. & Vance, C., 'Emissions Trading: Impact on Electricity Prices and Energy-Intensive Industries', *Ruhr Economic Papers* #81, 2008, p.5

the revenue that would be garnered from selling the otherwise required certificates at the market. The electricity price that a rational supplier therefore demands should cover production and opportunity costs, where in this case the opportunity cost originates from the certificates' value.

It bears noting that taking account of opportunity cost is not specific for the analysis of electricity prices. Rather, the concept of opportunity costs is deeply rooted in economic reasoning, and is applicable in many contexts.

Although opportunity costs are not incurred in the same sense as the actual costs associated with inputs to electricity production, such as natural gas, this kind of cost is nevertheless equally price-relevant. Irrespective of whether an emission allowance has been obtained via grandfathering or through an auction, the electricity producer always has the option of selling it at the exchange, rather than actually using it in the production process. That electricity prices need to reflect this option is independent of whether individual suppliers can exercise market power and of the allocation mechanism in place, be this grandfathering, auctioning or some mixture of the two. Thus, the suggestions by politicians, consumers and also cartel offices that electricity producers not include the value of grandfathered certificates in electricity prices is fundamentally at odds with free-market principles. Were the electricity sector forced to do so, rational electricity producers would certainly reduce production, thereby driving up electricity prices to the point that the sale of certificates would become the unattractive alternative relative to production. As a result, market laws ensure the inclusion of the certificates' value in the electricity price even in the presence of command and control measures.

What that means is that politicians have created a system that pretty much guarantees windfall profits to companies that are given allowances for free and then charge their customers for having to hold them. That isn't true for lots of manufacturing companies, who aren't able to pass the costs on as that would price them out of the market relative to competitors outside the ETS. But energy companies, in particular, do not have competition from outside the ETS. Few countries are able to import significant amounts of energy not just from outside their own borders but beyond the EU entirely.

There have been a number of attempts to estimate the size of the windfall profits that firms are making under the ETS. The study of the cost of the ETS mentioned in the Appendix, by Point Carbon for the WWF, estimated total windfall profits in five countries – Germany, the UK, Italy, Poland and Spain – over the period 2008–2012 at between €23 (£17, $31) billion and €71 (£53, $95) billion.[76]

Microsoft's net income in the fiscal year ending June 2010 was $18.8 (£12.1) billion. That is the same order of magnitude as the top end of Point Carbon's estimate of the windfall profits being made by electricity generators in those European countries. In other words, being given allowances for free and then charging your customers for them under the EU ETS has been an opportunity for profit on the same kind of scale as being the supplier of operating systems and office software for most of the world's computers.

One of the major targets for the corporate lobbying that is covered later in this book is securing free allocations of allowances. Politicians are torn between the possibility of getting hold of the revenue to fund their spending by auctioning the permits – the topic of the next section – and using them to buy the support of various industries. Energy companies have made most of the money so far but others are keen to get in on the act.

The American bills are particularly awful examples of how the free allocations can be used to buy political support by giving special interests the ability to fleece consumers. They carve up the allowances between favoured causes in an absolutely shameless way. Favoured industries, from electricity

---

76 Point Carbon Advisory Services, 'EU ETS Phase II – The potential and scale of windfall profits in the power sector', a report for WWF, March 2008, p.22

generators to research into low emission cars, specific industrial energy efficiency schemes to various transport projects,
all get billions of dollars' worth of free allocations. They all get
a piece of the pie, the $765 (£432) billion in revenue that the
CBO expect Kerry's American Power Act to produce over its
first decade in operation.[77]

The insistence that free allocations are a measure to
protect consumers is incredibly disingenuous – the cost will
be passed on regardless – and conceals a massive, venal
attempt to buy political support. Cap and trade around the
world has been built on support from industries making
handsome profits out of the schemes, not support from the
consumers who pay the price.

The first and biggest international tax

Governments have an answer to the problem of windfall
profits, but sure enough it isn't going to cut the burden on
families. They want to stop giving away the permits and start
selling them to companies through an auction. That won't
do anything to reduce the burden on consumers – in some
countries and industries it is likely to increase the share of
the carbon cost passed on to them. But it will mean that the
windfall goes to governments rather than companies, so you
can see why politicians like the idea.

The European Union hopes to increasingly auction allowances in the ETS. Auctioning will be the 'rule rather than the
exception' from 2013.[78] Most plans for new cap and trade
schemes also say that at least a significant portion of the
permits will be auctioned. The American Power Act contains

---

77 Congressional Budget Office, Letter to Honorable John F. Kerry, CBO estimate of the budgetary impact of the May 12, 2010, discussion draft of the
American Power Act, including subsequent corrections and changes to that
draft, 7 July 2010

78 European Commission, 'Climate Action: Auctioning', 18 November 2010,
http://ec.europa.eu/clima/policies/ets/auctioning_en.htm

a provision for allowances to increasingly be auctioned. Table 3.5 shows the schedule in the discussion draft.[79]

Table 3.5: Percentage of allowances auctioned under American Power Act

Vintage year	Percentage of allowances
2026	8.1
2027	21.5
2028	33.7
2029	47.1
2030	54.5
2031	54.5
2032	54.5
2033	54.5
2034	54.5
2035 and each calendar year thereafter	77.8

In theory, the proceeds will go to a 'Universal Trust Fund' and be used partly to reduce the public sector deficit and partly to provide a refund to taxpayers. There are two problems with that though, from a taxpayers' point of view. First, it is hard to see how the portion purportedly going to reduce the deficit is anything but an old-fashioned tax hike: more money going from electricity consumers to finance public spending. And the whole Universal Trust Fund provision doesn't kick in for the best part of two decades. By the time it is responsible for the majority of allowances, Kerry himself will be nearly ninety. There is no reason to think that a new generation of legislators in the 2030s won't start finding new causes they want to use the huge revenues of the cap and trade scheme to support.

In order to line up the supporters he needs and deliver the legislation now, Kerry has felt the need to give favours to a huge range of interest groups. Do we really think those interest groups won't fight their corner in just the same way in the future and continue to extract special treatment? And

79 Discussion draft, American Power Act, 'Part G – Disposition of allowances, Sec. 781 Allocation of emission allowances'

that others won't try to get in on the act and get some free allocations themselves?

If I was an American taxpayer, I wouldn't be spending too much time working out how I'm going to spend my Universal Trust Fund cheque, even if a bill like the American Power Act was passed.

Still, at least in theory, cap and trade is going to stop being a transfer to companies from their customers and start to become more like an old-fashioned tax. But remember that there are also provisions in the legislation to link the EU ETS and US cap and trade into a single transatlantic cap and trade scheme.

If cap and trade legislation hadn't stalled in the US Senate, then we would have had the first international tax beyond the borders of the EU. Politicians are trying to impose a coordinated levy on the bankers, but if the popular outrage at the passage of Waxman-Markey in the House hadn't stalled cap and trade in the Senate, the first targets for global taxation would have been ordinary families, through their electricity bills.

That stream of revenue represents a big opportunity for supranational government. The European Commission certainly sees the Emissions Trading System as a suitable source of revenue to free it from dependence on funding from national governments. A European Commission report uncovered by the *Daily Express* newspaper has argued that they need a tax that is 'closely linked to a fully developed key European policy' and one that is 'cross-border in nature and based on a system covering the whole territory of the Union'. They think a 'resource based on the auctioning of greenhouse gas emission allowances would fully respect' those principles.[80] In other words, they like the idea of a tax grounded in EU policy financing its institutions instead of money from member states that might not be generous enough to pay for their grand ambitions.

A wider, global tax including the United States would mean

---

80 Available here, p.29: http://followthemoney.eu/docs/budget-leak.pdf

a potential stream of revenue for global government. While national governments might guard the revenue jealously, there would be a huge pot of money from an international policy that those hoping to instate, to give just one example, major transfer payments from the developed to the developing world, could try to get hold of.

There have been a number of proposals for global taxes to finance perceived global goods. One that is a particular favourite of many radicals is the Tobin Tax – or Robin Hood tax as they like to call it these days – on financial transactions. While some governments have supported such a tax, they have rarely been those responsible for major financial centres and it has gone nowhere. The economics of a financial transaction tax are too obviously misguided. And the politics are difficult as it requires creating an entirely new tax from scratch. Patching together cap and trade schemes as they are established is a far more plausible proposition.

How much would auctioning permits for a cap and trade scheme covering the major economies of the developed world raise?

To work that out, we'll need to make a few assumptions about the scope of a new cap and trade scheme:

All the emissions are auctioned.

They achieve an auction value of just $15 per tonne. Most proponents of cap and trade would hope for a higher carbon price than that.

It covers about 4 Gt CO_2. Around a third of the nearly 12 Gt CO_2 that the developed world – for these purposes Europe, the US, Australia, New Zealand, Canada and Japan – emitted in 2008. It's somewhat less as a proportion of emissions in those countries than the share of UK emissions covered by the EU ETS now.

Even working on those very conservative assumptions, the value to governments of a developed world cap and trade scheme is $60 (£34) billion a year. If the carbon price rises and the scheme attains the kind of financial scale envisaged by the CBO for the United States, then the burden on consumers and the amount of revenue will also rise. Scale up the CBO's estimate of $120.9 (£68.2) billion a year in revenues in the US to the entire developed world in line with emissions and it suggests revenue of $265 (£150) billion in 2020.

Regardless of how you estimate it, a cap and trade scheme covering the entire developed world would generate a lot of revenue. Even the $60 billion dwarfs the current roughly $2 billion a year central UN budget, for example.[81] It could finance all sorts of ambitions to strengthen institutions like the United Nations and the G20 and global governance. Or national governments might keep hold of the money and it would simply be another tax hike. Regardless, the people who pay would be ordinary consumers facing higher prices, particularly through their electricity bills.

Fraud

Another difficulty facing a massive supranational regulation like cap and trade is that it interacts with other policies in ways that are difficult to predict. There are all sorts of unintended and unexpected consequences.

The combination of emissions trading and the Value Added Tax (VAT) has created huge opportunities for fraudsters in the EU, as the ETS has enabled carousel fraud on a vast scale.

The fraudsters take advantage of the way VAT works. Each company charges VAT on the goods it sells (its output) and pays it on the goods it buys (its input). It reclaims from the government the money that it pays in VAT, and therefore gives the government the net VAT it collects (output – input = value added).

Missing trader fraud is a pretty simple scam where a trader

81 General Assembly, 'Fifth Committee approves assessment scale for regular, peacekeeping budgets, texts on common system, pension fund, as it concludes session', Department of Public Information, GA/AB/3787, 22 December 2006

sells some goods, charges the customer for VAT and then runs off with the money instead of paying it to the Government. That is something that every country with a VAT has to police against.

The EU makes it much easier to carry that fraud on undetected. Fraudsters trade goods across borders in complicated chains between legitimate and phony businesses, and the firm that finally tries to claim money back from the Government may not be in on the scam at all. Here is a description from what is now Her Majesty's Revenue and Customs:[82]

VAT intra-community missing trader fraud (sometimes known as 'carousel' or 'acquisition' fraud) involves fraudsters obtaining VAT registration to acquire goods VAT-free from other EU Member States. They then sell on the goods at VAT-inclusive prices and disappear without paying over the VAT paid by their customers to the tax authorities.

This problem has been detected in many EU Member States. Most frauds of this type are currently concentrated on marketable goods with a high value and low transport costs, such as mobile phones and computer parts. Many known or suspected missing trader businesses are controlled by professional criminals.

The reason why the ETS has been such an opportunity for carousel fraudsters is that the fraud is much easier to carry out when it is possible to move around a valuable quantity of goods quickly and cheaply. As emission allowances can be moved at the click of a button, they are ideal.

At the same time, not all of the registries carefully checked people signing up to engage in emissions trading. The Danish registry seems to have been particularly lax: the *Daily Telegraph* have reported that 'hundreds of UK companies selling anything from hair loss treatments to electronics have mysteriously registered to buy and sell carbon permits

82 HM Customs and Excise, 'Measuring Indirect Tax Fraud', November 2001, p.2

in the Scandinavian nation [...] among them businesses with unreachable addresses and Hotmail, Gmail or Yahoo email accounts for company representatives'.[83] Many of those companies were apparently phony and used to carry out carousel fraud.

The European law enforcement agency Europol reported in December 2009:[84]

The European Union (EU) Emission Trading System (ETS) has been the victim of fraudulent traders in the past eighteen months. This resulted in losses of approximately 5 billion euros for several national tax revenues. It is estimated that in some countries, up to 90 per cent of the whole market volume was caused by fraudulent activities.

Five billion euros (£4.5, $7) is a huge amount of money to lose to criminals, and yet another heavy price to pay for cap and trade. Steps have been taken to stop emissions trading enabling carousel fraud, but the EUobserver in Brussels reported:[85]

One Europol official, Rafael Rondelez, who was involved with the investigation said that the 'missing trader' scam can happen to any good, particularly high-value items with high rates of taxation, such as carbon credits.

What makes the ETS such a beguiling enticement for criminals, he said, is that the item being traded – a carbon credit – is intangible.

'It makes it easier for fraudsters because it's an intangible good. Before, goods actually had to be transported from one member state to another. You had to prove that goods were really being transported. With this, it's just the click of a mouse.'

83 Mason, R., '"Carousel" frauds plague European carbon trading markets', *Daily Telegraph*, 30 December 2009

84 Europol, 'Carbon Credit fraud causes more than 5 billion euros damage for European Taxpayer', 9 December 2009

85 Phillips, L., 'EU emissions trading an "open door" for crime, Europol says', *EUobserver*, 10 December 2009

'It's an incredibly lucrative target for criminals,' he added, warning that there are other aspects of the ETS that are creaky.

'Beyond the missing trader scam, the ETS is attractive to fraudsters because in order to trade in EUAs [European Union Allowances] you have to register your company, but there are no strong regulations or checking principles as there is in banking to prevent such activities as money laundering.'

'You don't need to show identification, other documents, any sort of credibility,' he said.

Even if there were more stringent regulations, *'How can you control this, how can you check up on someone selling an intangible credit from Belgium to Denmark to Paris even with more rules?'* Mr Rondelez asked.

'It's an open door.'

The *Daily Telegraph* has reported three other more recent significant cases of fraud in the market.[86] In February 2010, there was another criminal attack on the system:

In another scandal to cause closures in some nations, online fraudsters targeted national registries through a 'phishing' scam in February 2010. The criminals first sent official-looking emails to market participants requesting their login details, which they then used to steal emission allowances and sell them on illegally.

In December 2010 one million allowances went missing thanks to a computer virus. In early 2011 the European Commission halted trading altogether across the EU after allowances worth up to £28 ($50) million were stolen, initially for a week but then extended, with registries gradually reopening as they established their secure credentials.

There are clearly a number of ways in which criminals can take advantage of cap and trade, even in countries without a VAT. Trying to ration carbon dioxide is such a major regulatory endeavour that there will always be the potential for

....

86 Mason, R., 'EU says half of countries trading carbon are poorly protected against fraud', *Daily Telegraph*, 21 January 2011

nasty surprises in the way that the new rules interact with other regulations.

And even if you trust your own politicians and regulators to keep the scheme honest, remember that they are planning to link the different cap and trade schemes into a single international system where failures in one jurisdiction can cause trouble for all the countries signed up. We almost certainly haven't seen the last of emissions trading fraud.

Volatility

As I mentioned at the beginning of this chapter, the purpose of an emissions trading scheme is to put a price on emissions. That way people only emit if it is really worth it, taking into account both the cash price they pay for fossil fuels and the wider cost to society from climate change. The idea is that businesses and households then invest to cut emissions and the size of their carbon bill.

But the scheme won't encourage investment efficiently if the price is too unstable. If the price lurches around too much it will put off investors who need reliable returns. As Oliver Tickell – a prominent environmentalist – put it: 'Wild fluctuations create a risk that deters some investors altogether and makes others demand a significant risk premium, pushing up the price of capital.'[87]

Unfortunately, the emissions price has rapidly fallen by a third or more a number of times since the ETS began in 2005.

In 2005 the price fell from €29 per tonne on 11 July to €18 per tonne on 22 July. It then slowly recovered to just under €30 again by 24 April 2006, before collapsing again to just over €14 by 28 April. It declined effectively to zero for the rest of Phase I, falling below €1 per tonne in February 2007 and then continuing to decline.[88] This complete collapse

----

87 Tickell, O., 'Carbon: a market we can't allow to fail', *The Guardian*, 29 January 2009

88 EEX Market Data

in the price has been attributed to many of the participating countries allocating an excessive number of allowances, with the United Kingdom a notable exception.

Figure 3.1: Emissions price, €/t CO$_2$, June 2005 to November 2007

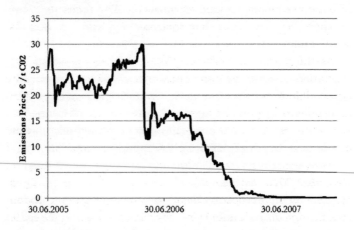

Figure 3.2: Emissions price, €/t CO$_2$, June 2008 to October 2009

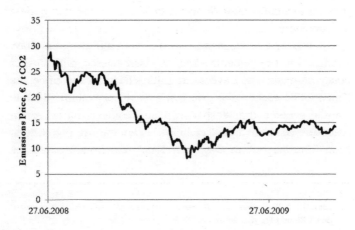

In 2008 the price fell from around €28 per tonne in July to around €15 in December. It declined further to just over €8 per tonne in February 2009. It has since recovered somewhat to a range between €13 and €15 per tonne. This two thirds fall in the price, and stabilisation at half the original price, is generally attributed to the fall in economic activity during the recession reducing demand for emission allowances.[89]

There are two principle reasons why the market is so unstable.

As the market is artificial, the product of a government regulation and not genuine consumer demand, it is highly susceptible to bursts of panic or euphoria at the prospect of governments stepping in to strengthen or weaken the scheme. When the failure of the negotiations at Copenhagen was announced, the price fell sharply. Bloomberg reported:[90]

European Union carbon-dioxide allowances for delivery in December 2010 declined 8.3 per cent to close at 12.45 euros ($17.82) on the European Climate Exchange in London. Today was the first day of trading since the summit concluded Dec. 19.

The agreed targets in the Copenhagen deal amount to a 'bunch of negotiation ranges' that investors had already factored in, Trevor Sikorski, an emissions analysts for Barclays Capital, said in a phone interview after returning to London from the Danish capital. 'It seems to be below even our modest expectations.'

All cap and trade schemes are vulnerable in this way. Even when the scheme itself isn't interfered with, other policy changes can have a dramatic effect on the price. As I mentioned earlier, the price under the US sulphur dioxide trading scheme that carbon cap and trade is modelled on has suffered a sustained collapse because other regulations have forced a cut in SO_2 emissions, reducing demand for

---

89 Ibid.

90 Carr, M. & Krukowska, E., 'Carbon Prices Tumble After Modest Climate Deal', Bloomberg, 21 December 2009

allowances. In the same way, other regulations designed to control CO_2 emissions could create a rapid fall in the ETS price. *Environmental Finance* reported in June 2011 that the Commission was pushing ahead with an efficiency directive that could dramatically depress carbon prices.[91] Companies making big bets on the future carbon price have to be very sure that the politicians are reliable.

But there is another, more fundamental, reason why the carbon price is so volatile. The supply of allowances is fixed, partly in order to try and limit political risk, but demand isn't. Demand for allowances is the product of how much companies are doing – whether they're producing electricity or steel – and the emissions intensity of that production – how much carbon dioxide they emit per megawatt hour of electricity or tonne of steel produced.

The rate at which companies cut their emissions intensity is unreliable. Firms can try to plan improvements but progress will always be a bit hit and miss. It will always be possible for major improvements in something like power plant design to come up that significantly reduce the cost of cutting emissions – reducing the value of allowances – or for an expected improvement to fail to live up to expectations – increasing the value of allowances.

Economic demand is even more unreliable. Governments rarely see recessions coming and with a fixed supply of allowances the price falls dramatically with demand. At the same time, the schemes may not properly allow for a recovery. In his book called – without a trace of irony – *Green Gold*, Tim Yeo MP argues:[92]

The ETS cap should now be tightened further to reflect the weakness of the European economy and the fall in emissions caused by the recession.

91 Nicholls, M., 'Fears grow over Commission's ability to support emissions trading', *Environmental Finance*, 30 June 2011

92 Yeo, T., *Green Gold*, Tory Reform Group, July 2010, p.52

It seems entirely possible that, having twice seen the carbon price crash, politicians and officials in Europe will follow Yeo's advice and adopt tighter caps just in time for an economic recovery, which will bring increased demand for allowances. That will cause a big spike in the carbon price, meaning huge pain for manufacturers and ordinary consumers, and political commitment to the ETS will really be tested. Volatility in the carbon price can go both ways and a rapid rise could be far more disruptive to the wider economy than the rapid falls we have seen so far.

Funnily enough, Paul Krugman, who I cited earlier as a supporter of these kinds of measures, has inadvertently produced a pretty good explanation of why the carbon price is inherently volatile. He wrote in the *New York Times* before the financial crisis about how a housing boom got started in those parts of the United States where it wasn't possible to build new houses:[93]

In Flatland, which occupies the middle of the country, it's easy to build houses. When the demand for houses rises, Flatland metropolitan areas, which don't really have traditional downtowns, just sprawl some more. As a result, housing prices are basically determined by the cost of construction. In Flatland, a housing bubble can't even get started.

But in the Zoned Zone, which lies along the coasts, a combination of high population density and land-use restrictions – hence 'zoned' – makes it hard to build new houses. So when people become willing to spend more on houses, say because of a fall in mortgage rates, some houses get built, but the prices of existing houses also go up.

The same thing happens in Britain: it is hard to build new houses so we get regular booms and crashes. In many markets it is relatively hard for supply to increase to sate new demand and in those markets prices tend to be relatively volatile. With cap and trade the supply is absolutely fixed,

---

93 Krugman, P., 'That Hissing Sound', *New York Times*, 8 August 2005

which means rises and falls in demand are entirely reflected in higher prices.

William Nordhaus has found that the volatility of prices in both the US SO_2 trading scheme and the EU ETS is similar to that of oil, where supply is also politically dictated and responds poorly to short term fluctuations in demand, and argued that 'high level of volatility is economically costly and provides inconsistent signals to private-sector decision makers'.[94] It is likely that oil and gas prices and the carbon price will often rise and fall together. An example of that happening can be seen in the recent recession, which led to declines in both prices. As gas prices and carbon prices both contribute to energy prices, the combined effect of the volatility in both markets will mean more pronounced swings in the bills facing businesses and households, and huge economic disruption.

Volatility in the carbon price is an unavoidable part of cap and trade. This doesn't just make emissions trading less efficient, by undermining the incentive for investors to put their money into reducing emissions, it also makes it harder for people to effectively manage their affairs as it makes their costs less predictable. More pronounced and frequent swings in the price of energy can be expensive and disruptive for manufacturing firms and mean sudden and unexpected hardship for families. That has to be understood as a significant, though difficult to quantify, additional cost of the ETS to consumers. The burden of the scheme is compounded by its unpredictability.

Rationing isn't a market solution, even if you can sell your ration book

Cap and trade has been a boon for plenty of special interests. Energy companies have enjoyed billions in windfall profits. International steelmakers have been paid hundreds of millions

94 Nordhaus, W., 'Economic Issues in a Designing a Global Agreement on Global Warming', Keynote address prepared for Climate Change: Global Risks, Challenges and Decisions, Copenhagen, Denmark, 10–12 March 2009, p.6

to cut production – and cut jobs. Some traders have probably enjoyed bumper profits, though some have undoubtedly also lost a fortune in the highly volatile carbon market, while the exchanges are making millions in fees. Even fraudsters have got away with billions by taking advantage of the ETS.

Hard pressed European consumers are financing all of that and dodgy schemes in developing countries, which we'll come on to in Chapter 8. Manufacturing industries are facing a new and unpredictable addition to their costs. Ordinary households are struggling to pay higher utility bills. That is the fate that politicians in other countries –the United States, Australia and Japan – have tried to line up for their citizens as well.

What the scheme is supposed to do, what we're supposed to get for our money, is put the right price on carbon dioxide emissions; ensure that everyone pays the wider price their emissions impose on society. All those trading fees and morally uncomfortable windfall profits are, at least, supposed to get politicians out of the business of deciding what that price should be, though they do then need to decide how much carbon dioxide the economy should be allowed to emit.

So the ultimate testament to the failure of the EU ETS is that the price has been so volatile that, as I mentioned earlier, British politicians are fixing it. For some time the energy company EDF Energy has been calling for a floor under the price, in other words a special tax to ensure that the price on carbon paid by energy firms never falls below a certain level.[95] I pointed out on a number of occasions, from private meetings to broadcast interviews and in reports, that those calls to fix the price were an indictment of the failure of the scheme. Defenders of cap and trade said that was just EDF Energy's lobbying, which was sure to be ignored by governments committed to the principle that the carbon market sets the carbon price. But now Britain's coalition government is introducing a floor with a target price of £30/t CO_2.

---

95   Reuters, 'EDF Energy calls for UK carbon floor price', 26 May 2009

That won't fix the problems with the scheme. The Institute for Public Policy Research has estimated it will mean 50–90,000 more households in fuel poverty by 2020 and won't even cut emissions because it is a unilateral policy, 'every ton of carbon that is priced out of the UK will be emitted elsewhere in Europe'.[96] The government might just be lining up a £350 ($620) million profit for canny EDF Energy,[97] who can pocket the money while changing their tune and are now saying that the floor price is 'just the first step' in getting the regulatory structure they need to make nuclear power work.[98] Credit Suisse has estimated that the new tax will add £7 ($11) billion to energy company profits overall.[99] So the floor price is far from a solution to the problems with the ETS, but it is a concrete admission that cap and trade itself just doesn't work efficiently.

It is a truly abysmal 'market solution' that requires price fixing after just half a decade in operation. If we don't trust the price produced by the carbon market then all of those traders and exchanges, all the windfall profits and all the administrative hassle associated with the scheme are a complete waste of money.

Cap and trade was intended to be an imitation of a US SO_2 trading scheme. In Europe we now have ample evidence that setting up a cap and trade scheme for CO_2 has been an expensive failure. In the United States the original SO_2 trading scheme, despite all the advantages it has over cap and trade for carbon, has lost a lot of its lustre. Putting in place new cap and trade schemes on a vastly more ambitious scale and linking them up into a new, global ration on energy would be utter folly.

....

96 Maxwell, D., 'Hot Air: the carbon price floor in the UK', IPPR, June 2011

97 Mason, R., 'Carbon windfall for EDF', *Daily Telegraph*, 7 August 2010

98 Mason, R. & Townsend, A., 'Britain is struggling to power the nuclear revolution', *Daily Telegraph*, 14 August 2010

99 McCabe, J., '£7bn windfall for UK utilities from carbon price floor', *Environmental Finance*, 28 June 2011

RENEWABLE ENERGY

In theory, if it works, cap and trade is pretty much all the climate change policy you need. It requires that emissions are cut to a given cap and produces the price necessary to get you there. You might need some accompanying green taxes to address sources of emissions that are too small for cap and trade to work, cars for example, but you shouldn't need more regulations on the sectors covered by cap and trade. So it is a bit odd that politicians who profess confidence in cap and trade also promote a range of other policies also designed to cut industrial emissions.

The biggest example is subsidies to renewable energy, which are enormously expensive but don't cut emissions at all. This is pretty well understood among those who work in the field, even dedicated green activists. *Der Spiegel* uncovered an email exchange between energy experts working for the German Green Party about that country's Renewable Energy Law (EEG) where one stated:[100]

'Dear Daniel, sorry, but the EEG won't do anything for the climate anyway.' Ever since the introduction of the emissions trading system, the Renewable Energy Law had become 'an instrument of structural change, but not an instrument to combat climate change'.

The basic issue is that every tonne of emissions that is avoided by using renewable energy just means one tonne less has to be cut elsewhere to fit under the cap in cap and trade. Renewable energy subsidies therefore don't cut

---

100 Waldermann, A., 'Climate Change Paradox: Wind Turbines in Europe Do Nothing for Emissions-Reduction Goals', *Der Spiegel*, 2 October 2009

emissions but just encourage cuts to be made in a particular way, and a particularly expensive way at that. *Guardian* columnist and environmentalist firebrand George Monbiot has also noted this problem with feed-in tariffs, one form of support for renewable energy targeted at things like solar panels and wind turbines on people's houses, though he resists applying the same logic to industrial renewable energy:[101]

Their total contribution to carbon savings, as a paper in the journal Energy Policy *points out, is zero. This is because Germany, like the UK, belongs to the European Emissions Trading Scheme. Any savings made by feed-in tariffs permit other industries to raise their emissions. Either the trading scheme works, in which case the tariffs are pointless, or it doesn't, in which case it needs to be overhauled. The government can't have it both ways.*

So in terms of addressing climate change, renewable energy subsidies are a spectacular waste of time. But they make a major contribution to the cost of climate change policy across the developed world. Even in those countries without cap and trade, renewable energy is a prohibitively expensive and inadequate alternative to conventional power.

Countries and states have set ambitious targets for the implementation of renewable energy and they are handing out eye-watering amounts of money in subsidies in order to try and meet those targets. The price is mostly paid by consumers in higher energy bills.

The final result is to shift our energy supply towards more expensive and less reliable sources. None of the renewable sources being rapidly expanded can reliably get us energy when we need it, where we need it. Having fossil fuel plants on hand to back the wind turbines and solar panels up is necessary, but adds even more to the cost of renewable energy and isn't particularly efficient in terms of emissions either.

....

101 Monbiot, G., 'Are we really going to let ourselves be duped into this solar panel rip-off?', *The Guardian*, 1 March 2010

Climate change policies, particularly renewable energy targets, are pushing us towards an energy 'affordability crisis'. That crisis could cause serious social problems and will bring a reckoning, sooner or later, for climate change policy everywhere, if we don't change course first.

Targets

There are targets for renewable energy production throughout Europe, the United States and Australia. Many of those targets are very ambitious and mature much sooner than the longer-term targets for cuts in greenhouse gas emissions by 2050, which means they have much more immediate implications for the economy, businesses and families.

European Union targets require sharp increases in the amount of power that countries get from renewable sources. Along with the main target for a reduction in EU greenhouse gas emissions to at least 20 per cent below 1990 levels by 2020, there is also a requirement for 20 per cent of EU energy consumption to be supplied from renewable sources by then.

Figure 4.1: Increase in use of renewables required as a share of total energy consumption, 2005–2020

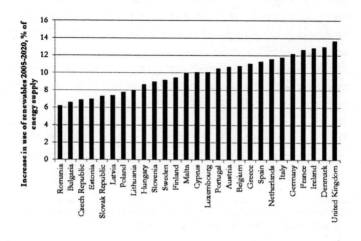

That means significant increases in many member states. Figure 4.1 shows the increase in the share of their total energy mix supplied from renewable sources required in each country, from 2005–2020.[102]

Table 4.1: US renewable portfolio standards

State	Amount	Year
Arizona	15%	2025
California	33%	2030
Colorado	20%	2020
Connecticut	23%	2020
District of Columbia	20%	2020
Delaware	20%	2019
Hawaii	20%	2020
Illinois	25%	2025
Massachusetts	15%	2020
Maryland	20%	2022
Maine	40%	2017
Michigan	10%	2015
Minnesota	25%	2025
Missouri	15%	2021
Montana	15%	2015
New Hampshire	24%	2025
New Jersey	23%	2021
New Mexico	20%	2020
Nevada	20%	2015
New York	24%	2013
North Carolina	13%	2021
Oregon	25%	2025
Pennsylvania	8%	2020
Rhode Island	16%	2019
Washington	15%	2020
Wisconsin	10%	2015

The United States also has renewable energy targets. The US Senate has sensibly junked a proposal for a federal renewable portfolio standard (RPS) in the past, but many states have

102 European Commission, 'Energy: Renewable Energy: Targets', 12 December 2009, http://ec.europa.eu/energy/renewables/targets_en.htm

put standards in place on their own. Twenty-six states have instituted an RPS with binding targets for increased use of renewable energy as a share of energy sales. Those states and their targets as of May 2009 are listed in Table 4.1.[103]

Another two states have set requirements for a certain absolute amount of capacity that should be in place. Those targets are less onerous than the portfolio standards for two reasons. Firstly, because they don't become more costly if the demand for energy rises and total energy supply rises in response. Maybe Texans and Iowans are preparing for more economic growth than Californians. Secondly, because if controls aren't in place, the targets can be achieved even if the plants don't produce anywhere near the amount of power that their capacity suggests. But meeting those targets may still impose significant costs. These are set out in Table 4.2.[104]

Table 4.2: US absolute renewable energy capacity requirements

State	Amount	Year
Iowa	105 MW	
Texas	5,880 MW	2015

Finally, five states have set voluntary goals for the adoption of renewable energy. Voluntary goals are less meaningful but could drive the development of more draconian policies. 'Voluntary' climate change policies are often how politicians make industry an offer they can't refuse, or allow businesses

103 US Department of Energy, 'Energy Efficiency & Renewable Energy: EERE State Activities and Partnerships: States with Renewable Portfolio Standards', http://apps1.eere.energy.gov/states/maps/renewable_portfolio_states.cfm
104 Ibid.

to get started and fight for position ahead of expected future binding targets. The targets are set out in Table 4.3.[105]

Table 4.3: US voluntary goals for adopting renewable energy

State	Amount	Year
North Dakota	10%	2015
South Dakota	10%	2015
Utah	20%	2025
Vermont	10%	2013
Virginia	12%	2022

Finally, Australia has implemented a Renewable Energy Target (RET) for renewable sources to provide 20 per cent of their electricity supply by 2020.[106] It is important to note that this is less stringent than the EU target, as electricity is just one part of energy use and relatively easy to supply from renewable sources, but it is broadly similar.

Meeting those targets won't come cheap. The International Energy Agency estimates that an additional $9.3 trillion in investment is needed, a 40 per cent increase above the baseline, to make the agency's plans, which include a major increase in the use of renewable energy by 2050, work out. Paying for that investment will be expensive. Estimates of the relative costs of different sources of energy have been produced by the US Energy Information Administration. Their results are shown in Figure 4.2.[107]

105 Ibid.

106 Department of Climate Change and Energy, 'Efficiency Renewable Energy Target', http://www.climatechange.gov.au/government/initiatives/renewable-target.aspx

107 Energy Information Administration, '2016 Levelized Cost of New Generation Resources from the Annual Energy Outlook 2010', December 2009

Figure 4.2: Total system levelised cost, 2016, $2008/MWh

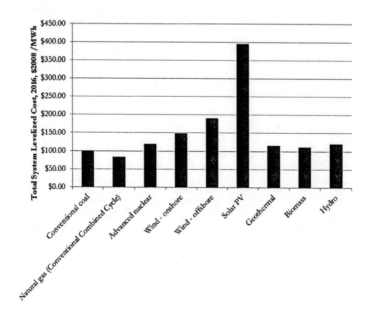

Onshore wind is about 50 per cent more expensive than conventional sources, offshore wind about twice as expensive and solar power is around four times as expensive.

In a paper for Global Vision and the TaxPayers' Alliance, leading British economist Ruth Lea looked at several estimates of the cost to Britain of meeting the EU's renewable targets.[108] A study by the energy consultancy Pöyry estimated that in 2020 the annual cost of meeting EU renewables targets would be around £150 ($270) to over £200 ($350) per household. Impact assessments by the Department for Business, Enterprise and Regulatory Reform (BERR) – a department that has since been taken apart but was responsible for the

108 Lea, R., 'The EU'S renewables policy: official cost estimates to Britain', Global Vision and the TaxPayers' Alliance, 11 December 2008

policies at the time – estimated that the average annual cost of meeting EU renewables targets could range from £55 ($100) to £120 ($210) per household for the twenty years up to 2030. The actual, overall cost of environmental targets in the energy sector could be far higher.

That means the politicians have had to work out regulations to get money into renewable energy, to require or encourage the investment needed. There are two principle ways they've done that. Mandating a market share for renewable energy and requiring energy companies to meet those targets or pay someone to do it for them. Or with more direct payments from themselves or the energy companies, often via feed-in tariffs that set out a certain guaranteed payment per kilowatt hour of energy produced. The first approach gives politicians more control over the rate at which the deployment of renewable energy takes place, the second gives investors more clarity over how much money they'll get.

Either way, renewable energy has been getting a lot of subsidy.

Mandates

In many states within the United States, in the United Kingdom, Italy and Australia, the government sets a market share for renewable energy and then requires energy companies to either produce that much power or pay those that do by buying certificates from them.

In the US that kind of policy is known as a renewable portfolio standard. It was summarised for a 2008 report by the Lawrence Berkeley National Laboratory:[109]

The design of an RPS can and does vary, but at its heart an RPS simply requires retail electricity suppliers (also called load-serving entities, or LSEs) to procure a certain minimum quantity

---

109 Wiser, R. & Barbose, G., 'Renewables Portfolio Standards in the United States: A Status Report with Data Through 2007', Lawrence Berkeley National Laboratory, April 2008, p.2

of eligible renewable energy. An RPS establishes numeric targets for renewable energy supply, applies those targets to retail electricity suppliers and seeks to encourage competition among renewable developers to meet the targets in a leastcost fashion. RPS purchase obligations generally increase over time, and retail suppliers typically must demonstrate compliance on an annual basis. Mandatory RPS policies are backed by various types of compliance enforcement mechanisms, and many – but not all – such policies include the trading of renewable energy certificates (RECs).

In the UK the terms are slightly different, but the basic mechanism is the same. This is how the energy regulator Ofgem describes the Renewables Obligation (RO):[110]

The RO is the main support scheme for renewable electricity projects in the UK. It places an obligation on UK suppliers of electricity to source an increasing proportion of their electricity from renewable sources.

A Renewables Obligation Certificate (ROC) is a green certificate issued to an accredited generator for eligible renewable electricity generated within the United Kingdom and supplied to customers within the United Kingdom by a licensed electricity supplier. One ROC is issued for each megawatt hour (MWh) of eligible renewable output generated.

[...]

Suppliers meet their obligations by presenting sufficient Renewables Obligation Certificates (ROCs). Where suppliers do not have sufficient ROCs to meet their obligations, they must pay an equivalent amount into a fund, the proceeds of which are paid back on a pro-rated basis to those suppliers that have presented ROCs. The Government intends that suppliers will be subject to a renewables obligation until 31 March 2037.

So the critical factor determining the generosity of subsidies to renewable energy generators is the value of the

---

110 Ofgem, 'Renewables Obligation', http://www.ofgem.gov.uk/Sustainability/ Environment/RenewablObl/Pages/RenewablObl.aspx

Renewable Energy Certificate (REC) or Renewables Obligation Certificate (ROC). For some context, the Energy Information Administration has estimated that US federal subsidies to natural gas and petroleum liquids are $0.25 per MWh, to coal they are $0.44 per MWh and to nuclear they are $1.59 per MWh.[111] The average wholesale market price of electricity on the NEPOOL Mass Hub in New England was just under $50 (£32, €36) in 2009.[112] So a subsidy of $50 or more means that renewable energy generators can roughly double their return on what they earn just selling their electricity on the open market.

As it is a single national policy, it is easiest to assess the value of the UK's Renewables Obligation. Onshore wind turbines, for example, can expect subsidies of more than £45 ($80) per MWh. Other technologies get even more generous treatment. Recently the Renewables Obligation was 'banded', which means some technologies, deemed to still be in the development stage, get more ROCs and therefore money. New offshore wind, in particular, gets two ROCs per MWh of electricity generated,[113] which means that it enjoys a staggering subsidy of over £90 ($160) per MWh.

The aggregate value, and cost to consumers, of the Renewables Obligation can be estimated by multiplying the size of the obligation by the buy-out price (a form of floor under the value of the obligation). Table 4.4 shows the value of the obligation in recent years and how it has grown rapidly to over £1.1 ($1.7) billion a year in 2009–10.[114]

---

111 Energy Information Administration, 'Federal Financial Interventions and Subsidies in Energy Markets 2007', 9 April 2008, Table 35. Subsidies and Support to Electricity Production: Alternative Measures

112 Energy Information Administration, 'Wholesale Day Ahead Prices at NEPOOL Mass Hub 2009', 10x Day Ahead Power Price Report/ICE Daily Indices, http://www.eia.doe.gov/cneaf/electricity/wholesale/wholesale.html

113 HM Treasury, 'Pre-Budget Report 2009: Securing the recovery: growth and opportunity', 9 December 2009, paragraph 7.18

114 Ofgem, 'Renewables Obligation – Interim Total Obligation Levels for 2007–08', 5 August 2008; Ofgem, 'Renewables Obligation - Total Obligation

Table 4.4: Renewables Obligation value

	2007-08	2008-09	2009-10
Size of the obligation, MWh	25,477,265	28,975,678	30,155,477
Buy-out price, £	£34.30	£35.76	£37.19
Value of the obligation, £	£873,870,190	£1,036,170,245	£1,121,482,190

The value of renewable energy certificates in the US varies considerably between different states. Figure 4.3, a rather confusing graph produced by the Lawrence Berkeley National Laboratories showing data from the company Evolution Markets, gives some idea of the kind of earnings per MWh possible.[115] The data is for the 'main tier' or 'class I', which basically means it should exclude well-established and relatively low-cost renewable sources like hydroelectric dams.

Figure 4.3: 'Main tier' or 'class I' REC price histories

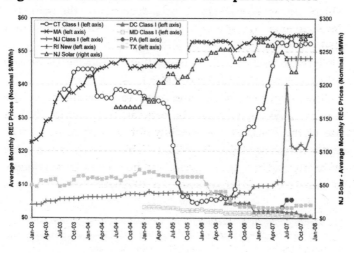

Levels for 2008–09', 18 August 2009; Ofgem, 'Renewables Obligation - Total Obligation Levels for 2009–10', 24 August 2010

115 Wiser, R. & Barbose, G., 'Renewables Portfolio Standards in the United States: A Status Report with Data Through 2007', Lawrence Berkeley National Laboratory, April 2008, Figure 14. REC Prices in RPS Compliance Markets (Main Tier and Class I)

There are three main groups shown in that graph: a number of states like Texas where subsidies are in the $0 to $10 (£6) range; others where the subsidies are in the $40 (£23) to $60 (£34) range; and finally New Jersey's subsidies for solar, which are remarkably high – requiring their own axis – at over $250 (£141) at the start of 2008.

Subsidies in the United States aren't as generous as they are in the UK, but renewable energy is getting very significant subsidies. In a number of states the subsidy is enough to double the return compared to the amount the generators could expect from selling the electricity on the market alone.

The state renewable energy mandates can impose serious economic costs. The Beacon Hill Institute, working with the John Locke Foundation, has produced estimates of the cost of the mandate in North Carolina. The legislation in North Carolina includes a cap that stops electricity companies passing on excessive costs to customers in order to satisfy the mandate. The Beacon Hill Institute study provides estimates of the costs with and without that cap, at almost $2 (over £1) billion:[116]

In the aggregate, the state's electricity consumers will pay $1.845 billion in cost recovery fees between 2008 and 2021, which will be added directly to their utility bills. In contrast, if the cost recovery caps were not in place, the REPS would cost North Carolinians $4.463 billion.

There are fresh proposals for a federal renewable energy standard, such as Senator Jeff Bingaman's proposed Renewable Electricity Promotion Act, which attracted dozens of co-sponsors. Energy companies would be required to source at least 11 per cent of their energy from renewable sources and up to 4 per cent from improving energy efficiency, for an overall standard of 15 per cent. In his 2011 state of the union address President Obama also took up that theme but

116 Tuerck, D. G., Head, M. & Bachman, P., 'The Economic Impact of North Carolina's Renewable Energy and Energy Efficiency Portfolio Standard', Beacon Hill Institute at Suffolk University, August 2009, p.2

included not just ordinary renewable sources, like wind and solar, but also nuclear power and natural gas. That means the US wouldn't enjoy the security and affordability of coal, but could be much less dramatic than outright renewable targets. Renewable Energy Focus USA reported in July 2011 that 'renewable energy advocates cheered during his state of the union address in January when he said that 80 per cent of US electricity should come from clean energy sources by 2035. But the cheers died down when he lumped traditional renewable alongside natural gas, nuclear and clean coal.' They reported Michael Wara, at the Program on Energy and Sustainable Development at Stanford University, saying, 'It's not clear that the CES will move the ball. If you include nuclear and gas, then that means we're already very nearly complying with the standard. When you factor in all the state RPS mandates, we already are. It's not clear that the standard represents additional ambition.'[117]

In Italy there is also a mandate for greater use of renewable energy. Green Certificates, Certificati Verdi, are awarded to generators for the first fifteen years of a plant's life.[118] At the time of writing they are worth around €80/MWh (£60, $110) for wind power,[119] but some sources get more certificates, such as offshore wind, which gets 10 per cent more. The subsidies are generous enough to have attracted the Mafia in Sicily, the *Sunday Telegraph* reported in September 2010:[120]

Attracted by the prospect of generous grants designed to boost the use of alternative energies, the so-called 'eco Mafia'

117 Carus, F., 'US Renewable Energy Industry on the Brink', *Renewable Energy Focus USA*, 1 July 2011

118 IEA, Global Renewable Energy: Policies and Measures, Finance Act 2008: Renewable energy provisions for the green certificates system, http://www.iea.org/textbase/pm/?mode=re&action=detail&id=4107

119 Gestore Mercati Energetici, http://www.mercatoelettrico.org/en/Esiti/CV/CV.aspx

120 Squires, N. & Meo, N., 'Mafia cash in on lucrative EU wind farm handouts – especially in Sicily', *Sunday Telegraph*, 5 September 2010

has begun fraudulently creaming off millions of euros from both the Italian government and the European Union.

And nowhere has the industry's reputation become more tarnished than Sicily, where windmills now dot the horizon in Mafia strongholds like Corleone, the town better known as the setting for the Godfather films.

'Nothing earns more than a wind farm,' said Edoardo Zanchini, an environmental campaigner who has investigated Mafia infiltration of the industry. 'Anything that creates wealth interests the Mafia.'

It isn't just Italy that has that problem, the same article reported:

Recent research by Kroll, the international corporate security firm, has discovered examples all over Europe of so-called 'clean energy' schemes being used to line criminals' pockets rather than save the planet. Some involve windmills that stand derelict or are simply never built, while others are used to launder profits from other crime enterprises.

'Renewable energy seems like a good thing, run by saintly people saving the world,' said Jason Wright, a senior director with Kroll, which performs background checks on renewable energy schemes on behalf of legitimate investors, and which has documented a sharp rise in the number of wind farms with suspect ownership.

In Australia the REC price hasn't stayed high like it has in many other countries. There have been persistent worries about it collapsing and not providing sufficient returns to justify new investment. In January 2011 the scheme was split in two, with large-scale generation certificates (LGCs) for actual renewable energy power stations and small-scale technology certificates (STCs) for smaller installations. That brings the Australians into line with practice in Europe, where smaller installations like solar panels and wind turbines on people's houses tend to enjoy much more generous and guaranteed support through the feed-in tariffs covered in the next section. In early March 2011 the LGC price was AUS$36 (£16,

$29) and the STC price was AUS$39 (£18, $32) (unless the Solar Credits multiplier applies).[121]

Figure 4.4: CBI 'balanced pathway' electricity generation projections

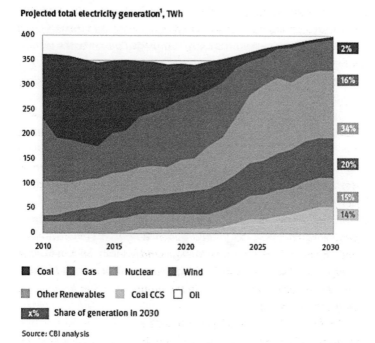

Projected total electricity generation[1], TWh

Coal | Gas | Nuclear | Wind

Other Renewables | Coal CCS | Oil

x% Share of generation in 2030

Source: CBI analysis

Mandates provide substantial subsidies to renewable energy generators. Establishing them entails choosing a certain set of technologies for special treatment. Many proponents of current climate change policies argue that they are trying to be technology-neutral, to establish a level playing field. But by setting out a certain set of technologies as 'renewable' and entitled to special treatment beyond the advantage they gain

121 Green Energy Markets, http://www.greenmarkets.com.au/

under a cap and trade regime, they start to decide not just that we should cut emissions, but how.

International organisations like the IEA, governments and lobby groups all set out their own plans for our energy supply, carving up demand by different sources instead of letting the market work. Figure 4.4, for example, shows a graph produced by the Confederation of British Industry showing their 'balanced pathway' plan for the UK's energy generation.[122]

With a bit of searching I could provide dozens more similar graphs, all with different shares allocated to nuclear, renewables, coal with CCS and gas. Many also include specific targets for energy efficiency savings. Such graphs are part of the political process that produces a mandate, setting out what share renewables must take in a country or state's energy supply by a certain date. Energy supply is, as we discussed earlier, absolutely fundamental to modern industrial economies. Trying to control it with long-term planning to the extent that mandates do is an exercise in enormous hubris. The plans could so easily be undone by demand savings not matching the expectations of the planners, or the relative costs of different technologies not turning out as expected. They will lead to a misallocation of resources on a vast scale if their choices are simply wrong.

And valuable mandates and obligations are just part of the subsidy provided to renewable energy.

Other subsidies

While there hasn't been a federal renewable portfolio standard, the federal government in the US does provide considerable support for renewable energy. The Energy Information Administration looked at the levels of support provided by the

---

122 Confederation of British Industry, 'Decision time: Driving the UK towards a sustainable energy future', July 2009, Exhibit 8. The 'balanced pathway' – generation

federal government to different sources of electricity in 2007 and their findings are shown in Table 4.5.[123]

Table 4.5: US electricity generation subsidy and support by fuel

Fuel/End Use	FY 2007 Net Generation (billion kilowatt hours)	Subsidy and Support Value 2007 (million dollars)	Subsidy and Support Per unit of Production (dollars/megawatt hours)
Coal	1946	854	0.44
Refined Coal	72	2156	29.81
Natural Gas and Petroleum Liquids	919	227	0.25
Nuclear	794	1267	1.59
Biomass (and Biofuels)	40	36	0.89
Geothermal	15	14	0.92
Hydroelectric	258	174	0.67
Solar	1	14	24.34
Wind	31	724	23.37
Landfill Gas	6	8	1.37
Municipal Solid Waste	9	1	0.13
Unallocated Renewables	NM	37	NM
Renewables (subtotal)	360	1008	2.8
Transmission and Distribution	NM	1235	NM
Total	4091	6747	1.65

Hydroelectric power – a well-established part of the energy mix but difficult to expand after the best sites have been used – doesn't require much support. But wind and solar – the big renewable energy sources that most plans really hope to expand – get massive subsidy. In addition to the support

....

123 Energy Information Administration, 'Federal Financial Interventions and Subsidies in Energy Markets 2007', [DATE], Table 35. Subsidies and Support to Electricity Production: Alternative Measures

available under state portfolio standards, they were getting around $25 (£12, €18) per tonne in support from the federal government in 2007. They have had considerably more since as part of the stimulus package.

These figures show how misleading headlines like the one produced by Bloomberg New Energy Finance, who claimed in July 2010 that renewables received just $43 (£27) to $46 (£29) billion in subsidy in 2009, against $557 (£300) billion spent subsidising fossil fuels in 2008.[124] Those figures are obtained in two ways. They cite a global figure when the lion's share of subsidies for fossil fuels is in the developing world – Iran's huge subsidy to keep the cost of petrol down doesn't compete with European or American subsidies for renewable energy.

They also don't adjust for the different contributions that the sources of power make to supply the energy we need. While some of the companies involved do quite well out of fossil fuel subsidies, the fuels are competitive without them. By contrast, renewable energy can only be sustained as part of our energy mix with spectacular amounts of subsidy, as Table 4.5 and the last section show very clearly.

Most countries spend more on national defence than they do on subsidising the ballet; without adjusting for what is produced in return those comparisons are meaningless. Once you adjust for the amount of electricity that the different sources produce, it becomes very clear that renewable energy is a massive subsidy junkie whereas fossil fuels broadly stand on their own two feet.

Things get even more extreme when you look at the feed-in tariffs that exist in a number of European countries and the support they provide to small-scale renewables. It is important to note that these payments normally replace, rather than add to, the earnings a plant can make from selling

124 Feinberg, S., 'Subsidies for renewables, biofuels dwarfed by supports for fossil fuels', Bloomberg New Energy Finance, 29 July 2010

electricity on the market. They are often still incredibly generous guaranteed prices.

Germany's feed-in tariff is the model for many such
schemes, while the structure of the scheme and the rates on
offer have changed the basic structure has been in place for
a decade. The different rates are somewhat complicated, but
here are a few important sections. First, onshore wind:[125]

Section 29

Wind energy

*(1) The tariff paid for electricity from wind-powered installa-
tions shall amount to 5.02 cents per kilowatt-hour (basic tariff).*

*(2) In derogation of subsection (1) above, the tariff paid in
the first five years after the installation is commissioned shall
amount to 9.2 cent per kilowatt-hour (initial tariff). This period
shall be extended by two months for each 0.75 per cent of the
reference yield by which the yield of the installation falls short
of 150 per cent of the reference yield. The reference yield is the
calculated yield for the reference installation pursuant to Annex
5 to this Act. The initial tariff shall increase for electricity from
wind-powered installations commissioned prior to 1 January
2014 by 0.5 cents per kilowatt-hour (system services bonus)
if it demonstrably fulfils the requirements of the Ordinance in
accordance with section 64(1) first sentence no. 1 from the date
of commissioning.*

The basic payment for onshore wind isn't that high, at
around €50 (£38, $67) per MWh. But in the early years, and
longer for some installations, the tariff pays more than €90
(£68, $121) per MWh.

There are also generous payments for offshore wind:[126]

Section 31

Wind energy – offshore

----

125 'Act Revising the Legislation on Renewable Energy Sources in the Electricity
Sector and Amending Related Provisions', which revises 'Act on granting
priority to renewable energy sources' (Renewable Energy Sources Act,
EEG), Section 29

126 Ibid., Section 31

(1) The tariff paid for electricity from offshore installations shall amount to 3.5 cents per kilowatt-hour (basic tariff).

(2) During the first twelve years after the commissioning of the installation the tariff shall amount to 13.0 cents per kilowatt-hour (initial tariff). For electricity from installations commissioned prior to 1 January 2016, the initial tariff paid in accordance with the first sentence above shall increase by 2.0 cents per kilowatt-hour. The period in accordance with the first and second sentences above in which the initial tariff is paid shall be extended in the case of electricity from installations located at least twelve nautical miles seawards and in a water depth of at least 20 metres by 0.5 months for each full nautical mile beyond 12 nautical miles and by 1.7 months for each additional full metre of water depth.

Again, the basic payment isn't that high, at €35 (£26, $47) per MWh. But for twelve years the subsidy is €130 (£98, $174) per MWh and that period is extended for plants further from shore or in deeper water. The most generous treatment goes to solar, though:[127]

Section 33

Solar radiation – installations attached to or on top of buildings

(1) The tariff paid for electricity from installations generating electricity from solar radiation which are exclusively attached to or on top of a building or noise protection wall shall amount to

1. 43.01 cents per kilowatt-hour for the first 30 kilowatts of output,

2. 40.91 cents per kilowatt-hour for output between 30 and 100 kilowatts,

3. 39.58 cents per kilowatt-hour for output between 100 kilowatts and 1 megawatt, and

4. 33.0 cents per kilowatt-hour for output over 1 megawatt.

(2) The tariffs shall be reduced to 25.01 cents per kilowatt-hour for electricity from installations in accordance with

127 Ibid., Section 33

subsection (1) no. 1 above with a maximum capacity of 30 kilo-watts where the installation operator or a third party is using the electricity himself in the immediate vicinity of the installation and can furnish proof of that fact.

(3) Buildings shall mean roofed building structures which can be independently used and entered by humans and are primarily designed for the purpose of protecting humans, animals or objects.

So solar panels get a guaranteed price of at least €330 (£249, $442) per MWh.

All of these generous subsidies mean economic trouble. Manuel Frondel, Nolan Ritter, Christoph M. Schmidt and Colin Vance wrote a Ruhr Economic Paper in November 2009 which looked at the record of Germany's feed-in tariff. They estimated that the cumulative, lifetime net cost of the solar PV that is likely to be installed by the end of 2010 would be over €53 (£40, $71) billion at 2007 prices. Wind power would add another €11 (£8, $15) billion to that burden even if operators switch off the feed-in tariff after five years, as market prices may then be higher.[128] Their overall verdict is damning:

We argue that German renewable energy policy, and in particular the adopted feed-in tariff scheme, has failed to harness the market incentives needed to ensure a viable and cost-effective introduction of renewable energies into the country's energy portfolio. To the contrary, the government's support mechanisms have in many respects subverted these incentives, resulting in massive expenditures that show little long-term promise for stimulating the economy, protecting the environment, or increasing energy security.

Britain recently introduced its own feed-in tariff, complementing the Renewables Obligation by focusing on smaller installations. Table 4.6 shows how much electricity companies

128 Frondel, M., Ritter, N., Schmidt, C. M. & Vance, C., 'Economic Impacts from the Promotion of Renewable Energy Technologies: The German Experience', *Ruhr Economic Papers* #156, November 2009

will have to pay to people who install the technologies in the first three years and for how long.[129]

Table 4.6: UK feed-in tariff

Technology	Scale	Tariff for new installations in... (£/MWh)			Tariff lifetime (years)
		2010-11	2011-12	2012-13	
Anaerobic digestion	<= 500 kW	115	115	115	20
Anaerobic digestion	> 500 kW	90	90	90	20
Hydro	<=15 kW	199	199	199	20
Hydro	>15-100 kW	178	178	178	20
Hydro	>100kw - 2MW	110	110	110	20
Hydro	>2MW - 5MW	45	45	45	20
MicroCHP pilot	<2 kW	100	100	100	10
Solar PV	<= 4kW (new build)	361	361	330	25
Solar PV	<= 4kW (retrofit)	413	413	378	25
Solar PV	>4-10 kW	361	361	330	25
Solar PV	>10-100 kW	314	314	287	25
Solar PV	>100kW - 5MW	293	293	268	25
Solar PV	Stand alone system	293	293	268	25
Wind	<=1.5kW	345	345	326	20
Wind	>1.5-15kW	267	267	255	20
Wind	>15-100kW	241	241	230	20
Wind	>100-500kW	188	188	188	20
Wind	>500-1.5MW	94	94	94	20
Wind	>1.5MW-5MW	45	45	45	20
Existing microgenerators transferred from the RO		90	90	90	to 2027

Data released by the regulator shows 58 per cent of the total installed capacity is retrofitted solar photovoltaics under 4kW, i.e. people putting little solar panels on their roof.[130] That means it will be getting a staggering £413 ($732) /MWh for twenty-five years.

---

129 Department of Energy and Climate Change, Table of tariffs up to 2013, available from: http://www.decc.gov.uk/en/content/cms/what_we_do/uk_supply/energy_mix/renewable/feedin_tariff/feedin_tariff.aspx
130 Ofgem, 'Feed-in Tariff Installation Report Dec 2010', 5 January 2011

The policy repeats all of the mistakes of the German feed-in tariffs. George Monbiot, an environmentalist radical enough to favour airships replacing planes for long distance travel, and a supporter of larger scale renewable energy, argues these policies are a massive rip-off:[131]

The government is about to shift £8.6bn from the poor to the middle classes. It expects a loss on this scheme of £8.2bn, or 95 per cent. Yet the media is silent. The opposition urges only that the scam should be expanded.

[...]

There appears to be a cross-party agreement to squander the public's money. Why? It's partly because many Tory and Lib Dem voters hate big, efficient windfarms, and this scheme appears to offer an alternative. But it's mostly because solar panels accord with the aspirations of the middle classes. The solar panel is the ideal modern status symbol, which signifies both wealth and moral superiority, even if it's perfectly useless.

If people want to waste their money, let them. But you and I shouldn't be paying for it. Seldom has there been a bigger public rip-off; seldom has less fuss been made about it. Will we try to stop this scheme, or are we a nation of dupes?

Italy does the same, with a special feed-in tariff as an alternative to the Green Certificates awarded to industrial renewable energy and only available to small plants with a capacity under 1 MW. Plants get the feed-in tariff for fifteen years, just like the Green Certificates. Table 4.7 shows the latest rates for its feed-in tariffs reported by the International Energy Agency. [132]

....

131 Monbiot, G., 'Are we really going to let ourselves be duped into this solar panel rip-off?', *The Guardian*, 1 March 2010

132 IEA, 'Global Renewable Energy: Policies and Measures', Finance Act 2008: Renewable energy provisions for 'all inclusive' feed-in tariff for small renewable plants, http://www.iea.org/textbase/pm/?mode=re&id=4469&action=detail

Table 4.7: Italian feed-in tariff

Source	Feed-in tariff, € /MWh
Geothermal	200
Tidal and wave	340
Hydroelectric	220
Biomass	280
Biogas	180
Wind	300

There is a separate scheme for solar plants, which get a twenty-five year guarantee of a €220 to €280 (£166, $295) / MWh subsidy on top of the electricity price.[133]

In Australia, between January 2000 and June 2009, households and owners of community-use buildings that installed solar panels could get rebates. The Australia Institute released a report on the programme in November 2010, this is their summary:[134]

The Australian government ran a renewable energy program in the 2000s that provided rebates to householders who acquired solar photovoltaic (PV) energy systems. Originally called the Photovoltaic Rebate Program (PVRP), it was rebranded the Solar Homes and Communities Program (SHCP) in November 2007. This paper evaluates both the PVRP and SHCP using measures of effectiveness and fairness. It finds that the program was a major driver of a more than

133 IEA, 'Global Renewable Energy: Policies and Measures', Feed-in tariff for solar thermodynamic energy, http://www.iea.org/textbase/pm/?mode=re&id=4106&action=detail

134 Macintosh, A. & Wilkinson, D., 'The Australian Government's solar PV rebate program', The Australia Institute, Policy Brief No. 21, November 2010

six-fold increase in PV generation capacity in the 2000s; however, the increase was off a low base and, in 2010, solar PV's share of the Australian electricity market was still only around 0.1 per cent. The data suggest there were equity issues associated with the program, with 66 per cent of all successful applicants residing in postal areas that were rated as medium-high and high on a socio-economic status (SES) scale. The program was also environmentally ineffective and costly. It will reduce emissions by 0.09 $MtCO_2$-e/yr over the life of the rebated PV systems (0.015 per cent of Australia's 2008 emissions) at an average social abatement cost of between \$257/tCO_2-e and \$301/tCO_2e. Finally, the program appears to have had a relatively minor impact as an industry assistance measure, with much of the associated benefit flowing to foreign manufacturers and most of the domestic benefit being focused outside of the high value added manufacturing areas.

In the face of 'a substantial blowout in costs' the Australian government terminated the programme on 9 June 2009.[135]

Traditionally, when governments have interfered and favoured one technology over another, they have been accused of 'picking winners'. They have tried to work out the most efficient way of satisfying a particular consumer demand or solving a particular thorny technical challenge. What is interesting about the approach with renewable energy is that they are doing the opposite, picking losers.

In a number of areas, the least competitive technologies get the biggest subsidies. It isn't just that low carbon sources of power get more money than fossil fuels; the most expensive low carbon sources get the most money. This is true in the banding of the Renewables Obligation in the United Kingdom and the different rates accorded to different technologies under feed-in tariffs. In the UK onshore wind gets a subsidy of about £45 per MWh, while someone putting a solar panel on their roof can get more than £400 per MWh.

---

135 Ibid., p.2

The effect is to invert the relative costs of different technologies and encourage investment in the most expensive ways of satisfying our demand for electricity. It is almost calculated to maximise the cost to the ordinary consumers who get the bill. And it destroys the market incentives that should exist to make energy steadily more affordable.

The argument for this approach is that the most expensive technologies are developing, and costs will fall rapidly as they are installed on a greater scale. It hasn't worked out that way so far. The UK Energy Research Centre reported in September 2010 that:[136]

The UK's ambitions for offshore wind reflect the size of the potential resource and difficulties associated with public opposition to onshore wind. They also reflect a widespread expectation in the late 1990s and early 2000s that costs would fall as deployment expands. However, in the last five years costs have escalated dramatically, with capital costs doubling from approximately £1.5m/MW to over £3.0m/MW in 2009.

Offshore wind is expensive because building things at sea is expensive. There is certainly no sign at all of the tiny wind turbines that people put on their roofs becoming competitive with the industrial electricity generation.

What if we did expect a dramatic improvement in the relative efficiency of the sources of energy that are currently the most expensive? That hardly makes a good case for a country to pay a fortune to install them now, locking in high costs. If I told you that laptops were going to halve in price tomorrow, you wouldn't run right out to buy one today. If we want to support the development of new sources of energy, it is far cheaper to support research directly, instead of mandating their purchase, now.

---

136 Greenacre, P., Gross, R. & Heptonstall, P., 'Great Expectations: The cost of offshore wind in UK waters – understanding the past and projecting the future', UK Energy Research Centre, September 2010

The real motivation appears to be a poorly defined sense that every technology has to have its place in our energy supply. To a certain extent that is right, there are circumstances, particularly in small communities too remote to be easily connected to the grid, where micro generation might make sense. But some sources of energy are, in almost all circumstances, inherently expensive. There is no sense in picking losers.

Unreliability

Despite all the expensive subsidies, in the first quarter of 2010 the amount of power Britain got from renewable sources fell by 7.5 per cent compared to the same period in 2009. The problem is that the power comes when the wind blows or when the sun shines, not necessarily when it is really needed. In the UK, companies are sometimes even being paid to turn their turbines off, because when the wind does blow it often doesn't coincide with periods of high consumer demand.

One example of this unreliability comes from the Hebridean island of Eigg, off the north-west coast of Scotland. They have won overall winner prize at the Ashden Awards for Sustainable Energy (Britain's 'green Oscars' apparently) for their 'refreshing' combination of extensively deploying wind, solar and hydro energy and limiting energy consumption in order to get 90 per cent of their energy from renewable sources.[137] Eigg is one of those places small and remote enough that renewable energy actually makes relative sense. The alternative probably isn't a cheap connection to the national grid, conditions are good on a windy island and a small population without any major industry can make do when output dips. But in summer 2010 mild weather, a rare heat wave by Hebridean standards, cut power from wind and hydro sources and forced the islanders to drastically ration energy

---

137 BBC News, 'Eigg wins green award amid forced return to diesel', 1 July 2010

use and fall back on diesel generators.[138] It doesn't bode well for renewable energy's ability to reliably provide energy in less advantageous locations and for populations of more than a hundred people.

The canonical example of a country that has supposedly integrated a huge amount of wind power into its network is Denmark. But actually that country has piggybacked off the huge hydroelectric capacity in Sweden and Norway. It has imported power from them when the wind stops and sold power at a loss when the wind blows. A study by Paul-Frederik Bach for the Renewable Energy Foundation (REF) found that even across an area as large as Germany and Denmark, it has sometimes been necessary to almost do without wind power's contribution entirely:[139]

The total installed wind power capacity in Germany and Denmark in December 2007 is estimated to have been between 23 and 26 GW. The sum of the individual wind power peak productions in the six control areas in December 2007 was 21,042 MW. However, the simultaneous or average production peak was 18,028 MW, or 14 per cent lower than the sum of the peaks in the individual areas.

The recorded minimum simultaneous, aggregate, wind power production was 252 MW, or about 1 per cent of the installed capacity.

Sometimes, wind power will produce very little over entire days:[140]

Calm periods with low wind power output occur simultaneously in Denmark and Germany. The minimum average wind power output during twenty-four consecutive hours in 2009 was 0.23 per cent of the maximum hourly production for Denmark, and 1.61 per cent for Denmark and Germany together.

---

138 Fryer, J., 'Will this eco island sink the green dream?', *Daily Mail*, 1 July 2010

139 Bach, P. F., *The Variability of Wind Power: Collected Papers 2009-2010*, Renewable Energy Foundation, 2010, p.28

140 Ibid., p.2

Larger countries, not as well connected to countries with as reliable and responsive a source of energy as Scandinavian hydroelectric power, need to tread very carefully. Wind power requires expensive backup, normally from gas plants which can't run nearly as efficiently when they are turning on and off regularly to adjust for the output from wind turbines. That means more cost and – for many countries – greater reliance on gas power, which in Europe's case often means imports from a potentially unreliable Russia even if shale gas is eroding that dependence.

The irony of calls to invest in renewable energy in order to build energy security and independence is that unreliable renewables have often meant a greater vulnerability to spikes in the gas price. If those calling for energy security were serious, they would advocate doing the same thing countries like China have: use coal (or nuclear to a certain extent). Coal supplies are plentiful. But coal plants aren't good at stepping in quickly when wind turbines stop turning and they are a high carbon enemy of the greens.

The affordability crisis

Expensive subsidies for renewable energy, combined with other measures like cap and trade, add up to sharp rises in electricity prices. In Europe climate change policies are already responsible for a substantial portion of prices. Britain is a good case study, as the government have adopted climate change policies particularly enthusiastically. In June 2008 the official BERR estimates suggested that a substantial portion of British bills were the result of climate change policy:[141]

Our current climate change policies (e.g. the Renewables Obligation, EU Emissions Trading Scheme, and the Carbon Emission Reduction Target) make up around 14 per cent of average domestic electricity bills and 3 per cent of average domestic

---

141 Department for Business, Enterprise and Regulatory Reform, 'UK Renewable Energy Strategy: Consultation', June 2008, paragraph 10.5.3

gas bills. On the industrial side, for an average medium-sized consumer, the Renewables Obligation, EU ETS, and Climate Change Levy together contribute around 21 per cent to industrial electricity bills and about 4 per cent to gas bills.

But that's just the start. It is widely understood that Britain will have to invest well over £200 billion in the energy sector by 2020, mostly to meet environmental targets. In a September 2010 report, Citigroup Global Markets set out the rough scale of the investment needed. Their estimates are shown in Table 4.8.[142]

Table 4.8: Citigroup Global Markets estimated utility capex spend by country, 2010–2020, € billion

Country	Replacement/renewal	Environmental Targets	Total
UK	91	229	320
Germany	90	87	177
France	150	60	210
Spain	55	53	108
Italy	100	23	123
Totals	470	330	800

The Department of Energy and Climate Change (DECC), who are responsible for making this happen, are retreating into overly optimistic delusion about the likely cost of all that investment. In July 2010, they released a report claiming that, with the efficiency measures they are planning, the increase in household energy bills can be limited to 1 per cent by 2020.[143] By contrast, the Citigroup Global Markets report argued that:[144]

....

142 Atherton, P., *The €1trn Euro Decade – Revisited: Costs up, risks up, but governments are still in denial*, Citigroup Global Markets, 29 September 2010, Figure 4. Total Required Capex 2010–2020 (€bn Euros)

143 Department of Energy and Climate Change, 'Estimated impacts of energy and climate change policies on energy prices and bills', July 2010

144 Atherton, P., *The €1trn Euro Decade – Revisited: Costs up, risks up, but governments are still in denial*, Citigroup Global Markets, 29 September 2010, p.22

Taking [the] higher savings [from reduced need to buy fossil fuels] figure would give a net additional revenue requirement of £16.4bn. Given that total revenue to the UK electricity sector in 2009 was £31bn, of which £15bn (48 per cent) was raised from retail customers and £16bn (52 per cent) from industrial and commercial. In total therefore we estimate that the UK electricity sector would need total revenue in 2020 of £47bn. If the split between retail and I&C customers were the same as 2009 then retail customers would [be] paying around £330 per household additional costs (2010 prices). This would represent a 52 per cent real terms increase in domestic electricity bills over their June 2010 level of £500 as calculated by Ofgem. This would take the dual fuel bill from today's £1,120 to £1,604 per annum.

Even with substantial improvements in efficiency, there will still be a big addition to bills:[145]

If gas demand can be reduced by 15 per cent that should save around £93pa for the average dual fuel customer. The dual fuel bill would then be £1,511 – which still represents a 35 per cent real increase. And it is worth noting that customers will be expected to fund the cost of the insulation work under the Green Deal, which could off-set the savings.

The basic issue is that we need to invest the huge amounts shown in Table 4.8. Those figures aren't really in dispute. The energy market regulator Ofgem has produced a similar estimate at around £200 ($354) billion.[146] Paying for that, and the returns that investors will want on such a massive risky commitment, will require a huge increase in energy bills.

The government claim they can fix the issue with dramatic efficiency improvements. If people cut their consumption of energy enough then their bills can be the same despite big rises in prices. The problem is that the £200 billion or more of investment still needs to be paid for. Unless we are expecting

---

145 Ibid.

146 Ofgem, 'Ofgem publishes a comprehensive review of Britain's energy supplies', press release R/39, 9 October 2009

to play the energy companies for fools and walk them into an obvious and massive loss, then all that investment will need to massively hike not just prices but bills. If the companies put a certain amount in, they need a certain return out.

More investment in energy efficiency means spending even more money now, and only really helps cut costs over time if it can substantially cut the amount of investment needed in the energy sector. Analysts and regulators clearly don't think that is credible enough to seriously shift their assumptions about the likely path of prices, and no amount of pixie dust from the politicians responsible, Chris Huhne MP at the time of writing, will conjure up a way of making investing £200 billion look cheap.

Such sharp increases in electricity bills have huge social and economic consequences. In Chapter 6, we'll look at the effect on manufacturing industry. But the more immediate effect on ordinary people is the higher bills that residential consumers have to pay.

Figure 4.5: Spending on electricity as a percentage of total expenditure, by income decile

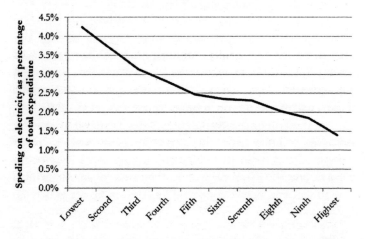

Rises in electricity bills hit poor and elderly families particularly hard. Figure 4.5 shows spending on electricity as a share of total expenditure in the UK by income decile, from the lowest to the highest earning.[147]

Figure 4.6 shows spending on electricity as a share of total expenditure in the UK by age of each household's reference person, from the youngest to the oldest.[148]

Figure 4.6: Spending on electricity as a percentage of total expenditure, by age of household reference person

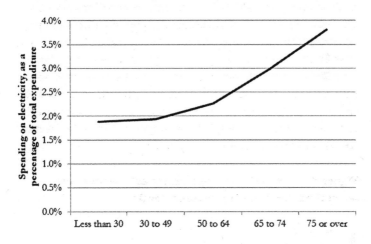

Electricity is a necessity. Making it more expensive will always hit the least fortunate hardest. Other developed countries will show a very similar pattern to that in Britain. If the Citigroup estimate is right, and environmental targets are on course to create substantial increases in prices, then that will make life a lot harder for lots of people. Some will die. There were an estimated 25,400 excess deaths in Britain over the 2009–10 winter, the latest winter for which

147 Office for National Statistics, 'Family Spending 2010', 30 November 2010, Table A8

148 Office for National Statistics, 'Family Spending 2010', 30 November 2010, Table A13

data is available.[149] Make it more expensive for people to turn up the thermostat or put on an electric heater and you are bound to increase that number. The same goes for air conditioning in hotter places.

Increasing energy prices will also worsen a number of other existing social problems. It will increase benefit dependency for example. You can already see that in the UK where elderly people are given a special Winter Fuel Payment of up to £250 ($443) for pensioners aged up to seventy-nine and £400 ($709) for those aged eighty or older, which is supposed to help with their energy bills.[150] The Winter Fuel Payment is a pretty inadequate way of addressing the problem of energy becoming unaffordable, though. It doesn't provide specific support for pensioners paying their energy bills but supports their overall income.

That means it isn't targeted on the key issue of whether people can afford to keep their homes at a reasonable temperature, and is easily outweighed by other rising bills. For example, council tax, which also hits the elderly hardest, has increased in England by £592 ($1,049) a year on an average Band D bill over the last decade.[151] The Winter Fuel Payment is not an efficient means of making energy bills more affordable and is poor compensation for the significant burden of climate change policies. It also costs taxpayers a fortune.

In other countries, similar affordability problems have translated into cuts in subsidy. Legislation has now passed the lower house of the German parliament – the Bundestag – to cut their renewable energy subsidies. The government's original plan was for around a 40 per cent cut in the feed-in

....

149 Office for National Statistics, 'Excess winter mortality in England and Wales, 2009/10 (provisional) and 2008/09 (final)', Statistical Bulletin, 23 November 2010

150 Directgov Winter Fuel Payment, http://www.direct.gov.uk/en/Pensionsand retirementplanning/Benefits/BenefitsInRetirement/DG_10018657

151 Department for Communities and Local Government, B and D council tax figures 1993–94 to 2010–11

tariff paid to renewable energy generators. By the time the cuts made it past the lobbyists and became legislation, they were less severe, but still involved double digit cuts.[152]

Spain and Italy are also making cuts. Italy is cutting its feed-in tariff by 18 per cent in 2011. In each four-month period there will be a 6 per cent cut. Apparently, markets expected 15 to 28 per cent, so solar companies are in some ways counting themselves lucky.[153] Spain is cutting revenue for operating solar plants by 30 per cent. Local trade groups have complained that they are being 'cheated' by these retrospective measures and face bankruptcy.[154] In the Czech Republic, they have applied a 26 per cent withholding tax on solar energy and increased the cost of buying land to install it on. Investors are furious and threatening legal action.[155] In Britain there hasn't been the same kind of general cut but some larger scale commercial solar operations are being cut – the trade association have complained even that move has 'ripped the guts out of the solar industry'.[156]

The massive cost of these policies creates an affordability crisis, so they aren't politically sustainable. That puts off investors and makes renewables even more expensive by increasing the cost of capital in the energy sector. The Citigroup report says:[157]

....

152 Solar PV Management, 'Bundesrat approve Renewable Energy Act Amendments', 12 July 2010, http://www.solar-pv-management.com/solar_news_full.php?id=73226

153 Rosenbaum, E., 'Italy Solar Tariff Cuts Not as Bad as Feared', *The Street*, 25 June 2010, http://www.thestreet.com/story/10792298/1/italy-solar-tariff-cuts-not-as-bad-as-feared.html

154 Sills, B., 'Spain May Cut Income 30% for Operating Solar Plants', Bloomberg Businessweek, 16 June 2010

155 Contiguglia, C., 'Withholding tax angers solar industry', *Prague Post*, 20 October 2010

156 Roca, M. & Morales, A., 'U.K. Cuts Subsidized Power Rates to Stem Solar-Farm Boom', Bloomberg, 9 June 2011

157 Atherton, P., *The €1trn Euro Decade - Revisited: Costs up, risks up, but governments are still in denial*, Citigroup Global Markets, 29 September 2010, p.10

We believe the consistency of government policy has been called into question in the past few months by events in Spain and Germany. The Spanish government has openly flirted with retrospective reductions in renewable power subsidies, although in the end only those subsidies for solar PV are likely to be reduced retrospectively.

Even more concerning the government in Germany has decided to impose a new tax on nuclear power to raise €2.3 billion per annum to help cut the government's budget deficit. What is so concerning about this new tax is that it demonstrates that governments can act arbitrarily and single out the utility sector as a source of cash when they have the need.

[...]

These actions by the Spanish and German governments have sent a shiver through investors in the sector. It is likely to have raised the cost of capital for future investment, and not just in the countries concerned.

Figure 4.7: Citigroup, European utilities required vs forecast spend

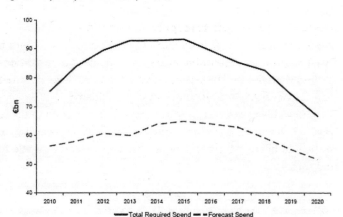

Figure 13. Required Spend vs Forecast Spend (€bn)

All that means investors are wary: at the time the Citigroup report was released the energy sector had underperformed the wider market by 26 per cent from March 2009. As a result, companies aren't investing enough to meet the targets, as shown in Figure 4.7.[158]

As the cost of these policies puts pressure on household budgets, there will be a backlash. If people are well informed about the consequences of climate change policy, they will demand cuts in expensive climate change policies. Unfortunately, politicians will probably try to blame others; accusing energy companies of rigging the market to guarantee excessive profits for example. The combination of rising prices and rising profits (to pay for all the investment required to meet renewable targets) will create fertile ground for opportunists to demand destructive measures like special windfall taxes that will put off investment in the entire sector, meaning more pain for consumers without actually stopping prices rising.

It is vital that people are aware of the price they are paying for climate change policies. That way, they will know what needs to be done as the bills rack up, and what would be counterproductive.

Renewable energy for transport and heating
Most renewable energy is consumed as electricity. It is much easier to produce renewable energy at a plant that is stationary and then deliver the power down the wires. Solar powered cars are never likely to be more than a curiosity.

Renewables are used in other settings though, in two key ways. Governments provide support for various sources of renewable heating for homes and businesses and biofuels to fuel cars.

....

158 Atherton, P., *The €1trn Euro Decade - Revisited: Costs up, risks up, but governments are still in denial,* Citigroup Global Markets, 29 September 2010, Figure 13. Required Spend vs Forecast Spend (€bn)

Support for renewable heating is still in its infancy compared to support for renewable electricity. There isn't nearly as much money in it, but it is already clear that it is a massive rip-off. The Renewable Energy Forum, the consultancy arm of UK think tank the Renewable Energy Foundation, has produced a report looking at the expected cost of the British subsidies through the Renewable Heat Initiative and find that they will be extremely expensive, representing very poor value.[159] Government estimates suggested that the average family could pay 14 per cent more on their gas bill (£94, $167, €124) and that the average medium-sized commercial gas consumer could pay 19 per cent more (£86,000, $150,000, €114,000) by 2020. The REF report that despite them pushing these policies the government's own estimates make it clear the measure won't represent good value:

DECC's estimates of the net benefit (benefits minus costs) are consistently negative and range from minus £1.2bn to minus £13.4bn (or minus £2.3bn to minus £14.5 billion if ancillary costs are included.

The scheme also doesn't look very good in terms of amount of subsidy needed per tonne of CO_2 emissions avoided. The subsidy cost is 'over £200 per tonne of CO_2 abated. While this compares favourably with the Feed-In Tariff (at over £440 per tonne), it is nearly double that of the Renewables Obligation (ca. £100 per tonne), which is itself widely regarded as an unreasonably costly measure.'

It has since been announced that the scheme will be funded through general taxation, rather than a further levy on energy bills, but that won't affect the basic cost of the scheme. It will just mean families and businesses pick up the bill in a different way.

Other countries have already implemented or are considering similar policies. Like feed-in tariffs, they often

---

159 Renewable Energy Forum, 'The Renewable Heat Initiative: Risks and Remedies', 2010

encourage the generation of energy at a scale, and in locations, where it just isn't efficient. That is why costs are high for both schemes.

There are some particular absurdities with renewable heating though. If people are given generous subsidies in return for producing energy to heat their own homes, they can produce more by opening the windows, setting the thermostat high and making other decisions that increase their household's heat consumption. To avoid that perverse incentive the government will just assume, or 'deem' the amount of energy generated. The subsidy won't be based on the actual amount of heat produced at all, and Ofgem have argued that creates a huge risk of money being lost to error or fraud:[160]

We are concerned about the potential for inaccuracy and fraud in the deeming process. If the vendor of the equipment is also responsible for determining the subsidy level there would be a temptation to exaggerate the property's heat requirement to make the deal more attractive.

All these problems and more mean that renewable heat incentives are a minefield and often represent extremely poor value.

Support for biofuels, generally intended for use as road transport fuel, is much more widespread and well established. But it arguably represents even worse value, with an even higher cost per tonne of emissions saved.

In the United States extremely generous subsidy is provided for corn ethanol. The subsidies were summarised by Ben Lieberman and Nicholas Loris for the Heritage Foundation in May 2008:[161]

Renewable fuels, and particularly corn-ethanol, have long enjoyed preferential treatment from the federal government.

....

160 Ofgem, 'Ofgem's response to DECC's consultation on the Renewable Heat Incentive', 23 April 2010

161 Lieberman, B. & Loris, N., 'Time to Repeal the Ethanol Mandate', Heritage Foundation, 15 May 2008

This includes a tax credit worth $0.51 per gallon. In addition, tariffs discourage imports of ethanol, including potentially cheaper sugar cane-based ethanol from Brazil.

Yet the ethanol industry still wanted more, and Congress, concerned about high gas prices, global warming and domestic energy production, enacted a mandate. The 2005 energy bill contained the first-ever requirement that renewable fuels be mixed into the gasoline supply. The 2007 energy bill increased the mandate substantially. The US is now committed to using 9 billion gallons in 2008, rising to 36 billion by 2022.

Similar biofuel subsidies exist in the EU. The EU's over-all renewable target is expressed as a share of the supply of energy, not electricity. That means countries need to encourage the use of renewable transport fuels to keep down the requirement for expanding renewable electricity. In Britain, the mechanism is the Renewable Transport Fuel Obligation, summarised by the Renewable Fuels Agency (which monitors the scheme) as follows:[162]

The Renewable Transport Fuels Obligation (RTFO), requires suppliers of fossil fuels to ensure that a specified percentage of the road fuels they supply in the UK is made up of renewable fuels. The target for 2009/10 is 3.25 per cent by volume.

Across the developed world, these policies are proving very pricy. The OECD has estimated that they cost $11 (£6, €9) billion in 2006 and that will rise to $25 (£14, €19) billion a year by 2015. They estimate that the policies cost between $960 (£542, €717) and $1,700 (£959, €1270) per tonne of CO_2-equivalent greenhouse gas emissions avoided.[163] That is outrageously expensive. But the heaviest price is paid in poorer countries.

The basic problem is that to make biofuels work on a significant scale you need to grow the crops somewhere. If we

------

162 Renewable Fuels Agency, 'About the RTFO', 30 July 2010
163 OECD, 'Biofuel policies in OECD countries costly and ineffective, says report', 16 July 2008

start burning what could be food in our cars, we are asking farmers to replace oil and keep feeding us at the same time. Often that means displacing agricultural land currently used to grow food, which means higher food prices.

In 2008 there was serious unrest in a number of countries as food prices rose dramatically. *The Guardian* reported on the scale of the issue:[164]

Rising food prices have pushed 100m people worldwide below the poverty line, estimates the World Bank, and have sparked riots from Bangladesh to Egypt. Government ministers here have described higher food and fuel prices as 'the first real economic crisis of globalisation'.

The BBC reported that 'at least four people were killed and twenty wounded when demonstrations against rising food prices turned into riots in southern Haiti'.[165]

An internal report by the World Bank, leaked to *The Guardian*, argued that biofuel policies were the main culprits. The newspaper reported that:[166]

President Bush has linked higher food prices to higher demand from India and China, but the leaked World Bank study disputes that: 'Rapid income growth in developing countries has not led to large increases in global grain consumption and was not a major factor responsible for the large price increases.'

Even successive droughts in Australia, calculates the report, have had a marginal impact. Instead, it argues that the EU and US drive for biofuels has had by far the biggest impact on food supply and prices.

[...]

'Without the increase in biofuels, global wheat and maize stocks would not have declined appreciably and price increases

164 Chakrabortty, A., 'Secret report: biofuel caused food crisis', *The Guardian*, 3 July 2008

165 BBC News, 'Food riots turn deadly in Haiti', 5 April 2008

166 Chakrabortty, A., 'Secret report: biofuel caused food crisis', *The Guardian*, 3 July 2008

due to other factors would have been moderate,' says the report. The basket of food prices examined in the study rose by 140 per cent between 2002 and this February. The report estimates that higher energy and fertiliser prices accounted for an increase of only 15 per cent, while biofuels have been responsible for a 75 per cent jump over that period.

It argues that production of biofuels has distorted food markets in three main ways. First, it has diverted grain away from food for fuel, with over a third of US corn now used to produce ethanol and about half of vegetable oils in the EU going towards the production of biodiesel. Second, farmers have been encouraged to set land aside for biofuel production. Third, it has sparked financial speculation in grains, driving prices up higher.

Other reviews of the food crisis looked at it over a much longer period, or have not linked these three factors, and so arrived at smaller estimates of the impact from biofuels. But the report author, Don Mitchell, is a senior economist at the Bank and has done a detailed, month-by-month analysis of the surge in food prices, which allows much closer examination of the link between biofuels and food supply.

Even if the effect is not as stark as that report suggested, the potential for biofuel policies in the developed world to impoverish the world's poorest is clear. The alternative is to increase the amount of land under cultivation, but that often means making inroads into environmentally precious wilderness land. There are some hair-raising claims in George Monbiot's book *Heat* about the impacts of existing biofuels on forests: millions of hectares being cleared, horrendous fires and animals threatened with extinction. He also raises the possibility that forest clearances undermine any emissions savings.[167]

Even if all his warnings about the environmental consequences of these fuels are wrong, and those sorts of warnings are certainly subject to exaggeration, increasing the use of

---

167 Monbiot, G., *Heat*, Penguin, 2006, pp.159–160

biofuels will necessarily either put new pressure on agricultural land, increasing food prices or the wilderness. We can't grow them on the moon.

To a certain extent, the pressure can be alleviated by improvements in agricultural yields, getting more out of the same quantity of land. That might produce a surplus that can be put to use as biofuels. There are a few problems. It is asking a lot to expect improvements in yield to feed an expanding population and replace a significant portion of the huge amounts of energy we get from burning petroleum in our cars at the same time. And one of the problems created by global warming is supposed to be declining crop yields. While that may be offset by greater concentrations of carbon dioxide increasing plant growth, if one of the symptoms of climate change is a threat to agricultural production it hardly makes sense to base your policies on their being an agricultural surplus.

Many of the huge improvements that we have seen in agricultural productivity have come from farms making heavy use of fossil fuel energy. As I mentioned earlier, the economic historian Edward A. Wrigley has written about the move from pre-Industrial farms that were net producers of energy to modern farming that uses large amounts of fossil fuel energy to enable a vast increase in the amount of food that can be produced from a given amount of land.[168]

That means trying to reduce greenhouse gas emissions by switching to biofuels may be counterproductive. A study by David Pimentel, of Cornell University, and Tad W. Patzek, from the University of California, found that:[169]

Ethanol production using corn grain required 29 per cent more fossil energy than the ethanol fuel produced.

....

168 Wrigley, E. A., *Continuity, chance & change: the character of the industrial revolution in England*, Cambridge University Press, 1988, p.73

169 Pimentel, D. & Patzek, T. W., 'Ethanol Production Using Corn, Switchgrass, and Wood; Biodiesel Production Using Soybean and Sunflower', *Natural Resources Research*, Vol. 14, No 1, March 2005

Ethanol production using switchgrass required 50 per cent more fossil energy than the ethanol fuel produced.

Ethanol production using wood biomass required 57 per cent more fossil energy than the ethanol fuel produced.

Biodiesel production using soybean required 27 per cent more fossil energy than the biodiesel fuel produced (Note, the energy yield from soy oil per hectare is far lower than the ethanol yield from corn).

Biodiesel production using sunflower required 118 per cent more fossil energy than the biodiesel fuel produced.

In other words, it takes more energy, and requires burning more fossil fuels, to produce the biofuel than that produced by your car. Other studies are more optimistic. The Congressional Budget Office has cited research suggesting that using biofuels reduces emissions 20 per cent compared to using petroleum.[170] But Pimentel & Patzek argue that a 'review of the reports that indicate that corn ethanol production provides a positive return indicates that many inputs were omitted'.[171] In other words they don't take account of all the ways fossil fuels have to be burned in order to produce ethanol.

Whether or not biofuels do cut emissions now, there is a catch-22 as higher yields tend to come from more intensive farming and at the price of higher emissions intensity. So attempts to produce biofuels while avoiding starving the poor or encroaching further on the wilderness will risk undermining the whole point of using them in the first place. Technological improvements – better crops; better tools; better methods – will steadily make things easier but expecting them to simultaneously outweigh a rising population and a major shift towards energy crops is simply unrealistic. If there is a dramatic technological revolution that makes biofuels a

170 Congressional Budget Office, 'Implications of Ethanol Use for Food Prices and Greenhouse-Gas Emissions', April 2009

171 Pimentel, D. & Patzek, T. W., 'Ethanol Production Using Corn, Switchgrass, and Wood; Biodiesel Production Using Soybean and Sunflower', *Natural Resources Research*, Vol. 14, No 1, March 2005

useful means of affordably cutting emissions then that is the time to start using them, not now.

The environmentalist movement has had a rather complicated relationship with biofuels. While some like George Monbiot have attacked them as the expensive disaster they are,[172] too many others hold them up as the way forward. *The Independent*, which prides itself on its environmentalist credentials, might be the best example of the confusion. A blogger, going by the pseudonym Mr Eugenides, compared two leader columns by the paper, before and after Britain had adopted biofuel mandates.[173] On 7 November 2005 they wrote that:[174]

At last, some refreshing signs of intelligent thinking on climate change are coming out of Whitehall. The Environment minister, Elliot Morley, reveals today in an interview with this newspaper that the government is drawing up plans to impose a 'biofuel obligation' on oil companies. This would require major firms such as BP and Shell to blend a fixed proportion of biofuels with the petrol and diesel they sell on Britain's garage forecourts. This has the potential to be the biggest green innovation in the British petrol market since the introduction of unleaded petrol a decade and a half ago.

The beauty of biofuels – petrol made from sugar beet and diesel made from oilseed rape – is that they are 'carbon neutral'. The quantity of CO_2 they produce when burned has already been absorbed by the crops used to make them. There is no reason why a biofuel quota should not work.

By 15 April 2008, the newspaper had changed its tune to a dramatic extent, with Chief Reporter Cahal Milmo writing that:[175]

....

172 Monbiot, G., 'The western appetite for biofuels is causing starvation in the poor world', *The Guardian*, 6 November 2007

173 Mr. Eugenides, *How journalism works*, 15 April 2008

174 'A welcome proposal - but no magic bullet', *The Independent*, 7 November 2005

175 Milmo, C., 'Biofuel: the burning question', *The Independent*, 15 April 2008

From today, all petrol and diesel sold on forecourts must contain at least 2.5 per cent biofuel. The government insists its flagship environmental policy will make Britain's thirty-three million vehicles greener. But a formidable coalition of campaigners is warning that, far from helping to reverse climate change, the UK's biofuel revolution will speed up global warming and the loss of vital habitat worldwide.

Amid growing evidence that massive investment in biofuels by developed countries is helping to cause a food crisis for the world's poor, the ecological cost of the push to produce billions of litres of petrol and diesel from plant sources will be highlighted today with protests across the country and growing political pressure to impose guarantees that the new technology reduces carbon emissions.

Al Gore is even worse, and admitted only in November 2010 that he endorsed ethanol subsidies as a cheap electoral ploy after years of recommending them. He told a green energy business conference in Athens that it was all about securing the support of voters in critical early Democratic Party primaries:[176]

One of the reasons I made that mistake is that I paid particular attention to the farmers in my home state of Tennessee, and I had a certain fondness for the farmers in the state of Iowa because I was about to run for President.

The politicians who instituted the subsidies could be forgiven for feeling a little put out. They tried to give the environmentalists what they wanted, and then the activists turn on them and attack the human and environmental consequences of generous support for biofuels. Now those subsidies are locked in, entrenched by the farm lobby in the United States and political inflexibility in Europe. As I mentioned at the start of this book, the EU Commissioner responsible said that: 'There is no question for now of

---

176 Wynn, G., 'US corn ethanol "was not a good policy": Gore', Reuters, 22 November 2010

suspending the target fixed for biofuels... You can't change a political objective without risking a debate on all the other objectives'.[177] In the United States, the farm lobby won't let go of ethanol mandates lightly. Those environmentalists who weren't properly critical of biofuels bear a heavy responsibility for the disastrous waste that has been instituted on their behalf and is now entrenched.

Unsustainable renewable energy

Renewable energy is plagued by old problems. While the wind and the sun are free, using them to supply energy when and where we need it to power a modern economy is extremely expensive. There are some narrow circumstances where renewable energy could make sense as part of the energy mix, and it might become efficient enough in the future, but right now renewable energy needs costly subsidies.

Of course, people might think those subsidies are worth it in order to cut greenhouse gas emissions. But renewable energy doesn't cut emissions in any country with cap and trade as it just displaces other, cheaper, reductions in emissions. Even if a country avoids making the same mistake as the European Union, and doesn't combine these policies, renewable energy is still just one more way of cutting emissions, and an expensive one. It would take a sociologist to explain why politicians and activists fetishise windmills and solar panels so much. It might be that they are very visible. You can stand next to an array of solar panels or a wind farm for a great photo opportunity.

Renewable energy does also have intangible costs beyond the dollars, pounds and euros discussed here. I touched on the impact of biofuels on biodiversity and food prices in poor countries earlier. There is also the disruption to landscapes from so many wind turbines. This is a contentious issue. Politicians have sometimes moved to bend planning law

177 AFP, 'EU defends biofuel goals amid food crises', 14 April 2008

in order to facilitate renewable energy developments. Many communities hugely resent the imposition of wind turbines but activists claim they are being unreasonable and the wind-mills are actually quite attractive.

The truth is probably that there is nothing inherently ugly about wind farms, but they do constitute a very obtrusive development often sited on land that is appreciated for being relatively untouched. New York is a beautiful city but that doesn't mean we want to build skyscrapers over the Lake District or Yosemite. Disturbing the wilderness, killing birds and innumerable other environmental issues are the result of trying to gather energy from an extremely diffuse source – the wind or sunlight – instead of digging it out from under the ground.

Coal, gas or nuclear power plants are just as disruptive as wind farms but you don't need as many of them, and there-fore they don't have nearly the same geographical footprint as most sources of renewable energy. When experts are asking questions like 'What if we covered 10 per cent of Britain in wind farms?'[178] and still finding it would only be able to supply a small portion of our total daily energy use, it becomes appar-ent how widely spread those turbines would have to be. In his book *Blue Planet in Green Shackles*, Czech President Václav Klaus asks how many wind turbines it would take to replace the nuclear power plant at Temelín in the south of the Czech Republic. He finds that you would need 4,750 of them. That would take 8.6 million tonnes of raw material and, if they were built next to each other, they could stretch from Temelín to Brussels.[179]

So renewable energy isn't just an expensive way of cutting emissions, it also isn't a particularly pleasant one. Then

178 MacKay, D., 'Sustainable Energy – without the hot air', 3 November 2008, p.33
179 Klaus, V., 'Blue Planet in Green Shackles, What Is Endangered: Climate or Freedom?', Competitive Enterprise Institute, 2008, Appendix C

politicians make things worse by searching out the most expensive renewables they can find. Rigging the market so that every technology is subsidised till it is competitive means that there is no incentive to choose the option that gives best value. That is a spectacular rip-off for ordinary consumers who pay unnecessarily high energy bills for no good reason because the subsidies are picking losers. Poor families pay the highest price and these policies force too many into poverty and dependence on benefits.

There is a human cost to high energy prices. We are paying a heavy price for indulging the obsession of activists and politicians with expensive renewable energy.

GREEN TAXES AND TRANSPORT

Tim Yeo MP, Chairman of the House of Commons Energy and Climate Committee, is in favour of individual carbon trading, along with some other British politicians; cap and trade not just for power plants and factories but for every single consumer.[180] It is a truly incredible idea. That everyone walks around with their own little carbon ration card for every purchase they make. It is easy to see the problems. The administrative costs would be huge, it would require a highly intrusive Government database logging our purchases and a comprehensive scheme (and any scheme like that which wasn't comprehensive would distort decision making) might not even be possible. So the idea has generally stayed on the drawing board.

Regulations like cap and trade are used with big emitters like power plants. Cars, aeroplanes and other smaller scale sources of emissions generally get taxed instead. Everything from driving to work to flying abroad for a much needed holiday is more expensive thanks to green taxes.

There is a theory that justifies green taxes. They are supposed to be what is known as a Pigovian tax and correct for externalities, problems for wider society created by doing things like driving that create greenhouse gas emissions. Actual green taxes need to be tested against that theory though, to see if the blackboard economics has translated into policy practice. If green taxes are just used as an excuse to jack up taxes and finance wasteful spending, then they are one more part of the rip-off.

---

180 Yeo, T., *Green Gold*, Tory Reform Group, July 2010, p.45

Pigovian taxes and the social cost

Green taxes are justified in theory by the need to correct for negative externalities.

Anything done by an individual or a company within an economy will have positive and negative effects on others that they are not charged or compensated for by the market. Someone going to university will pay a certain fee and gain a certain reward in the form of skills and credentials they can exchange for a higher income. Their studies may also produce positive social effects for which no one is charged. The students' education may make them better citizens who are better able to hold politicians to account through the ballot box. That would mean there was a positive externality to going to university.

By contrast, someone who burns petrol in order to power their car will pay a price for the petrol and the car and will get a certain return in the form of greater mobility. They will also create carbon dioxide emissions, and as we think those emissions contribute to climate change we expect that to have a negative effect on wider society. That means there are negative externalities to burning petrol in order to drive.

If government intervenes and places a tax on an activity that creates a negative externality, or provides a subsidy to an activity that creates a positive externality, then it can theoretically improve efficiency by better aligning private incentives with the social good. The taxes or subsidies should be equal to the harm or benefit that is placed on society so that each individual's actions reflect the costs and benefits to society. People should then produce an efficient amount of the positive or negative externality.

There are problems with that idea even in theory. Nobel Laureate Ronald Coase pointed out the biggest problem in 'The Problem of Social Cost'.[181] He established that, in a hypothetical world with zero transaction costs, the market

---

181 Coase, R. H., 'The Problem of Social Cost', *Journal of Law and Economics*, October 1960

would perfectly correct for externalities. If someone suffered as the result of a negative externality they would offer to pay the person creating it to stop. If they placed a greater value on preventing the externality than the person producing the externality did on pursuing the activity that created it, then they would pay the person producing the externality enough that they would stop. On the other hand, if the value they placed on stopping the activity was less than the value the person creating the externality placed on being able to continue to do so then they would not offer enough, and the externality would continue to be created.

Coase identifies the limits of this reasoning himself. The Coase Theorem, as his theory has since become known, only works in a world of zero transaction costs. There are innumerable reasons why it is often extremely difficult, if not impossible, for the rest of society to pay someone for producing a public good or not producing a negative externality. Global warming offers a clear example. The potential harms to each individual created by someone else burning a litre of petrol are infinitesimally small, but the externality is significant on a global scale. It would be utterly impractical for everyone to club together and put in their tiny fraction of a penny in order to pay someone to drive less.

However, attempts to correct for externalities through Pigovian green taxes are also subject to transaction costs. There are a variety of reasons why politicians might get interventions intended to correct for externalities wrong. They have to work out the right level for the tax or subsidy; they need to ensure the intervention itself is efficient (administering a tax may be costly, for example, or it could hurt the economy); they may need to balance a series of positive and negative externalities created by a single activity; rent seekers may distort an intervention so that it serves their private interests rather than the social good. With those problems, governments need to avoid rushing to subsidise every public good and tax every negative externality.

In the case of green taxes, we can test the theory against the practice; at least whether they have got approximately the right price. Too many politicians and activists seem to see the challenge as setting the highest green tax they can, if people are still driving then the tax isn't high enough. But that is just arbitrary and unfair. The IPCC has acknowledged that economic theory implies 'if taxes were used, then they should be set equal to the SCC [social cost of carbon]'.[182] In other words, the tax paid for emitting greenhouse gases equivalent to one tonne of carbon dioxide should be set equal to the value of the harms to others, now and in the future, created by the contribution a tonne of carbon dioxide will make to climate change. If it's a Pigovian tax, you should pay for the costs you impose on others, no more or less.

It is important to note at this stage that the term 'social cost of carbon' does not mean that only carbon dioxide is considered. Other greenhouse gases are also significant, and many contribute considerably more to the greenhouse effect for a given volume of gas. For that reason, the social cost of carbon is normally expressed as a value per ton of carbon dioxide (/t CO_2) or carbon (/t C) equivalent, i.e. the costs imposed by burning a tonne of carbon dioxide or enough of another greenhouse gas to have the same effect.

Establishing the correct social cost of carbon is extremely important, as this determines the size of the price that should be imposed on those who produce carbon dioxide emissions. Get the social cost of carbon too high and a tax set equal to it will create an unfair and inefficient burden. Set it too low, too much carbon dioxide will be emitted and society will face a greater climate change risk than is desirable. For that reason, the social cost of carbon has been studied by quite a range of academics, some of whose work I have already touched on.

....

182 IPCC, 'History and present state of aggregate impact estimates', *Climate Change 2007: Working Group II: Impacts Adaptation and Vulnerability*, 20.6.1

Dozens of studies have produced hundreds of estimates vary-
ing from the extremely low to the extremely high. Fortunately,
several studies have worked through the different estimates
and calculated averages which represent a reasonable guide
to the middle ground in the debate over the social costs of
greenhouse gas emissions.

The IPCC included, in their most recent 2007 report, a
review of the existing peer-reviewed literature which found a
mean social cost in 2005 of \$12 (£7, €10)/t CO_2.[183]

That report suggests it is 'very likely' this is an underestimate of the true value as non-quantifiable impacts of global
warming will be missed. However, there is little evidence of
such a bias in the peer-reviewed literature. On the contrary,
Richard Tol – who has studied this issue for the IPCC – found
that there was 'a downward trend in the estimates of the
social cost of carbon – even if the IPCC would like to believe
the opposite'.[184] If further study is leading, on average, to
lower estimates of the social cost of carbon then it is hard to
sustain the idea that the true value should be expected to be
significantly higher. Do we think that the literature is somehow appreciating the full spectrum of potential harms from
global warming less over time? All that research on climate
change and we know less?

Tol has confirmed that result in his most recent survey:[185]

Estimates of the economic effects of greenhouse gas emis-
sions have become less pessimistic over time. For the studies
listed here, the estimates become less negative by 0.23 per
cent of GDP per year in which the study was done (with a
standard deviation of 0.10 per cent per year). There are several
reasons for this change. Projections of future emissions and
future climate change have become less severe over time – even

183 IPCC, 'Climate Change 2007: Synthesis Report - Summary for Policymakers'
184 Tol, R. S. J., 'The Social Cost of Carbon: Trends, Outliers and Catastrophes',
   Economics, Vol. 2, 12 August 2008, p.9
185 Tol, R. S. J., 'The Economic Effects of Climate Change', *Journal of Economic*
   Perspectives, Vol. 23, No 2, Spring 2009, p.36

though the public discourse has become shriller. The earlier studies focused on the negative effects of climate change, whereas later studies considered the balance of positives and negatives. In addition, earlier studies tended to ignore adaptation. More recent studies – triggered by Mendelsohn, Nordhaus, and Shaw (1994) – include some provision for agents to alter their behavior in response to climate change.

He does argue that the newer estimates might be too optimistic. All we really know is that the estimates of the harms of climate change are still very uncertain – for all the reasons discussed in Chapter 2 – and the true value could be significantly higher or lower.

This is how Tol summarises the peer-reviewed literature:[186]

The best available knowledge – which is not very good – [suggests a] government that uses the same 3 per cent discount rate for climate change as for other decisions should levy a carbon tax of $25 per metric ton of carbon (modal value) to $50/tC (mean value).

That estimate uses the social cost per tonne of carbon, which can be converted to the social cost per tonne of CO_2 by a ratio of 100:27.29 (1 tonne of CO_2 contains 0.2729 tonnes of carbon). The mean value of $50/t C is therefore equivalent to $13.65 (£7.70)/t CO_2. Not much different to the estimate produced for the IPCC report.

As well as these surveys, there are two estimates based on studies of the costs and benefits of cutting emissions mentioned earlier are worth looking at. William Nordhaus's model suggests a social cost of around $28/t C, or $7.64 (£4.20)/t CO_2, in 2005.[187]

An estimate has also been produced by the British government's Department for the Environment, Food and Rural Affairs (DEFRA) – before its responsibilities for responding

....

186 Ibid., p.46

187 Nordhaus, W., *A Question of Balance: Weighing the Options on Global Warming Policies*, Yale University Press, 2008, p.91

to climate change were handed to the new Department of Energy and Climate Change – which builds on the work of the Stern Review but attempts to provide an estimate better suited to policy appraisal.

The DEFRA 'Shadow Price of Carbon' in 2007 is £25.50 ($51)/t CO_2. Of course, that is subject to all the problems with the Stern Review outlined earlier.

The social cost of greenhouse gas emissions is widely expected to rise over time as the quantity of existing greenhouse gases in the atmosphere rises. For that reason, DEFRA quote different social costs for different years, as shown in Table 5.1.[188]

Table 5.1: 550ppm SPC using 1990–2005 market exchange rate and GDP deflator (£/t CO_2)

	2007	2008	2009	2010	2011	2012	2013	2014	2015
Shadow price of carbon	25.5	26	26.5	27	27.6	28.1	28.7	29.2	29.8

These social cost estimates can be used to assess new policies, by seeing if proposed green taxes match up to the social cost of carbon, and also to test existing policies to see whether they meet the Pigovian standard of aligning private incentives with the social good. Studies for the TaxPayers' Alliance have used those estimates to compare green taxes and regulations to the social cost of carbon. The same method has been used by Britain's Department of Transport in its assessment of aviation taxes, which summed it up as follows:[189]

The steps involved are:

take the most recent available Greenhouse Gas Inventory estimates of UK carbon dioxide emissions from all domestic flights and departing international flights;

---

188 Price, R., Thornton, S. & Nelson, S., *The Social Cost Of Carbon And The Shadow Price Of Carbon: What They Are, And How To Use Them In Economic Appraisal In The UK*, DEFRA Economics Group, December 2007
189 Department for Transport, 'Aviation Cost Assessment 2008'

indicatively account for the non-CO$_2$ climate change effects of air travel, applying a multiplier value of 1.91. To reflect the degree of uncertainty around this value, a sensitivity range of 1 to 4 will also be presented; then

multiply this by the appropriate monetary value based on the government's Shadow Price of Carbon, again using a sensitivity range to reflect the uncertainty; and

compare this range of values with the air passenger duty/ aviation duty and aviation gasoline duty receipts for the year concerned.

The most recent TaxPayers' Alliance report found that the burden of green taxes and regulations, net of road spending, in 2008–09 was £26.4 ($48.9) billion in the UK. That was up £1.7 billion from £24.7 billion in 2007–08. The rise was driven by an increasing price on emissions under the EU's Emissions Trading Scheme and an increase in the cost of the Renewables Obligation.

Depending on which 'per tonne' estimate of the social cost of carbon is used, the total cost of Britain's emissions was between £2.8 ($5.2) billion and £16.2 ($30.0) billion in 2008, the estimate under the IPCC social cost was £4.6 ($8.5) billion. There was little change between 2007 and 2008 as falling emissions were balanced out by a rising social cost per tonne.

Green taxes were therefore excessive by between £10.2 ($18.9) billion and £23.6 ($43.8) billion in 2008–09, the estimate under the IPCC social cost was £21.8 ($40.4) billion. Excessive green taxes and regulations therefore cost between £408 ($756) and £944 ($1,750) per household, the estimate under the IPCC social cost was £872 ($1,617) per household. Again, the extent to which the cost of climate change policies is excessive has risen from between £8.4 billion and £21.8 billion in 2007–08, and £20.1 billion under the IPCC social cost.[190]

....

190 Sinclair, M., *Ending the green rip-off: Reforming climate change policy to reduce the burden on families*, TaxPayers' Alliance, December 2009

It is possible to use official statistics to produce an updated figure similar to the ones in those reports. The Office for National Statistics has reported British environmental taxes raised £41.4 billion in 2010,[191] or £30.1 billion if you take out Air Passenger Duty which addresses emissions which aren't fully included in the national total and the £9.2 billion a year the government spends on roads.[192] Our total greenhouse gas emissions in that year were 582.4 Mt CO_2.[193] Adjusting for inflation,[194] the social cost of our emissions in that year was only £16.9 billion even at the high DEFRA shadow price of carbon. While that is only a back of the envelope calculation, it suggests that we paid around £13.2 ($20.5) billion a year at least in excessive green taxes in 2010.

The method used in the TPA studies, and by the Department for Transport, is not entirely uncontroversial. In response to one of the TaxPayers' Alliance reports on this subject, Paul Ekins wrote for the Green Fiscal Commission, a campaign for higher green taxes, that:[195]

The argument in the TPA report that any environmental tax in excess of the best estimate of environmental damage is 'excessive' is simply wrong. It is in principle as legitimate to raise revenues from green taxes (above their 'optimal' rate) as it is from any other taxes, and whether or not to do so is one of the more complex judgements of tax policy.

In a trivial sense this is clearly correct. There is no reason why the government can't tax motor fuel, home energy use or anything else at any level if they choose to do so for reasons entirely unrelated to their impact on potential climate change.

....

191 Office for National Statistics, 'Environmental Accounts 2011', June 2011, Table 3.1: 'Government revenues from environmental taxes'

192 HM Treasury, 'Public Expenditure Statistical Analyses 2011', July 2011, Table 5.2: Public sector expenditure on services by sub-function, 2006-07 to 2010-11. Combined national and local roads total.

193 DECC, '2010 Provisional UK Figures', 31 March 2011

194 HM Treasury, 'GDP deflators at market prices', 29 March 2011

195 Green Fiscal Commission, 'The burden of green taxes – The TaxPayers' Alliance is wrong', Press Response, 28 August 2008

Even if those taxes are levied on emitting activities in addition to other taxes such as Value Added Tax, as they generally are. What they can't do, though, is legitimately sell those new taxes as Pigovian green taxes. If emitting activities are systematically overtaxed, that suggests that – in the UK at least – government has proved incapable of effectively delivering Pigovian taxation. They would need some other concrete reason to single people out for fiscal punishment.

In theory, many proposals to increase green taxes are supposed to be part of a shift from other taxes rather than an increase in the tax burden. 'Pay as you burn, not pay as you earn' or the 'polluter pays'. That rhetoric is almost tempting so long as you forget that the polluters in question are people driving to work, heating their home, taking their family on holiday or working in industry.

In reality, if green taxes aren't actually being matched to the harms created by climate change, then they are being used to impose a higher tax burden. Politicians are using them because competitive pressures or popular demand mean other taxes need to be cut and they don't want to cut spending to make the sums add up; or because wasteful spending has outpaced their ability to raise the money from existing taxes leaving big deficits. Either way, if green taxes provide a politically expedient way of raising extra revenue then they will mean higher taxes and less pressure to restrain wasteful spending.

Apart from the energy sector struggling under the regulations discussed in earlier chapters, driving and flying are the two activities that bear the greatest burden. The only major source of emissions not being hit by heavy green taxes or regulations is agriculture, which instead gets generous subsidies in most developed economies. The generous treatment agriculture gets is more evidence that climate change policy is not applied neutrally but just hits those industries without adequate political support.

It is worth looking in more depth at the taxation and

regulation of driving and flying; the modes of transport that dominate domestic and international travel respectively.

Driving

Motorists tend to get hit particularly hard by green taxes. They were being taxed heavily before climate change came along but it provided a fresh impetus, a new excuse. Motor fuel is actually subsidised in many developing countries, which accounts for most global fossil fuel subsidies as mentioned in Chapter 4, but in just about every developed economy there are heavy gas taxes.

In the United States, data on the amount charged in each state is recorded by the American Petroleum Institute.[196] In July 2010, the most recent data at the time of writing, they found that gas taxes vary between under 30 cents (20p) per gallon in Alaska and nearly 70 cents (45p) per gallon in California.

In Europe, the taxes are much higher. The European Commission's Market Observatory for Energy records the scale of indirect taxes on benchmark Euro-Super 95 petrol in different European countries and in every one the rate is over a euro per gallon, in some it is well over two euros and fifty cents a gallon (£2.14, $3.32), like the Netherlands and the United Kingdom.[197]

To put it all in metric terms, in the US states gas taxes vary between about 6.5 cents (4p) and nearly 18 cents (12p) per litre.

European taxes on petrol vary between around 35 (30p, 46 cents) and 70 euro cents (60p, 93 cents) per litre.

We can test those taxes against the scale of the externality created by global warming. Burning a litre of petrol produces

....

196 American Petroleum Institute, State Gasoline Tax Reports, July 2010
197 European Commission, Energy: Market Observatory, Duties and taxes, 26 July 2010

around 0.0023 tonnes of carbon dioxide.[198] As mentioned earlier, the mean estimate of the social cost found in the peer-reviewed literature was found by Tol to be \$13.65 (£7.70)/t CO_2. That implies the social cost of burning a litre of fuel is just over 3 cents (under 2p) per litre.

Figure 5.1: European indirect taxes on Euro-Super 95 by country, €c/l, July 2010

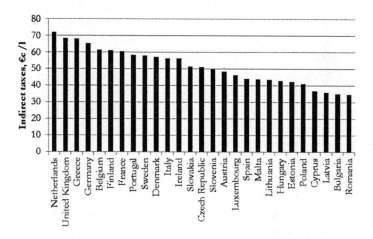

Existing taxes in the United States, let alone in the European Union, are much higher than that. Even if you use a more ambitious estimate of the social cost, like the DEFRA shadow price based on the flawed Stern Review, it will be a bit of a challenge to justify even the exceptionally low taxes in Alaska. Motorists, at least, are already paying a price higher than can be justified by the threat of climate change.

When this is pointed out, those promoting higher taxes on motorists tend to stop talking about climate change quite

---

198 Select Committee on Environment, Food and Rural Affairs, Letter to the Committee Chairman from Mr John Healey MP, Economic Secretary, HM Treasury, Minutes of Evidence, 6 November 2003

quickly. Some change tack completely and claim that taxes on motor fuel aren't really about climate change at all, they're just one more way of raising revenue.

The problem with that approach is that if motorists are singled out for taxation, without the justification of correcting for negative externalities, it means distorting the economy. It is not just unfair but inefficient as higher taxes move the price away from the right value, producing the right incentives, at the social cost of carbon.

While most of the green taxes have been around since before we were worried about carbon dioxide emissions, the threat of global warming has been used endlessly to promote hiking them. Environmentalists can't have it both ways. They can't spend decades arguing for higher taxes on motorists to fight climate change then decide those taxes are really just one more way of raising revenue when pressed on whether the tax is proportional to the economic objective.

In the UK in 1993 Fuel Duty was charged at 28.32 pence on a litre of unleaded petrol. At that stage an 'escalator' was introduced which saw the rate rise significantly above inflation for some years. By 2008 the rate had nearly doubled to 50.35 pence per litre. This followed Ken Clarke's announcement in a statement to the House of Commons in 1993,[199] which I cited earlier:

I have now decided to strengthen the March commitment by increasing road duties on average by at least 5 per cent in real terms in future Budgets. This will complete Britain's strategy for meeting our Rio commitment.

Similarly, recent increases in the Vehicle Excise Duty tax on car ownership were justified on the basis of road transport's contribution to carbon dioxide emissions. If motoring taxes aren't really green taxes then politicians should stop using climate change as an excuse to hike them.

....

199 Hansard, 30 November 1993, Column 938

Another option is to add other problems associated with motoring, other negative externalities, until you get to the total social cost needed to justify high motoring taxes. Politicians and activists bring in noise and air pollution, road injuries and fatalities and most importantly, congestion, for example. Table 5.2 shows an example of this kind of account of the externalities associated with driving.[200]

Table 5.2: Estimate of road transport externalities, pence/vehicle km

Externality	Low estimate, pence/vehicle km, 1998	High estimate pence/vehicle km, 1998
Operating costs	0.42	0.54
Accidents	0.82	1.4
Air pollution	0.34	1.7
Noise	0.02	0.05
Climate change	0.15	0.62
Congestion	9.71	11.16

However, simply adding externality after externality in an attempt to arrive at an optimal total tax on petrol has a number of problems. Many of the externalities in the list above are already controlled by other regulations. Noise and air pollution are created by a vast spectrum of industrial and commercial activity from factories to night clubs. They are controlled by regulation which limits acceptable levels of noise and particulate emissions in different geographical areas. New roads are subject to planning controls based on the amount of traffic they are likely to carry and many developments are subject to planning controls based on the amount of traffic

....
200 Leicester, A., 'The UK Tax System and the Environment', Institute for Fiscal Studies, November 2006 http://www.ifs.org.uk/comms/r68.pdf, p.25

they will create. Equally, emissions standards for new vehicles and the requirement to fit catalytic converters control particulate emissions.

There is clearly extensive regulation designed to control road traffic accidents: driving tests, speed limits, speed cameras and installations such as speed bumps. Many of these impose substantial costs on drivers and others are paid for as part of the process of building and maintaining roads. With most of the costs controlled in some other manner, motorists would need to be unfairly singled out for other, localised externalities to be subject to taxation as well. Factories, for example, need to control noise and particulate emissions along with other externalities to safe levels but are not taxed as well. To correct twice for the same externality just in the case of motorists would be disproportionate and unfair. Pigovian taxes and regulation are substitutes as different methods of achieving the common objective of controlling externalities. To put both in place is to arbitrarily burden motorists.

The costs of congestion, except for the cost of building and maintaining roads, are internalised within the body of road users and create an incentive to travel in other ways or less. Taxes on motor fuel are also probably not the best measure to correct for the externality of congestion. Evidence to the Mirrlees review by the Institute for Fiscal Studies think tank described Fuel Duty as a 'very blunt instrument' for addressing the problem of congestion.[201] Congestion is by far the biggest element in high estimates of the social cost of driving, but it is far from clear that it is fair or effective to respond to congestion with taxes, particularly on motor fuel.

Studies that aim to comprehensively assess the external costs of driving also tend to focus purely on the negative

---

201 Institute for Fiscal Studies, 'Don't expect much extra revenue from green taxes, says study prepared for the Mirrlees Review', press release, 10 July 2008

externalities and ignore the positive externalities associated with driving. These positive externalities include the fact that motorists reduce the strain on overcrowded public transport networks. In the UK for example, trains only account for seven per cent of passenger travel and buses and coaches six per cent, against 85 per cent who travel by car or van.[202] If motorists all decided to leave their cars at home there is no way even a massively upgraded public transport network could cope. By relieving congestion on public transport motorists do a significant public good.

Road users also encourage the development of greater road transport infrastructure. While motorists may be inconvenienced by other drivers when they create congestion on the roads they also depend on them. If there were fewer motorists the broad network of service stations, mechanics, driving instructors and other services that support driving would be less comprehensive. This network effect is the other side of the coin to the problem of congestion and can be just as important.

Finally, motorists allow economic activity to be more dispersed. The ability to drive to work quickly from a huge range of places means that homes, places of work and services do not need to be concentrated on top of each other. This eases pressure on public services such as water and sewerage. Even getting to work, instead of sitting on benefits at other people's expense, is easier with a car. One study by Paul Ong at the University of California Transportation Centre found that if car ownership was more expensive that reduced the chance of welfare claimants finding work:[203]

This study examines the role of car ownership in facilitating employment among recipients under the current welfare-to-

....

202 Office for National Statistics, Neighbourhood Statistics, Key Statistics 15: Travel to work

203 Ong, P. M., 'Car Ownership and Welfare-to-Work', The University of California Transportation Center No 540, 26 February 2001

*work law. Because of a potential problem with simultaneity,
the analysis uses an instrumental variable constructed from
insurance premiums and population density for car ownership.
The data comes from a 1999–2000 survey of TANF recipients in
the Los Angeles metropolitan area. The empirical results show
a significant independent contribution of car ownership on
employment. The presence of an observed ownership is associated with a 12 percentage point increase in the odds of being
employed. Moreover, the results indicate that lowering insurance premiums by $100 can increase the odds of employment
by 4 percentage points.*

Granted that study looks at LA, where getting around without a car is notoriously difficult. It is common sense though,
that making driving more expensive will reduce the range
within which people can look for work at a given income, shifting the balance towards choosing to remain unemployed. It will
make the journey to work more costly or more time consuming
and plenty of people just won't be able to find a job they are
practically able to get to. Others will just be put off and, at the
margin, more will stay home on benefits. The same is true of
anything that makes working more expensive and not working
more attractive by comparison. If people can't travel then they
are less likely to be matched up to the best job possible.

If cars are taxed on the basis of an incomplete attempt to
assess every externality they create or, worse, just an account
of every negative externality, then the final result will be a
deeply inefficient intervention in the market that could easily
make things worse, rather than better. If you take the principle of Pigovian taxation to that kind of extreme it becomes an
arbitrary exercise. Jim Manzi wrote in September 2009:[204]

*Start with the point that we tax an activity, not a substance.
Let's take the example of burning a gallon of gasoline by driving
to work rather than riding your bike. This action creates social*

204 Manzi, J., 'The Socialism Implicit in the Social Cost of Carbon', *The Daily
Dish*, 1 September 2009

cost in the form of AGW. But it also creates other social costs, such as, for example, local air pollution, congestion, noise and increased risk of accidents for others. Why would we privilege a unit of social cost created by AGW over that same unit of social cost created by any of these other effects? If I die from cancer because I inhaled some of your fumes or I die from flooding because of increased global temperatures, I am in each case equally dead. But it also creates social benefits. You spend less time travelling, get to work earlier and produce more output that day; because you can not capture all of the social utility of your labour, this creates incremental social benefit. You also have more time at home, and use this time with your kids to improve their educational outcomes, which creates social utility in later years. And so on, ad infinitum. In order to set the tax, we don't just need to know the costs created by AGW (which is a pretty tall order), but rather all of the social costs and benefits created by the activity, which is far harder.

[...]

In order to achieve the 'fairness and social optimality' that we started with when discussing the AGW effects of carbon, we are logically led to demanding that the government measure the social value of almost every economically significant action, and then set up incentives to manage the population so as to achieve social goals. Because this is an impossible analytical task, in practice this means the purely political management of society based on relative power. What is this but unadulterated socialism in a green dress?

If you drop the other externalities and just look at climate change and the cost of road building, which it seems fairer to charge motorists for, then it is hard to justify the current levels of taxation. I produced research for the TaxPayers' Alliance comparing them and found road taxes were excessive in Britain to the tune of £18 ($33) billion a year in 2008.[205]

---

205 Sinclair, M., 'Excessive Motoring Taxes', TaxPayers' Alliance, 20 January 2011

Figure 5.2 shows the results. While the picture may be less extreme in other European countries, it will be similar. Even if the balance is different in some parts of the United States, and road building accounts for more or all of the tax levied, the threat of climate change can't justify significant increases in the tax for the reasons already shown.

Figure 5.2: Road transport taxes and social costs, UK, 2008

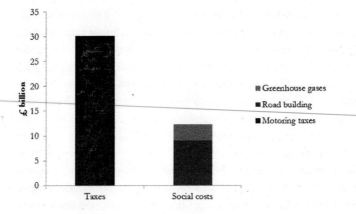

Green taxes on motorists are often wildly excessive, but that is just the start. Politicians are promoting all sorts of other policies in order to address the same issue. The whole point of Pigovian taxes is that once they are set at a sufficient level that is it, private incentives are then aligned with society's best interests and they will only emit if it is best for them to do so. To take other actions as well as green taxes means correcting for the same externalities twice, three times or more with motorists and taxpayers paying a heavy price. These are some of the measures that are being proposed or are already heaped on top of green taxes in an effort to limit road transport emissions:

Subsidies for alternative modes of transport; trains, buses and bikes. I'll cover some of those subsidies later in this chapter.

Subsidies for low emissions cars. Again, they are covered later in this chapter.

Emissions standards for vehicle manufacturers. These can lead to particularly absurd results with some specialist manufacturers. Aston Martin is producing a restyled version of the Toyota iQ city car called the Cygnet purely in order to reduce its average fleet emissions and make it easier to comply the EU targets.[206] It is hard to see how the new cars, which won't exactly substitute for an Aston Martin supercar, will really cut emissions.

Higher parking charges for relatively high emissions vehicles. In October 2009, Richmond-upon-Thames council in London became the first in the world to apply higher parking charges to cars with higher emissions. Vehicles that emit 186 g /km of CO_2 or more pay 25 per cent more. Some extremely low emissions vehicles get a discount but the measure is expected to mean a significant hike in charges overall.[207]

Road pricing. Advocates, like Tim Yeo MP, claim it will allow cuts in taxes on drivers[208] but local authority leaders have argued it could cost £23 ($41) billion a year to run a national road pricing scheme.[209] Motorists would need to pay for that – almost as much as is currently raised from taxes on motor fuel – just for the scheme to break even and before it starts funding other objectives like high speed rail, returns to investors and tax cuts. More modest schemes might work better so long as they are a substitute, and not yet another complement to excessive motoring taxes.

Mandates for biofuels. As discussed earlier, in the chapter on renewable energy, burning agricultural produce in our

206 Mooney, C., 'Aston Martin Cygnet is real, coming next year', *Top Gear*, 11 October 2010

207 Sky News, 'World First For "Green" Charge On Parking', 1 October 2009

208 Yeo, T., *Green Gold*, Tory Reform Group, July 2010, p.47

209 Hope, C., 'General Election 2010: Lib Dems back plans for road pricing across country', *Daily Telegraph*, 3 May 2010

cars rather than eating it means either pushing up food prices or encroaching on the wilderness.

It is very clear that the burden on motorists is excessive. They are being singled out for taxation as an easy target and also facing a range of burdensome regulations.

But even wildly excessive green taxes haven't stopped people driving. High fuel prices might partly explain why Europeans drive smaller cars (if you've ever tried to drive a big car round the narrow roads of a city like London you'll understand there are other reasons as well) but cars and lorries are still how most people and goods get around. In a refusal to take no for an answer, characteristic of so much current climate change policy, politicians have piled on other regulations and expensive subsidies.

Still people persist in driving. Pushing them into smaller cars comes at a price as safety can be compromised. A number of studies in the United States have found that the CAFE emissions standards there increased casualties by encouraging the use of lighter vehicles. A study by the US National Highway Traffic Safety Administration found that reducing a vehicle's weight by 100 pounds increases the estimated fatality rate by up to 5.63 per cent for light cars weighing less than 2,950 pounds, 4.70 per cent for heavier cars weighing over 2,950 pounds and 3.06 per cent for light trucks.[210] Sam Kazman, General Counsel at the Competitive Enterprise Institute, has summarised a few studies which showed that would translate into significant numbers of casualties:[211]

CAFE's tradeoff of safety for fuel economy is widely documented. A 2002 National Academy of Sciences study concluded that CAFE's downsizing effect contributed to between 1,300 and 2,600 deaths in a single representative year, and to ten

210 Kahane, C. J., 'Vehicle Weight, Fatality Risk and Crash Compatibility of Model Year 1991–99 Passenger Cars and Light Trucks', National Highway Traffic Safety Administration, October 2003

211 Kazman, S., 'First, Do No Harms to Motorists: Six Reasons Not To Raise CAFE Standards', CEI OnPoint No 114, 12 June 2007

times that many serious injuries. A 1989 Brookings-Harvard study estimated that CAFE caused a 14 to 27 per cent increase in occupant fatalities – an annual toll of 2,200 to 3,900 deaths. A 1999 USA Today analysis concluded that, over its lifetime, CAFE had resulted in 46,000 additional fatalities.

And the emissions cuts from switching people to smaller cars are limited in the context of wildly ambitious targets to cut emissions; it can't produce ongoing cuts in emissions.

Driving is just very convenient. Motorists are able to drive where and when they want to go, whereas passengers on a train are forced to accept its route and timetable. In highly congested cities with dense populations, public transport networks can be competitive, but most people living in rural areas or the suburbs have to drive. Figure 5.3 shows the share of the working population who drive to work plotted against population density in 376 local authority areas in England and Wales, and the pattern is pretty clear.[212]

Figure 5.3: Population density and driving to work

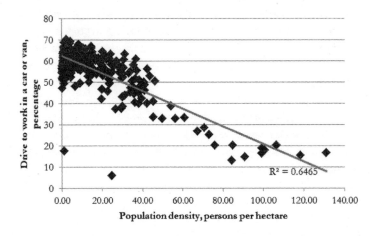

---

212 Office for National Statistics, Neighbourhood Statistics, Travel to work (KS15); Population Density (UV02)

That is also why attacks on motorists tend to produce such meagre emissions reductions. People need to drive to get to work or access services, they just have to bear higher taxes on motoring. That is why those taxes are able to raise so much revenue; an effective green tax that actually changed behaviour wouldn't raise much money.

Motoring taxes impose a huge burden on families that can't be justified by the threat of climate change. Attacks on the convenience and freedom of driving are an unfair response to road transport emissions. They need to end.

Flying

Aviation creates quite a small share of global emissions. A report for the IPCC in 2000 projected emissions from aircraft would rise substantially, but would remain a low share of the global total:[213]

Emissions of carbon dioxide by aircraft were 0.14 Gt C/ year in 1992. This is about 2 per cent of total anthropogenic carbon dioxide emissions in 1992 or about 13 per cent of carbon dioxide emissions from all transportation sources. The range of scenarios considered here projects that aircraft emissions of carbon dioxide will continue to grow and by 2050 will be 0.23 to 1.45 Gt C/year. For the reference scenario, this emission increases 3-fold by 2050 to 0.40 Gt C/year, or 3 per cent of the projected total anthropogenic carbon dioxide emissions relative to the mid-range IPCC emission scenario (IS92a).

Emissions at high altitudes are thought to have a greater effect on the climate than emissions at ground level. The IPCC also has estimates of the contribution of aviation to climate change now and in 2050:[214]

---

213 IPCC, *Aviation and the Global Atmosphere*, Cambridge University Press, 1999, p.6
214 Ibid., p.8

For the reference scenario, the radiative forcing by aircraft in 2050 is 0.19 Wm-2 or 5 per cent of the radiative forcing in the mid-range IS92a scenario (3.8 times the value in 1992).

Five per cent of the human contribution to global warming by 2050 is a little more significant, but still pretty marginal. With aviation expected to continue to make up such a small share of global emissions, stopping people flying isn't critical to limiting climate change. Aviation is a bigger share of emissions in the developed world though, and easy to paint as a luxury. That's why environmentalists are attacking flights.

Few countries tax flights particularly heavily. As airports are paid for through charges to airlines, there isn't the same need for governments to pay for infrastructure. At the same time, it is often easy for passengers to choose routes for long haul flights that avoid aviation taxes, which creates an incentive for countries to keep their taxes relatively low. Airline passengers aren't hit anything like as hard as motorists are by green taxes.

Britain is the sad exception to that rule. The government here levies Air Passenger Duty on flights. The rate is between £11 ($19) and £55 ($97) – depending on the distance – on each passenger flying from a UK airport for a standard economy ticket. Passengers in first or business class pay between £22 ($39) and £110 ($195).[215] Rates are continuing to rise despite the Department for Transport releasing a study in 2008 which showed the taxes crossed the line in February 2007 and became excessive even on the DEFRA Shadow Price of Carbon, which is much higher than most academic estimates of the social cost of carbon as I mentioned earlier. That study concluded that:[216]

Government took action in February 2007 to double the Air Passenger Duty rates, which reflects the framework now in operation in the UK; this will therefore be in the actual data of future emissions cost assessments. As demonstrated in the illus-

....

215 HM Revenue and Customs, Air Passenger Duty, September 2010, 2.1.2 Rates of duty from 1 November 2009

216 Department for Transport, Aviation Cost Assessment 2008, p.9

trative scenario B, this has a marked impact on the results of the emissions cost assessment. Under this scenario, aviation would cover its climate change costs with an excess of some £0.1 billion.

Once again, high green taxes can't be justified by the problem they are supposed to address. Taxes on aviation have risen since, becoming even more excessive, and further hikes are expected.

Britain's aviation taxes aren't even effective at cutting emissions. While there have been attempts at reform recently, when the tax was doubled in 2007, it did more to cut the difference in price between flying to New York or Sydney than to actually put people off flying. As a result, the best academic study of the change suggested it had 'the perverse effect of increasing carbon dioxide emissions, albeit only slightly'.[217]

The European Union is going to include aviation in its cap and trade scheme and will require airlines to hold emissions permits from 2012. A report from the House of Lords European Union Committee in 2006 provided a range of estimates of the potential impact on fares, which are shown in Table 5.3.[218]

Table 5.3: Potential fare increases from including aviation in the EU ETS

Length of flight	Range of fare increases depending on assumptions, € per round trip
Short haul (e.g. Amsterdam–Paris)	0.2 to 4.6
Medium haul (e.g. Munich - Palma de Mallorca)	0.4 to 9.0
Long haul (e.g. Gatwick - Newark USA)	1.0 to 6.9

---

217 Mayor, K. & Tol, R. S. J., 'The impact of the UK aviation tax on carbon dioxide emissions and visitor numbers', Working Paper FNU-131, April 2007

218 House of Lords, European Union Committee, 'Including the Aviation Sector in the European Union Emissions Trading Scheme', Report with Evidence, 21st Report of Session 2005–06, 9 February 2006, Table 1. Estimates of impacts of ETS on air fares

Those estimates, even at the high end, are probably just the start. Environmentalist pressure groups are already calling for the cap to be tightened, which could sharply increase costs.

Advocates of cap and trade for aviation also envision it going global, just like the plans to link the main EU and US cap and trade schemes. Major airlines, through the Aviation Global Deal Group which includes companies like British Airways, KLM and Air France, released a plan to control aviation emissions in September 2009.[219] Their plan called for a global aviation cap and trade scheme.

Industry estimates reported in *The Guardian* suggested the average passenger could pay an extra £10 ($18) for a return ticket under their scheme.[220] The Aviation Global Deal Group talked up how auctioning the emissions would make billions available to help developing countries but, looking at their plans, they only envisioned 10 to 30 per cent of the permits being auctioned.[221]

With most of the allowances given out for free, most of the £10 each passenger paid for a ticket would go straight to the airlines as a windfall profit. The airlines say that they hope to 'contribute towards a pragmatic, fair and environmentally effective global policy solution for addressing CO_2 emissions from international aviation',[222] but they've just found a great excuse to take more money from ordinary holidaymakers and businesspeople without offering a better service.

The airlines in the Aviation Global Deal Group aren't the only ones pushing for a global cap and trade scheme for airlines. The International Air Transport Association, the global aviation trade association, released a report in 2009

....

219 Aviation Global Deal Group, 'A sectoral approach to addressing international aviation emissions', 9 June 2009

220 Milmo, D., 'No immediate increase in flight taxes, transport secretary says', *The Guardian*, 9 September 2009

221 Aviation Global Deal Group, 'A sectoral approach to addressing international aviation emissions', 9 June 2009, paragraph 43

222 Ibid., paragraph 2

which avoided explicitly calling for cap and trade but did argue for a cap – from 2020, with emissions halving by 2050 – and that any policy should be global in scope.[223]

The international shipping industry has done the same, again calling for global cap and trade to cover their industry.[224] When you talk to industry groups about this, they argue that they will not make windfall profits as they will not be able to pass the carbon cost on to their consumers. But in a global scheme there are no foreign competitors to restrain rises in prices and the basic economic logic set out in Chapter 3 suggests that the carbon price will be passed on to consumers at some point in what is a highly competitive market. That will mean more expensive flights, adding to the burden that green taxes impose on families taking a well-earned holiday, and more expensive international shipping pushing up the cost of imported goods.

Cap and trade is likely to prove particularly inefficient at controlling emissions from aviation. The industry is notoriously prone to booms and busts as people tend to increase the amount they fly a lot in a growing economy but cut back sharply in a recession. That means demand from airlines for emissions allowances will increase and decrease sharply as the economy does better or worse. With the supply of emissions capped, fluctuations in airline demand will cause rapid booms and busts in the emissions price. That volatility will make the scheme less effective the same way it does in existing cap and trade schemes, by undermining the incentive the scheme is supposed to create to make expensive investments in new equipment.

....

223 International Air Transport Association, 'A global approach to reducing aviation emissions: First stop: carbon-neutral growth from 2020', November 2009

224 Joint report by the Australian Shipowners Association; Royal Belgian Shipowners' Association; Norwegian Shipowners' Association; Swedish Shipowners' Association; and the Chamber of Shipping of the UK, 'A global cap-and-trade system to reduce carbon emissions from international shipping', September 2009

As well as taxing flights and putting in place new cap and trade schemes, politicians are starting to block the construction of new airport capacity. Just like with flight taxes Britain is leading the world.

London Heathrow is a key hub airport. It hosts around 60 million international passengers a year, more than any other airport in the world.[225] That makes it a huge asset to London and the UK. Anyone who can get to Heathrow has access to an unparalleled range and frequency of flights to destinations all around the world. Flights are more convenient and more affordable, as they are more direct.

The owners of the airport, BAA, want to add another runway. That would help keep Heathrow competitive and reduce congestion. It would also mean fewer flights had to circle over London before a slot became available for them to land – good news in terms of cutting emissions. The Labour government had approved the new runway but the new Conservative and Liberal Democrat coalition has blocked it. Their coalition agreement stated simply: 'We will cancel the third runway at Heathrow.'[226]

The opposition to the new runway was made of two groups.

There are those who aren't against an expansion of air travel but don't want to see an expansion of Heathrow itself. Their feelings are understandable. Long years of operating beyond capacity have left the airport with a bad reputation and it probably isn't the site that you would choose if you were building a new airport from scratch today. Lots of people live under the flight path. However, like it or not, it is Britain's international hub and establishing a new one is impractical and prohibitively expensive.

---

225 Airports Council International, International Passenger Traffic Monthly Ranking: August 2010, 11 November 2010
226 HM Government, 'The Coalition: our programme for government', May 2010, p.16

There are network effects with air travel; the more routes you have into an airport already the more it makes sense for airlines to introduce new ones. Passengers travelling on a new route can connect to more places once they arrive in London. Heathrow's existing traffic and connections make it the best place for airlines to expand new services.

Establishing a new hub on an artificial island in the Thames estuary, as the Mayor of London Boris Johnson has suggested, would be a long and difficult political and commercial process even if it could be built. The website *The Daily Mash* satirised the plan well:[227]

Boris Johnson's plan to build an artificial island in the Thames and then put an airport on it has been backed by the majority of Britain's 12-year-old boys.

According to Johnson's '£500 squillion' plan, the island will be surrounded by laser cannons and thousands of deadly sharks to keep out terrorists and girls.

No airport but Heathrow is going to be a British competitor to continental hubs in Paris and Frankfurt any time soon. Putting the third runway on hold while we wait for a new airport that isn't much more than an idea at the moment will mean flights from the UK will become more expensive and longer.

The other group trying to stop the runway were out to stop people flying. They carry banners that say 'cheap flights cost the Earth' (expensive flights taken by environmentalists going to climate summits in Bali are okay) and work to stop working-class families with the temerity to want to enjoy a summer holiday in Spain.

If environmentalists are able to block airport infrastructure in other countries, they will probably adopt a similar strategy and work with opposition from local groups opposing expansion at a specific airport.

....

227 '12 year-old boys back Boris Johnson airport plan', *The Daily Mash*, 22 September 2008

The attack on aviation is only just beginning. Compared to motorists, airline passengers face a relatively light burden right now but that may not last. Politicians have ambitious plans to leap straight to a global cap and trade scheme. If such a scheme were put in place – and producing revenues for governments, subsidies for industry and fewer flights to satisfy the environmentalists – over time it would be a recipe for airline passengers to be charged more and more.

In the end, the question comes down to your attitude to flying. If you see it as just one more consumer good then it is easy to attack flights as a carbon intensive luxury. On the other hand, if you appreciate aviation as the incredible opportunity for people to see the world that it is, you will have little time for attempts to demonise it for the small contribution planes make to climate change.

Journeys that used to take weeks or months now take hours. International travel has been radically democratised. Whether people use that liberty to see new cultures, experience something remarkable or just have fun is up to them. The opportunity is still a remarkable technical and economic achievement that it would be an awful shame to give up.

Back in 2007, *Guardian* columnist Jonathan Freedland wrote about taking the train instead of flying to France:[228]

Except there's a catch. The truth is, I don't feel I'm making any sacrifice at all. Because I hate flying.

[...]

Even before kids came along, I hated flying. Irrational, I know, but I find it frightening: the loss of control, the sheer helplessness up in the sky. I can make my palms sweat just thinking about it.

Another *Guardian* columnist has described our taste for international travel as 'binge-flying'.[229]

---

228 Freedland, J., 'Ground rules', *The Guardian*, 3 August 2007

229 Hastings, M., 'Binge-flying culture is just beginning. The only way to stop it is a severe tax', *The Guardian*, 7 May 2007

Of course, plenty of people don't like the actual experience of flying. That doesn't mean they don't appreciate how wonderful the opportunities it presents are. We definitely shouldn't trust people who have found in climate change an excuse to vent their dislike of mass air travel. Air travel is great and we should celebrate it. Any policy that attempts to curb people's taste for travelling abroad should be imposed with a heavy heart. Too many environmentalists seem to quite enjoy clamping down and there is a real threat that policies implemented at their behest will make flying more expensive and rarer. We shouldn't let that happen.

Alternative transport

There are two main forms of alternative, low carbon transport that get subsidies: electric cars and trains, particularly high speed rail.

It seems quite likely that eventually, as the technology develops and oil becomes scarcer, we will move towards some form of electric or hydrogen-fuelled car. At some point it will just be cheaper. Right now though, electric cars are expensive and impractical. Trying to force them into action is a bad idea, just as it would have been to subsidise the combustion engine car in the late nineteenth century when it couldn't compete with the train.

The *New York Times* commissioned five authors to look at the prospects for electric cars. Only one thought their time had really come, the bureau chief of *Automobile* magazine.[230] By contrast, and reflecting the views of the other commentators, Maryann Keller, an industry analyst, told the newspaper that:[231]

Electric vehicles are neither practical replacements for modern internal combustion engine vehicles nor are they affordable without massive subsidies from state and federal

230 Kitman, J., 'A Game Changer', *New York Times*, 7 October 2010
231 Keller, M., 'Impractical Novelties in the US', *New York Times*, 7 October 2010

governments. High price and limited range make pure electric vehicles a novelty until technology progresses to overcome these challenges.

Christopher R. Knittel, an associate professor of economics at the University of California, Davis, set out two of the key problems:[232]

First, a shift to electric vehicles will require a fundamental change in how we 'replenish' vehicles. Gone will be gas stations, replaced by either 440 volt quick charge stations that will still require at least thirty minutes to charge the batteries, or battery exchanges similar to the propane tank exchanges that exist today.

Will consumers be willing to only charge at night, or wait thirty minutes to charge during the day? The frustrated faces I see when consumers have to wait for one car to finish refuelling at gas stations suggests not. Adding to these frustrations is the fact that the range of the Leaf is roughly 100 miles, far shorter than today's gasoline-powered vehicles, requiring more frequent recharging.

To charge an electric car up, even if you are happy for it to take hours and only need to charge overnight, many households will need a dedicated line. For rapid charging, to get the battery to 70–80 per cent of capacity in 20–40 minutes, special and expensive equipment is needed.

Public charging networks could also prove very expensive.

First the slow-charging networks needed to give people the confidence they won't run out of juice and be unable to find a charging point. Citigroup Global Markets have pointed out that plans to build 100,000 charging points in Israel are expected to cost €300–400 (£227–302, $402–536) million, and that is a compact country with around 2 million cars. Scaling that up to a bigger country like Germany, France or the United Kingdom could requires billions of euros in infrastructure investment.[233] Let alone trying to make it work in the United States.

Then you need some rapid charging or battery swapping stations to make long journeys practical, so you don't add hours to people's journey time if they want to undertake a journey beyond their electric car's range. Citigroup Global Markets expects that could also cost hundreds of millions of euros even if you don't need as many rapid charging outlets or battery swap stations.[234]

The other problem that Christopher R. Knittel set out is the cost:[235]

Second, batteries are expensive. They are so expensive that for most uses, even accounting for the added cleanliness of the Leaf, the full lifetime cost of the Nissan Leaf will be greater than a comparable gasoline-powered sedan.

Heavy state and federal subsidies may make the Leaf privately economic for some of us. The key question, however, is whether these subsidies are a good investment, either for the environmental or more generally? That is, could that money be better spent elsewhere? The answer appears to be yes.

There are extensive subsidies for electric cars. Citigroup Global Markets report government rebates and tax incentives aimed at stimulating sales worth over €5,000 (£3,800, $6,700) in France, Spain, the United Kingdom, China, Japan and the United States.[236] As Peter van Doren from Cato pointed out, those subsidies are a very expensive way of cutting emissions unless you already have a grid running on renewable energy:[237]

And there would not be carbon-emission advantages from

233 Brown, M., Atherton, P. & Lawson, J., 'All Hail the Electric Car', Citigroup Global Markets, 23 September 2009, p.23

234 Ibid., p.24

235 Knittel, C. R., 'Use Subsidies Elsewhere', *New York Times*, 7 October 2010

236 Brown, M., Atherton, P. & Lawson, J., 'All Hail the Electric Car', Citigroup Global Markets, 23 September 2009, Figure 9. Overview of government position and incentives for selected European & Other countries

237 van Doren, P., 'Batteries Matter', *New York Times*, 7 October 2010

*electric cars unless all the new electricity used for cars were
renewable. With natural gas-fired generation, the cost of carbon
emission reduction from electric cars would be well over $100
per ton, much higher than any carbon tax recommended by
economists. Thus, the electric car is not a cost effective answer
to all our problems and would not exist without government
tax subsidies.*

If we had solved the problem of how to generate huge
amounts of affordable, low carbon electricity then electric cars
might be a reasonable way forward. We haven't. As I showed
in the chapter on renewable energy, it is still exceptionally
expensive and an inadequate substitute for power from fossil
fuels. That means that, for now, electric cars are a niche product for those who drive short distances, probably in cities,
and are willing to pay a premium.

Another problem that governments will find if they try to
shift people onto electric cars is that their revenues depend
on the internal combustion engine. It is much cheaper to fill
up on electricity than it is on petroleum, but the low fuel costs
of electric cars are mostly the result of high taxes on petrol.
Without those taxes, in the UK for example and with oil at $70
a barrel, an efficient Golf diesel would be cheaper to fuel for
100 kilometres than a Nissan Leaf electric car is in the day. But
if government policies encourage people to shift away from a
highly taxed fuel they might lose out on revenue. That wouldn't
be such a bad thing, but governments could respond by imposing new taxes, even some kind of levy on electricity used to
charge cars.[238] Investors have to be wary of a product that only
makes sense because it is getting favourable fiscal treatment.

For longer journeys, environmentalists are promoting high
speed rail as an alternative to driving or flying. Unfortunately,
proposals for high speed rail tend to have one of two problems. They either try to make rail work where populations are

238 Brown, M., Atherton, P. & Lawson, J., 'All Hail the Electric Car', Citigroup
Global Markets, 23 September 2009, p.13

too dispersed and railways can't compete with the flexibility of cars, or are introduced as an upgrade where there are already decent train services and higher speeds don't provide sufficient benefits to justify the cost.

In the United States, the Obama administration have plans to build lots of high speed routes that it is hard to imagine many people ever using. Michael Barone has made that point forcefully:[239]

Take the proposed line between Orlando and Tampa. Who would ride? Locals can drive the distance in 90 minutes; it would take longer to drive to the station, wait for the train, ride on it for a little less than an hour. And then, what would you do to get to your final destination? Tampa and Orlando are sprawling metro areas, with few destinations within walking distance or reasonably priced taxi service of any possible train station. As for tourists, don't they all rent cars, for exactly these reasons? They rent cars at the airport (Orlando and Tampa airports have pretty nifty setups, much more convenient than, say, San Francisco or Los Angeles or Detroit). Why would they want to get on a train and then rent a car? An Orlando-Tampa train would look nice on the map, paralleling Interstate 4, but I think it would be useful only for people looking for a quiet place for an hour's meditation.

Or consider the proposed Los Angeles-San Francisco metro area line. These are even huger metro areas and travellers between them have a wide variety of destinations. There are multiple major airports in each of these metro areas – LAX, Burbank, Orange County, Ontario in southern California; SFO, San Jose and Oakland in northern California. High-speed rail is not going to beat planes for travel times, and it seems unlikely that there will be as many choices between different destinations in each metro areas as planes currently provide.

The United States is just too big a country, with its population too spread out, for high-speed rail to really work. And

239 Barone, M., 'High-speed rail: not much in other continent-sized countries', *Washington Examiner*, 20 August 2010

plans for high speed rail risk endangering slow moving but economically vital freight rail services. The Wall Street Journal has reported that:[240]

To save time and money, government officials want new high-speed rail routes to operate on the vast system of train corridors that already crisscross the US, unlike European and Asian countries that have built dedicated tracks for high-speed rail.

But Norfolk Southern Corp., Union Pacific Corp. and other railroad companies are balking at sharing their tracks or rights-of-way with trains that would run between 90 and 200-plus miles an hour. They argue that mixing high-speed passenger trains with slower freight trains would create safety risks, prevent future expansion and cause congestion.

Cargo would be pushed to their competitors—trucking firms—the railroads argue, just as freight loads are picking up after the recession. Weekly average carloads in August were the highest since November 2008, according to the Association of American Railroads, the industry's main trade group.

State and railroad officials are struggling to hammer out partnership deals required to release the funds. The Federal Railroad Administration has distributed just $597 million out of $8 billion in stimulus funds awarded by the administration in January to jump-start high-speed rail. An additional $286 million is expected to go out the door soon, the FRA said. Even when states and freight railroads have reached agreements, disagreements remain over the speeds at which the passenger trains will be allowed to travel.

Those freight trains are important but they are a part of an economy powered with fossil fuels, not a challenge to it. Some European commentators are a bit confused. In his book *Green Gold*, Tim Yeo MP breathlessly cited an investment in that freight network as evidence that 'more and more

---

240 Levitz, J., 'High-Speed Rail Stalls', *Wall Street Journal*, 21 September 2010

countries are [...] recognising the advantages of high speed rail'. He reported that:[241]

In America, Warren Buffett has just made his biggest ever investment – in a railway business.

Can you guess what carbon-intensive commodity Warren Buffett's trains are going to be moving?

Coal.

Brad Plumer at *The New Republic*, wrote in an article titled 'Buffett Bets Big On Coal', that:

Specifically, the BNSF railway serves a lot of coal fields in the West, including Wyoming's vast Powder River Basin, and hauls enough coal on its routes to supply about 10 per cent of the electricity in the United States. So Buffett's essentially betting that coal's going to remain a major part of the US energy mix for quite some time, even as the country moves to cut carbon emissions.[242]

On those routes where high speed rail makes more sense, decent routes already exist, even if they aren't as fast as France's TGV. The Northeast Corridor in the United States has the Acela Express which reaches speeds of 150 miles per hour. The London to Birmingham route that is the proposed site of Britain's second high speed rail line (the first links the Channel Tunnel to London) already has trains running at up to 125 miles per hour. The gains from going even faster are limited and expensive.

The HS2 Action Alliance, a group campaigning against the new 'HS2' route the government is planning, have pointed out a number of problems with the business case for the line, which claims high speed rail will produce benefits sufficient to justify the huge cost. No account has been taken in the business case of the potential for people to work while travelling,

241 Yeo, T., *Green Gold*, Tory Reform Group, July 2010, p.12
242 Plumer, B., 'Buffett Bets Big On Coal', *The Vine*, 3 November 2009

the demand forecasts are too optimistic and the line isn't fairly compared with alternatives.[243]

Analysts Daniel J. Graham and Patricia Melo produced a report on the economic benefits of high speed rail for the HS2 Limited company tasked by the government with establishing the case for high speed rail. They found that the economic benefits of speed itself, by bringing regional economies together, would be 'very small indeed'.[244] Proponents of the line now talk about it primarily as a way of getting more capacity to reduce overcrowding; more rail not high speed rail.

Unfortunately on that score it doesn't do too well. Lots of major towns such as Coventry and Stoke-on-Trent will get a worse service. Others like Milton Keynes will wait years for the scheme to complete in 2026, with overcrowding getting worse and worse.[245] It just isn't worthwhile to keep up the same service on the existing line, and the new line will only serve a limited set of destinations. There are then further problems with how the line connects into London, dumping huge numbers of passengers on the already overcrowded London Underground lines out of Euston station. The government promises it will overcome all these problems but the money just isn't there, it will make the financial case even worse. The 51M group of local authorities opposing the scheme have set out a far more affordable alternative.[246]

It doesn't do much for the environment either. In a report for the House of Commons Transport Select Committee the consultancy Oxera wrote that:[247]

....

243 HS2 Action Alliance, 'Review of the February 2011 consultation business case for HS2', June 2011

244 Graham, D. J. & Melo, P., 'Advice on the Assessment of Wider Economic Impacts: a report for HS2', 25 February 2010

245 Stokes, C., 'HS2 Capacity Analysis', TaxPayers' Alliance, 30 March 2011

246 Stokes, C., 'Optimised Alternative to HS2 – The Scope for Growth on the Existing Network', 51M, May 2011

247 Oxera, 'Review of the Government's case for a High Speed Rail Programme', 20 June 2011, p.15

Given the very limited anticipated substitution from air to rail (6 per cent) and car (7 per cent), the substantial volume of new trips (22 per cent) suggested for HS2, and the lower rates of emission from slower trains, the classic rail options could well involve lower overall emissions.

The main argument you hear from proponents of high speed rail is an appeal to train envy. Continental European countries have trains that go up to 200 miles per hour and Japan has the bullet train, surely Britain and America can't afford to be left behind?

In Britain's case, as I mentioned, we already have fast intercity services with routes capable of speeds of 125 miles per hour. Dense populations mean that you don't need very high speed rail to get good journey times.

In the United States, the comparison is just unfair. The distances that you need to cover are too great for trains to really compete with planes. As Michael Barone has pointed out, other continent-sized countries like Canada, Brazil, Australia and Russia don't have high speed rail either.[248] China does, but it is concentrated in densely populated coastal regions and some of the projects may not represent good value.

There are two problems that invariably come up with high speed rail. First, demand will be overstated. Danish researchers have looked at the issue and found that nine out of ten rail projects overestimated demand and the average overestimation is 106 per cent.[249] Second, it will be a rich man's train paid for with poor people's taxes. Long-distance trains are overwhelmingly used by people on high incomes.[250] It is very

248 Barone, M., 'High-speed rail: not much in other continent-sized countries', *Washington Examiner*, 20 August 2010

249 Flyvbjerg, B., Skamris Holm, M. K. & Buhl, S. L., 'How (In)accurate Are Demand Forecasts in Public Works Projects – The Case of Transportation', *Journal of the American Planning Association*, Vol. 71, No 2, Spring 2005

250 Rorh, C., Fox, J., Daly, A., Patruni, B., Patil, S. & Tsang, F., 'Modelling Long-Distance Travel in the UK', RAND Europe, NHS 2002/5, income data

capital intensive, and looks like a pretty bad investment for countries already struggling with large government deficits.

Other modes of transport obviously have their part to play. Electric cars may well become more important over time, but they aren't practical or economical today. Trains are great but only in their niches. They are great at moving a lot of people and reducing strain on the roads into congested cities. In that role, they tend to already have quite high market share.

Cars – powered by internal combustion engines – are the dominant mode of transport for domestic, short-range transport. For longer journeys, and particularly international travel, there is no effective substitute for a plane. High taxes and draconian regulations won't stop that, they will just make travel more expensive for ordinary people, whether they are getting to work or taking a welcome break.

Inefficient and unfair green taxes

The logic of green taxes can sound like common sense. If people are imposing costs on wider society they should pay for them. Unfortunately, trying to translate that simple principle into practical policy ends in disaster. It gives politicians a licence to single out motorists, in particular, and impose wildly excessive taxes on them.

The sheer amount of revenue raised from green taxes is testament to the fact that they are serving as a cash cow for governments and not really as a tool to change behaviour. If green taxes worked, if they actually encouraged people to drive less or otherwise use less petrol, then they wouldn't raise much money at all. People pay the taxes because they need to drive to work; they pay them because they want a large car to accommodate their family. Of course, some people drive a fast car with a big engine just as a luxury, but there aren't enough people like that for a change in their behaviour to make a significant difference to the amount of carbon dioxide we emit overall.

Politicians could devise ever more specific taxes in an attempt to target unnecessary gas-guzzling, but it tends to be middle-class families who need to drive who get hit in practice and the actual emissions savings from being such a killjoy are limited.

Attacks on aviation are unnecessary and unfortunate. Flying is an incredible liberation and the way it has been democratised, opened up to ordinary people, is remarkable. Clamping down on the opportunities that cheap, convenient long-distance travel creates would be very sad. With flying projected to continue to make up a small portion of global emissions, and planes constantly getting more efficient, there is no need to stop people taking those opportunities.

Electric cars are still a niche product and the substitutes for cars and planes just aren't sufficient. Trains are great for certain journeys and where they can work effectively they are generally quite well developed already. But they can't compete with the flexibility of cars for journeys between cities with dispersed populations, and they can't compete with planes over genuinely long distances. Trying to press trains into action where they aren't competitive is an easy way to waste a lot of money.

Motorists deserve a better deal and green taxes should go down, not up. Transport policy needs to be directed more at delivering convenient and affordable travel, not quixotic attempts to drive people onto non-existent substitutes for cars and planes.

GREEN JOBS

When politicians try to sell ambitious green policies these days, they tend to talk less about climate change than they do about the boon they claim their initiatives will be for the economy. Jonathon Porritt, environmentalist and former head of Britain's Sustainable Development Commission, recommended that approach when he told an audience at the London School of Economics:[251]

Obama sells that in, not on the back of say 'we've got to do something about climate change, 'cause otherwise your teddy's going to sink under the waves', he doesn't do teddys sinking under the waves okay, what he does is jobs. And what he says is: guess how many new jobs we can generate through this investment?

In September 2009, Senators John Kerry and Barbara Boxer introduced a 'Clean Energy Jobs and American Power Act'. Back in March 2009, when Representatives Henry Waxman and Edward Markey announced their legislation, they both focused first on jobs when promoting the bills. Representative Waxman started with:[252]

This legislation will create millions of clean energy jobs, put America on the path to energy independence and cut global warming pollution.

And Representative Markey with:[253]

....

251 Porritt, J., 'LSE Sustainability in Practice lecture', co-hosted by the Grantham Research Institute on Climate Change and the Environment, 4 February 2010
252 Committee on Energy and Commerce, 'Chairmen Waxman, Markey Release Discussion Draft of New Clean Energy Legislation', 31 March 2009
253 Ibid.

This legislation will create clean energy jobs that can't be shipped overseas, reduce our dependence on foreign oil and make America the global leader in energy technology.

The same strategy is used in Europe. In a joint article the climate change ministers of Germany, France and the United Kingdom, arguing for a new 30 per cent cut in emissions by the 2020 European target, said that:[254]

At the same time we have a tremendous opportunity: to reinforce our own economic recovery, to improve our energy security and to tackle climate change through the development of decarbonised energy sectors, opening up new sources of employment and exports.

The reason politicians now put so little weight on climate change when they try to promote climate change policies is that they know it doesn't sell. The Institute for Public Policy Research, a British centre-left think tank, released findings from a focus group which looked at how to motivate consumers to buy green products in September 2009.[255] The very first of their main recommendations was 'don't focus on climate change'. They found that many of the people in their focus groups regarded the issue as boring or 'faddy' and an excuse to hike their taxes. Many also resented being made to feel guilty about a lifestyle they had worked hard to earn. Greens were viewed as 'over-virtuous', 'self-righteous' or 'smug' and frequently hypocritical.

When people did move to improve the energy efficiency of their home for example, it was generally because they wanted to save money. This response was particularly telling:[256]

If I was to build a house tomorrow, it would have anything energy saving that I could possibly ram in it to make it as

254 Huhne, C., Borloo, J-L. & Röttgen, N., 'Benefits of 30% emissions cut for European Union', *Financial Times*, 15 July 2010

255 Platt, R. & Retallack, S., 'Consumer Power: How the public thinks lower-carbon behaviour could be made mainstream', IPPR, September 2009

256 Ibid., p.19

energy efficient as I could – and then I could have my Audi TT. (Female, York, with children)

The public are interested in saving energy where that can save them money, not so that they can emit less, but so they can do more.

Just as telling people it will save them money is the best way to sell loft insulation, not grand claims about the dangers of climate change, politicians want to claim their policies will make people better off, not that they are a necessary sacrifice. Those claims are going to be hard to sustain.

Figure 6.1: Energy as a percentage of total production costs, selected industries

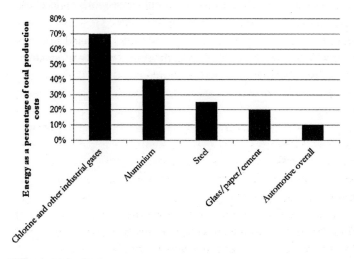

Effect on industry
Rising energy prices don't just affect bills for residential customers, they also increase costs for business. Energy is a substantial part of many manufacturers' costs. Figure 6.1 gives a rough idea of energy's share in the total costs of a number of major industries.[257] As it shows, there are a

257 Industry sources

number of major energy intensive industries that will have to go where energy is cheap. They will find it impossible to compete otherwise. Other manufacturing firms will face a situation like that in the automotive sector, where energy is one cost among many but enough to make a difference to where industry is located at the margin.

You will sometimes hear politicians or activists referring to 'old industries' as if we are talking about some kind of hang-over from the Industrial Revolution that was never going to last anyway. It is easy for the mix of Wall Street or City of London analysts and Silicon Valley serial entrepreneurs who run the green industries, to feel contemptuous of old-fashioned metal bashing or chemicals firms. Environmentalists see their cause as a moral issue, and those working in energy intensive industries are on the wrong side.

Figure 6.2: Index of production, manufacture of chemicals and man-made fibres

The reality is that the energy intensive industries are inno-vative, successful and major employers. You can see that looking at the pattern of output over the years, even in the relatively post-Industrial British economy. Since 1970 output in the chemicals industry in Britain has more than doubled, as you can see in Figure 6.2.[258]

There is no way energy intensive industries will be able to remain competitive located in a country where climate change policies are dramatically increasing energy costs. They would be at an insurmountable disadvantage compared to rivals in countries not imposing the same burden on their manufacturers.

In his book *Power Grab*, Chris Horner of the Competitive Enterprise Institute gives the example of Acerinox, the parent company of North American Stainless, which created steel jobs in Kentucky in order to avoid the costs of European climate change policy:[259]

Those jobs were exported here in 2004 by North American's European parent company, Acerinox, after Chief Executive Officer Victoriano Muñoz announced he could no longer justify long-term, capital- and energy-intensive investments while burdened with the new environmental regulations imposed in Europe.

The Energy Intensive Users Group (EIUG) and the Trades Union Congress (TUC) recently released a report looking at the scale of the likely rise in industrial energy bills in the UK. They commissioned the consultants Waters Wye Associates who estimated that industrial firms could face an increase in their total energy bill of between 18 and 141 per cent.[260] That is clearly a huge risk to the viability of their businesses.

In response to that report, a number of major British employers sounded the alarm.[261] The Managing Director and CEO of Tata Steel Europe, Kirby Adams said:

....

258 Office for National Statistics, CKZG: IOP: DG: Mfr of chemicals & man-made fibres: CVMSA

259 Horner, C., *Power Grab*, Regnery Publishing, p.4

260 Waters Wye Associates, 'The Cumulative Impact of Climate Change Policies on UK Energy Intensive Industries – Are Policies Effectively Focussed?', A summary report for The Energy Intensive Users Group and the Trades Union Congress, July 2010, p.33

261 Energy Intensive Users Group, 'Climate change policies threaten the future of the energy intensive sector', 27 July 2010

Many of the taxes and costs identified in this report are UK-specific and will reduce the competitiveness of Corus' British operations. Moreover, the very significant cumulative nature of the additional costs likely to come in under European legislation will damage the competitiveness of all EU steelmakers and limit their ability to fulfil their crucial role in a low carbon future.

In May 2011 they announced the loss of 1,500 jobs in Scunthorpe and Teesside, after raising rising energy costs with the government.[262]

Chief Executive Officer of GrowHow, Paul Thompson, said:

The fertiliser industry has been identified by the EU's own study to be the sector most exposed to the risk of 'carbon leakage'. Despite our substantial recent investment to reduce greenhouse gas emissions by more than 40 per cent, the combined effect of these climate change policies will almost certainly make this a reality in the UK.

The Chief Executive of Ibstock Brick Limited, Wayne Sheppard, said:

We want to invest more in the UK, but we are competing for funds from our parent company with our other plants in Europe and around the world. The UK's climate change policies are seriously out of line with other countries' more pragmatic approaches.

Of course, you can write these comments off as self-promoting. But it is common sense that if you significantly increase energy prices that will make manufacturing firms that have to spend a lot on energy less competitive. Over time investment and jobs will move to countries that don't impose the same burden.

In a study for the think tank Civitas, Ruth Lea and Jeremy Nicholson used the INEOS Chlor plant in Runcorn as one example of how many jobs hang on energy intensive industries, and their ability to compete. As they pointed out, it isn't just significant in itself but has a wider importance because

---

262 Fortson, D., 'Industry rebels on carbon targets', *Sunday Times*, 22 May 2011

the chlorine and caustic soda it produces has so many uses in other industries:[263]

It is used as a disinfectant and a purifier, and in the manu-facture of plastics (Polyvinyl chloride, PVC), solvents, agro-chemicals and pharmaceuticals. It is also an intermediate in manufacturing other substances where it is not contained in the final product. Products relying on chlorine's unique proper-ties include household items such as bleach and disinfectant to bullet-resistant vests, computer hardware, silicon chips and automotive parts.

That's why an industry study suggested 46,000 jobs would be lost directly within ten years if the plant closed and a further 87,000 would be threatened in the wider economy. Jim Ratcliffe, founder of INEOS, has warned the government that he could be forced to close it if something isn't done about mounting energy costs.[264]

Overall, and according to the EIUG/TUC report, energy intensive sectors currently employ 225,000 workers in Britain[265] and again far more jobs will be at risk than that if the factories move abroad.

The Civitas study also looks at existing cases where high energy prices have cost jobs, though climate change policies have only recently become the driving force behind those high prices so the earlier spikes were normally not down to policy.[266]

There is no doubt that high energy prices have already been a factor behind industry closures. In 2003 the energy intensive Britannia Zinc works near Bristol was closed, with a loss of 400 jobs. And in May 2006 the EIUG reported that

---

263 Lea, R. & Nicholson, J., 'British energy policy and the threat to manufac-turing industry', Civitas, p.13

264 Fortson, D., 'Industry rebels on carbon targets', *Sunday Times*, 22 May 2011

265 Waters Wye Associates, 'The Cumulative Impact of Climate Change Policies on UK Energy Intensive Industries – Are Policies Effectively Focussed?', A summary report for The Energy Intensive Users Group and the Trades Union Congress, July 2010, p.3

266 Lea, R. & Nicholson, J., 'British energy policy and the threat to manufac-turing industry', Civitas, p.11

the UK gas price spike of 2005–06 had contributed to 6,000 jobs lost over the previous eighteen months in the glass sector; several paper mills had also been closed. In addition, brick capacity had been cut back and manufacturers of chlorine and ammonia-based fertiliser had reduced production. In July 2006 EIUG reported that even where production was continuing investment was being reduced, thus cutting back the potential capacity and potential contribution of these businesses to employment and GDP.

Anglesey Aluminium's plant closed last year, following the ending of its deal to buy competitively priced electricity from the nearby Wylfa nuclear power station, which had recently passed into state ownership. Under EU law the electricity deal with the now state-owned Wylfa was classified as 'state aid' and therefore deemed illegal. Of Britain's two other primary aluminium plants, the one at Lynemouth in Northumberland uses electricity from its own coal-fired power station. This power station will require the fitting of costly scrubbers in order to comply technically with the EU's Large Combustion Plants Directive even though they will have no improved environmental impact because the air quality is already controlled using another, more sophisticated, procedure. Such extra costs will inevitably undermine the economic viability of the plant.

It is important to note that high energy prices are not just damaging energy intensive industrial businesses. It was reported last year that high electricity prices, then quoted as the third highest in Europe, were a factor in forcing companies to locate power-hungry data centres outside Britain. Uncompetitive energy prices are therefore undermining the British economy across a wide spectrum of businesses.

It isn't just energy intensive industrial jobs that are at risk. Green taxes and regulations are now even starting to threaten some British service industries. Regulation called the Carbon Reduction Commitment (CRC) is a particular source of trouble. It requires all firms using 6,000 MWh of energy or more a year, but not covered by other regulations, to buy allowances from the government for the emissions implied by the energy they use. The revenue from selling those allowances was going to be recycled back to the firms in the scheme, with those doing the most to improve their energy efficiency getting the most generous treatment. Even with the money being recycled, the burden of complying with the complex CRC regulation was expected to be significant. But that pot of money was too appetising for a government struggling to get its finances in order and in the recent Spending Review they announced that they would be keeping the revenue. That turned the CRC into a stealth tax worth £1 billion a year by 2014–15.[267]

The problem is that most of those companies get their energy in the form of electricity, which is already more expensive thanks to cap and trade and other climate change regulations. Double taxation is apparently old hat; in Britain we almost had double cap and trade. Instead we just have yet another tax on business energy costs.

The combined effect on bills is significant for service companies that use substantial amounts of energy. The organisers of the DatacenterDynamics' London conference reported that the new stealth tax is a threat to Britain's competitiveness as a location for data centres:[268]

UK-based Romonet, which researches energy and cost points within the data centre, told DatacenterDynamics London, which will soon host its annual conference, that the changes could have wide implications for the data centre industry.

Romonet CTO Liam Newcombe said the large collocation and hosting data centre operators would be most affected, having to find a possible additional £500,000 in OPEX costs. 'The change

267 HM Treasury, Spending Review 2010, October 2010, Table 3: Spending Review AME policy measures

268 Jones, P., 'Carbon Reduction Commitment 'stealth tax' puts UK data center industry in doubt', DatacentreDynamics, 26 October 2010

in the recycling payments will clearly have a substantial impact on the UK data centre sector,' Newcombe said.

No longer is CRC simply a complex regulatory burden that will cost a lot of money in compliance and reporting. It is now an expensive tax as well. A medium-sized collocation data centre can expect to add £500,000 to its annual OPEX for the purchase of allowances in addition to the compliance costs.

For some operators, this could be enough to halt new projects in the UK, and for some businesses, it could lead to a drop off in business, as clients investigate offshore options offering lower energy costs.

'This change to CRC will, in combination with the already high cost of electricity in the UK, cause some operators to build new facilities in other countries instead. This is likely to be particularly true for outsourcers and cloud (computing) providers who are able to deliver services from remote data centres with little overhead,' Newcombe said.

Other firms echoed those sentiments. That is more investment, more jobs, more tax revenue and more prosperity being driven abroad by the combined burden of climate change policies. Ironically scientists have even claimed that research into alternative energy is threatened. The Culham Centre for Fusion Energy faces an estimated £400,000 a year bill which a senior scientist told *The Guardian* was 'perverse'.[269]

Europe in general and Britain in particular are the already ailing canaries in the mine as other Western countries follow our example and put in place more and more expensive climate change policies. Increasing the cost of energy makes it harder for firms to compete and will drive production abroad. The green jobs promised by politicians would need to be delivered on an incredible scale to make up for rises in energy prices putting so many jobs at risk. Unfortunately, all the signs are that many of the promised green jobs aren't going to materialise.

....

269 Sample, I., 'Environmental tax threatens green energy research in UK', *The Guardian*, 30 May 2011

Markets of the future

In the article I quoted from earlier, the German, French and British climate change ministers went on to talk about the economic opportunity they saw in climate change policy. They argued that making the 2020 emissions target tougher, which would increase the carbon price produced by the ETS, would bring improved economic growth:[270]

The key question Europe faces is: do we have the vision to grasp this opportunity and to lead the world in creating this new low-carbon model for economic growth?

We are convinced that Europe has the capability – but it does not yet have the right incentives for changing investment patterns.

A key barrier is the EU's current emissions target, a 20 per cent reduction from 1990 levels by 2020, a target that seems now insufficient to drive the low-carbon transition.

After all, the recession by itself has cut emissions in the EU's traded sector by 11 per cent from pre-crisis levels. Partly as a result, the current price of carbon is far too low to stimulate significant investment in green jobs and technologies.

If we stick to a 20 per cent cut, Europe is likely to lose the race to compete in the low-carbon world to countries such as China, Japan or the US – all of whom are looking to create a more attractive investment environment by introducing low carbon policy frameworks and channelling their stimulus packages into low-carbon investment.

In an article for *The Guardian*, Jeremy Leggett, founder and Chairman of solar energy company Solarcentury, made a similar argument in a crasser way:[271]

When Britain and Germany raced to scale up their aircraft industries for war in the 1930s, the British competed rather

---

270 Huhne, C., Borloo, J-L. & Röttgen, N., 'Benefits of 30% emissions cut for European Union', *Financial Times*, 15 July 2010

271 Leggett, J., 'Surrendering our future', *The Guardian*, 25 October 2007

well. Recovering from a late start, we rapidly produced machines capable of winning the Battle of Britain.

Today, the two nations are on the same side in a differ-ent battle, but Germany alone is mobilising as fast as it did seventy years ago. Our common enemy is global warming, and it is already at our gates. But while our German allies are turn-ing out the renewable energy equivalents of Messerschmitts by the factory-load, Britain is again slow to spring into action. Worse, as we learned yesterday, officials responsible for UK mobilisation have told the Prime Minister it is impossible for us to build modern-day Spitfires in any number.

Finally, Tim Yeo MP – never one to miss a bad environmen-talist argument – says that climate change policy needs to be more urgent to make Britain more competitive:[272]

We must persuade the public that it is in Britain's economic interests to move to a low carbon economy faster than other countries, not least to give us a competitive edge.

Environmentalist activists and politicians throughout the developed world, from Eastern Europe to the United States, make a similar case. We aren't just going to get the relatively small number of green jobs installing and operating new green technologies like wind turbines and solar panels, we are going to make them. That's the only way to make the sums add up and support rhetoric claiming green jobs will be a significant source of net new employment.

Unfortunately, putting in place tougher emissions targets, regulations like cap and trade and renewable energy subsi-dies, can only make you a bigger customer for green goods, it can't make you a bigger supplier. Buying hundreds of copies of Microsoft Office can't make you Bill Gates, it can make you poor.

Not every country can become a big net exporter of green capital goods. High domestic demand might increase the chances of a country building up internationally successful

---

272 Yeo, T., *Green Gold*, Tory Reform Group, July 2010, p.66

green industries but there are a range of other factors, plenty of them potentially far more important:

How high are costs? Including labour costs and, ominously for countries pushing up industrial bills through their climate change policies, energy costs.

How strong is the scientific and engineering skills base? Politicians will flatter themselves that, with the right programmes, they can ensure that their country has that skill base, but in reality countries that already have an established workforce in similar industries will do well.

Are there existing companies working in similar industries? Countries with a well-established and successful industry producing capital equipment, particularly in the energy sector, are likely to do well.

With that in mind, it is possible to make some educated guesses about the countries likely to prove most competitive in the markets for solar panels, wind turbines and other green consumer goods. The two major economies you would expect to do well are China, thanks to its low costs, and Germany, thanks to its established expertise and industry in electrical engineering and capital goods. Germany might have the upper hand at the leading, high-tech edge of the green industries and China might do better as the technologies mature and the challenge moves to keeping costs down. Other countries like Japan, South Korea and the United States might also be able to compete in some areas.

I'm not trying to play at being a market analyst here. The point is just that the amount of subsidy on offer for domestic installation of renewable energy is not the critical factor in where the production of capital goods takes place. Unless a country becomes protectionist and refuses to let its utility companies buy equipment on the international market, which would drastically increase the cost to consumers, strong domestic demand can easily be satisfied by foreign suppliers.

Germany is a good test case of the potential for developed economies to build lasting green industries supplying the world. The Germans have the established expertise and industrial capacity to do very well out of a huge expansion in the amount electricity companies spend on capital equipment, to meet climate change policy targets and mandates. Their domestic subsidies, particularly for solar power, have been incredibly generous for a long time.

They have been very successful but as solar panels, for example, have become more of a commodity their position has been eroded by competitors in Asia and the promise of huge numbers of green jobs looks increasingly hollow.

In August 2009, Benny Peiser, Director of the Global Warming Policy Foundation, translated the following from an article in the *Financial Times Deutschland*:[273]

The young German solar industry faces an unprecedented wave of bankruptcies. After many cell manufacturers suffered losses in the first half of the year, industry experts fear the collapse of many solar ventures. 'A large part of the German solar cell and solar module manufacturers will not survive,' says UBS analyst Patrick Hummel.

Although Germany is the world's largest growth market for solar panels, industry sales and profits are collapsing. The situation is paradoxical: Lush state feed-in laws ensure a demand boom in solar energy systems. But Germany's solar cell and module manufacturer hardly benefit. According to the industry magazine Photon, *the real benefactors of Germany's green laws are Asian competitors, especially from China.*

Last week, the world's market leader, Germany's Q-Cells, declined to provide a revenue forecast for the current year. The group suffered a high loss in the hundreds of millions, while sales fell in the first half by almost 40 per cent to 366 million euros. The Bosch subsidiary Ersol too suffered a sharp decline in sales in the first six months of 2009. The loss was even more severe, by more than 200 per cent, to a

---

273 Krümpel, M., 'Solarindustrie droht der Kollaps', *Financial Times Deutschland*, 16 August 2009

minus of almost 16 million euros, the company announced on Friday.

Germany's solar cell and module manufacturers are ensnared in cost trap: Their Asian rivals can always produce solar systems much cheaper – by an average of one third, according to calculations by the investment bank UBS. Moreover, the Chinese government promotes an aggressive pricing policy. As a result, prices are falling rapidly. And while the Asian manufacturers are back with their production capacity almost fully utilised, Q-Cells and Ersol have put their workers on short-time.

You can see the effect in the Q-Cells share price, shown in Figure 6.3, which has been steadily falling for some time.[274]

Figure 6.3: Q-Cells share price, 5 years to July 2011

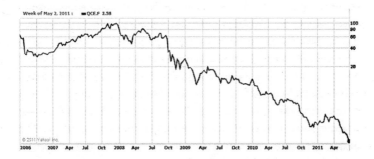

All this doesn't mean that the green industries will entirely locate themselves in China and other low cost locations. Just as in so many other industries, specialist manufacturing and research and development is as likely to stay in the developed world. It just means that the green industries are like any other and there is no good reason to think that forcing huge investment to meet climate change targets will give a country a lasting competitive advantage, or produce a lasting

274 All share price histories downloaded from Yahoo Finance

boost to employment. Some countries could do well out of a major increase in utility capital expenditure, but they will profit from other countries' expansion of renewable energy, not their own.

At the same time, there are lingering questions over the whole sector, particularly with some European countries cutting subsidies in response to the affordability crisis.

Some other solar panel manufacturers haven't done as badly as Q-Cells but they have hardly been delivering a barn-storming return to shareholders. Market leader First Solar, with plants in a number of countries but most of its capacity in Malaysia, has been pretty flat too.

All around the world green jobs have turned out to be a mirage. In November 2010 the Orange County Register reported that:[275]

Despite a $535 million loan guarantee from the federal government, Solyndra, a maker of solar panels in the south-east San Francisco Bay Area city of Fremont, will close one of its manufacturing plants, lay off forty permanent and 150 contract workers, delay expansion plans of a new plant largely financed with the government-guaranteed loan and scale back production capacity more than 50 per cent.

Despite the hype and tax money, Solyndra seems unable to compete with Chinese manufacturers, whose prices are lower. This is the latest bad news for the company touted by Mr Schwarzenegger and President Barack Obama as one of the green industry's supposed shining lights. President Obama visited Solyndra in May, calling the operation 'a testament to American ingenuity and dynamism'.

But, truth be told, Solyndra is more of a testament to taxpayers' hard-earned money pledged to guarantee 73 per cent of the cost of building its new facility. Closure of its older plant, located nearby, is a testament to the reality that, even

275 Orange County Register, 'Editorial: Green jobs cut despite government subsidy', 10 November 2010

if massively underwritten by taxpayers, renewable energy operations aren't certain to find a profitable niche in the open market.

Shortly after the President's visit, the company announced in June that weak demand in capital markets, high costs and 'a prodigious cash burn', as GreenEnergyReporter.com put it, forced withdrawal of plans for an initial public stock offering. In July, its CEO was replaced. The company found itself 'struggling to justify the early hype by bringing down costs from $3 per watt to $2 per watt by 2013', GreenEnergyReporter.com reported.

It isn't just solar; there is a similar situation in the wind market. Vestas is the biggest supplier of wind turbines and in 2009 it supplied about an eighth of the market with just over 23,000 employees worldwide.[276] If we assume that they are roughly representative of the industry, then global wind turbine manufacture employs fewer than 200,000 people. Given that there are nearly 320,000 people working in financial services in London alone,[277] wind turbine production is making a pretty limited contribution to global employment. Of course, the idea is that the market will grow as more countries shift to using greater renewable energy, and there are other industries connected to or dependent on wind power, but even with substantial growth it is a pretty small pie with so many different countries trying to take a piece.

In October 2010, Vestas announced substantial job losses, with 3,000 staff expected to go, in response to a sharp decline in profits. The jobs being axed were primarily in Denmark:[278]

Net profit fell 23.6 per cent to €126 million and EBIT fell 24 per cent to €185m. Revenues decreased 5 per cent to €1,722m and shipments of wind turbines dipped 27 per cent to 719 wind turbines.

....

276 Vestas, Financial figures and outlook (Q3 2010); Employees (30 September 2010)

277 TheCityUK, Key facts and figures about UK financial services

278 Renewable Energy Focus, 'Vestas' Q3 profit falls 23.6% - lays off 3000', 26 October 2010

Explaining what had happened, the CEO of Vestas, Ditlev Engel told the *FT* Energy Source blog that:[279]

The announced changes primarily affect our factories and organisation in Denmark, as the production costs in Northern Europe are too high.

Yet again, extensive, market-leading subsidies haven't been able to purchase a lasting competitive advantage.

There is no evidence to support the contention that countries really can build sustainable, exporting industries on regulations dictating a high cost of carbon. Cap and trade, renewable energy subsidies and the other policies I've looked at so far in this book can ensure an economy buys lots of solar panels or wind turbines, not that it sells them. Claims that it is possible to secure massive numbers of green jobs with aggressive climate change policies are empty political rhetoric.

Net green jobs

In order to work out whether or not climate change policies are good for employment, we ultimately need to work out the net number of jobs created or destroyed. Is the number of jobs created in the green industries more or less than the number of jobs destroyed in the wider economy?

There have been a number of studies that have attempted to answer that question. Professor Gabriel Calzada, at King Juan Carlos University, produced a study in May 2009 that looked at Spain's experience with renewable energy subsidies. He found that the number of jobs lost paying for the subsidies significantly exceeded the number created:[280]

Optimistically treating European Commission partially funded data, we find that for every renewable energy job that

....

279 Stacey, K., 'Vestas' CEO answers your questions', *Financial Times* Energy Source, 3 December 2010

280 Calzada, G., 'Study of the effects on employment of public aid to renewable energy sources', Universidad Rey Juan Carlos, March 2009, p.1

the State manages to finance, Spain's experience cited by President Obama as a model reveals with high confidence, by two different methods, that the US should expect a loss of at least 2.2 jobs on average, or about nine jobs lost for every four created, to which we have to add those jobs that non-subsidised investments with the same resources would have created.

Essentially, Professor Calzada compared the amount of employment that the major EU Commission-financed Monitoring and Modeling Initiative on Targets for Renewable Energy (MITRE) project estimated would be created in renewable energy, to the amount that was paid in subsidies. He found that renewables had received €28.7 billion in subsidies, nearly €600,000 for each of the roughly 50,200 jobs created.

That is then compared with estimates of resources per worker in the wider economy:[281]

This forcible loss of resources incurred by renewable energy programs must be compared with the average resources per worker allocated in the private sector. The parameter that most closely approximates it is the average stock of capital per worker, whose mean between 1995 and 2005 in Spain was 259,143 Euros.

Professor Calzada then looks at it from another angle, comparing average subsidy per worker and average productivity, and comes to the same result. An Italian study produced by Carlo Stagnaro and Luciano Lavecchia for the Istituto Bruno Leoni comes to similar results, though it lamented the low quality of the data available on green jobs and is a bit more cautious about the implications of the results. That study found the amount of capital that created one green job would create 4.8 jobs if invested in the wider economy.[282]

The National Renewable Energy Laboratory in the United States, run for the Department of Energy by the Alliance for

281 Ibid., p.28
282 Lavecchia, L. & Stagnaro, C., 'Are Green Jobs Real Jobs? The Case of Italy', Istituto Bruno Leoni, May 2010, p.39

Sustainable Energy according to the front cover of the report, produced a response. Chris Horner, in his book *Power Grab*, revealed that a draft of that response was run by the left-wing campaign group the Center for American Progress and industry lobby the American Wind Energy Association for comment and assistance;[283] politicians, activists and special interests working together.

Some of the criticisms in the National Renewable Energy Laboratory response to Professor Calzada's work were incredible. For example, they attacked the study for not following a 'traditional' method that is obviously flawed:[284]

Traditional methods applied in jobs and economic impacts analyses rely on input-output models to estimate job creation or loss. These models measure how changes in demand for specific goods and services affect economic activity and jobs within the specific area of study. At the most basic level, jobs analyses rely on a straightforward estimate of gross economic impacts from new investments in specific energy technologies under different scenarios. Such efforts in the United States suggest that, in some cases, the project-level job creation impacts of wind power are greater than that of conventional energy generation resources, including coal and natural gas (Tegen 2006, Lantz and Tegen 2008).

Here are some examples of the kind of study they're talking about. The following studies were cited by a Deutsche Bank report which argued that stimulus funds should be focused on renewable energy:[285]

[The] Apollo Alliance estimates that every $1 million invested in the US in energy efficiency projects creates 21.5 new jobs, as

283 Horner, C., *Power Grab*, Regnery Publishing, p.50

284 Lantz, E. & Tegen, S., 'NREL Response to the Report Study of the Effects on Employment of Public Aid to Renewable Energy Sources from King Juan Carlos University (Spain)', White Paper, NREL/TP-6A2-46261, August 2009

285 DB Advisors, 'Economic Stimulus: The Case for "Green" Infrastructure, Energy Security and "Green" Jobs', November 2008

compared to only 11.5 jobs for new natural gas generation. The University of California Berkeley's Renewable and Appropriate Energy Laboratory also finds that renewable energy tech-nologies create more jobs per average megawatt of power generated and per dollar invested than coal or natural gas.

The problem is obvious, our policy choices aren't redirect-ing investment from coal and gas to wind and solar. They are requiring that we invest a lot more in the energy sector, capital that then can't be invested elsewhere. Look at the estimates in Table 4.8. That shows the amount that Citigroup Global Markets thinks needs to be invested in the energy sectors of the major European economies to meet environmental targets and it increases the total amount of investment needed in the sector.

Studies that look at whether we can get more employment out of the energy sector miss the point. The sector isn't a job creation scheme. Its vital economic function is to power the rest of the economy at an affordable price. Robert Michaels and Robert Murphy made this point in a paper for the Institute for Energy Research:[286]

Energy is the lifeblood of the economy. The primary objec-tive of the energy sector is to supply cost-effective energy to the broader economy, allowing it to grow and increase the standard of living of its citizens. Artificially pumping up employment in the energy sector per se – and thereby driving down productivity, while driving up costs to the broader economy – is counterpro-ductive to overall net job creation and economic growth. It is a sign of increased efficiency if more energy can be produced and delivered with fewer workers, because this expands the over-all output potential of the economy. Yet the green jobs studies that we analyse in this report reach the opposite conclusion, and favour energy sources that require more workers to yield a given amount of energy. By analogy, the number of workers in the US devoted to agriculture has steadily declined over the last

---

286 Michaels, R. & Murphy, R. P., 'Green Jobs: Fact or fiction? An assessment of the literature', Institute for Energy Research, January 2009

century, and this is a healthy sign of progress in the US economy.
Government efforts to reverse the trend, and force more workers
back into agriculture, would not 'create jobs' in the long-run, but
would simply raise food prices and shrink other sectors.

We would employ a lot more people in the energy sector if
we powered our homes and factories by running around and
around in circles holding a children's pinwheel rigged up to
a generator. But we aren't playing some kind of game where
the objective is to find the most labour intensive source of
energy possible.

Imagine we had done that in agriculture, and instead of
using combine harvesters we still harvested crops by hand.
More people would work on the farms, but food would be a
lot more expensive and we would all be worse off. There would
be fewer jobs making iPods, clothes, computers, books, or
whatever else people choose to spend their money on instead
at a time when food takes up a smaller share of the budget.

Renewable energy is extremely expensive and requires a
huge amount of capital expenditure. That means generating
it is more of a burden on the rest of the economy, where most
people are employed. For that reason, increasing the amount
of renewable energy we use will tend to mean sacrifices in
employment and prosperity.

As Professor Calzada's study is absolutely right to point
out, there are serious economic costs to tying up huge
amounts of capital in renewable energy. One possible consequence is that it might not be invested in other sectors where
it would do more to boost employment. His report isn't the
final word on the consequences for employment of supporting renewable energy but it serves the important purpose of
pointing out that there are huge costs to ploughing capital
into the energy sector in order to develop renewable energy.
The authors of the Italian study put it well:[287]

---

287 Lavecchia, L. & Stagnaro, C., 'Are Green Jobs Real Jobs? The Case of Italy',
    Istituto Bruno Leoni, May 2010, p.40

The only scope, and we dare to say the only result, of our study is to show that green investments are an ineffective policy for job creation.

The Obama administration wasted their time going after Professor Calzada's work. Their attack was weak. Its other criticisms included that Prof. Calzada's study failed to take sufficient account of the potential of renewable energy subsidies to ensure Spain captures lucrative export markets, for failing to buy that myth, and for focussing only on employment, which is both inaccurate – the study looks at the subsidy cost of Spanish renewable energy in detail – and irrelevant – it never claims to be a complete survey of the effects of renewable energy subsidies.

Spain and Italy were never going to be the definitive test of the potential of climate change policy to deliver green jobs anyway. The best case was always Germany. If any developed economy could really do well out of the growth of capital expenditure in the energy sector, where businesses would be able to take full advantage of the new market for massive quantities of wind turbines and solar panels, it was Germany.

It looks like even Germany has seen lower employment thanks to its renewable energy subsidises. In the November 2009 Ruhr Economic Paper by Manuel Frondel, Nolan Ritter, Christoph M. Schmidt, and Colin Vance that I quoted earlier, they survey the evidence on net green jobs in Germany:[288]

Taking account of adverse investment and crowding-out effects, both the IWH (2004) and RWI (2004) find negligible employment impacts. Another analysis draws the conclusion that despite initially positive impacts, the long-term employment effects of the promotion of energy technologies such as wind and solar power systems are negative (BEI 2003:41). Similar results are attained by Fahl et al. (2005), as well as

---

288 Frondel, M., Ritter, N., Schmidt, C. M. & Vance, C., 'Economic Impacts from the Promotion of Renewable Energy Technologies: The German Experience', *Ruhr Economic Papers* #156, November 2009

Pfaffenberger (2006) and Hillebrand et al. (2006). The latter analysis, for example, finds an initially expansive effect on net employment from renewable energy promotion resulting from additional investments. By 2010, however, this gives way to a contractive effect as the production costs of power increase.

In contrast, a study commissioned by the BMU (2006:9) comes to the conclusion that the EEG's net employment effect is the creation of up to 56,000 jobs until 2020. This same study, however, emphasises that positive employment effects critically depend on a robust foreign trade of renewable energy technologies (BMU 2006:7). Whether favourable conditions on the international market prevail for PV, for example, is highly questionable, particularly given negligible or even negative net exports in recent years. While the imports totalled 1.44 Bn €, the exports merely accounted for 0.2 Bn € (BMU 2006:61). Actually, a substantial share of all PV modules installed in Germany originated from imports (BMU 2006:62), most notably from Japan and China. In 2005, the domestic production of modules was particularly low compared with domestic demand. With 319 MW, domestic production only provided for 32 per cent of the new capacity installed in Germany

In 2006 and 2007, almost half of Germany's PV demand was covered by imports (Sarasin 2007:19). Recent newspaper articles report that the situation remains dire, with the German solar industry facing unprecedented competition from cheaper Asian imports.

Hence, any result other than a negative net employment balance of the German PV promotion would be surprising. In contrast, we would expect massive employment effects in export countries such as China, since these countries do not suffer from the EEG's crowding-out effects, nor from negative income effects.

All the evidence suggests that climate change policies are counterproductive as a means of promoting employment. Draconian climate change regulations tend to lead to a net reduction in employment.

Some countries will do well out of tough climate change

targets, but they probably won't be the ones setting or abiding by those targets themselves. It will be the countries where the equipment needed to meet the targets can be made at the lowest cost. It will be those who supply the expensive wind turbines and solar panels, not the mugs who buy them.

Exporting emissions

If ambitious attempts to curb greenhouse gas emissions hurt energy intensive industries and force firms to relocate production in countries that don't embrace radical climate change policy, it doesn't do much to cut emissions. As more and more industries are affected by rising energy prices and shift to countries that don't impose such a burden, more and more emissions will be exported. Climate change policies become utterly pointless. The only thing that politicians achieve is driving investment and jobs abroad.

As Nigel Lawson put it in a lecture to the Centre for Policy Studies in November 2006:[289]

In reality, if the Kyoto approach were to be pursued beyond 2012, which is – fortunately – unlikely, the price increase would in practice be mitigated in the global economy in which we now live. For as energy prices in Europe started to rise, with the prospect of further rises to come, energy-intensive industries and processes would progressively close down in Europe and relocate in countries like China, where relatively cheap energy was still available.

No doubt Europe could, at some cost, adjust to this, as it has to the migration of most of its textile industry to China and elsewhere. But it is difficult to see the point of it. For if carbon dioxide emissions in Europe are reduced only to see them further increased in China, there is no net reduction in global emissions at all.

---

289 Lawson, N., 'The economics and politics of climate change: an appeal to reason', A Lecture to the Centre for Policy Studies, 1 November 2006, p.11

It is hard to work out the extent to which industries are exporting emissions in order to avoid climate change policy. Decisions about where to locate industrial capacity are always the result of a range of factors and it is difficult to really disentangle how much of a difference rising energy costs have made at the margin.

There are estimates of the scale of Britain's consumer emissions, though. That is the amount that is emitted producing goods for British consumers, whether that production is in Britain or abroad. When we talk about a country's emissions we normally use their producer emissions instead, the quantity of emissions produced in Britain. The difference between the two captures the extent to which emissions have been exported to countries like China as more and more of our manufactured goods are made there.

Figure 6.4: British consumer and producer emissions, 1992–2004, Mt CO$_2$

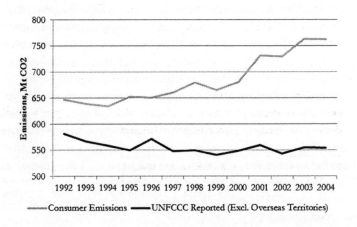

The difference between the emissions we report to the UNFCCC agency, our producer emissions and our consumer emissions, is stark. The figures in Figure 6.4 are from a study produced by researchers at the Stockholm Environment Institute and the University of Sydney for the Department for Environment, Food and Rural Affairs.[290] While our producer emissions have been slowly falling, consumer emissions have been rising steadily. Much of the progress that politicians think they have made in cutting emissions is entirely illusory. It is just the result of industry moving abroad.

The problem of exporting emissions is likely to mount in the coming years as climate change policies really bite and a higher carbon price drives high emitting industries abroad.

That calls into question the whole point of the ambitious unilateral targets and caps that developed countries are putting on their emissions. Those limits necessarily only cover producer emissions, which a national government can actually regulate, and they might be met just by the carbon price shifting production out, doing nothing to cut global emissions. Dieter Helm has raised exactly this point:[291]

This international dimension raises perhaps the most important aspect of the 20 per cent overall target: it is based on production of carbon within the EU, and not on consumption. Thus the EU can achieve its targets if it switches carbon production that would have taken place within the EU to overseas, and then imports back the goods and services which would have caused the emissions internally.

Policies like cap and trade and draconian targets to reduce emissions were never meant to work without an international deal. The British government's Impact Assessment for the

....

290 Wiedmann, T., Wood, R., Lenzen, M., Minx, J., Guan, D. and Barrett, J., 'Development of an Embedded Carbon Emissions Indicator – Producing a Time Series of Input-Output Tables and Embedded Carbon Dioxide Emissions for the UK by Using a MRIO Data Optimisation System', Report to the UK Department for Environment, Food and Rural Affairs by Stockholm Environment Institute at the University of York and Centre for Integrated Sustainability Analysis at the University of Sydney, June 2008

291 Helm, D., 'EU climate-change policy – a critique' from Helm, D. & Hepburn, C. (eds), *The Economics and Politics of Climate Change*, Oxford University Press, October 2009, p.6

Climate Change Act 2008, which set our binding targets to cut emissions, accepted that the 'economic case for the UK continuing to act alone where global action cannot be achieved would be weak'.[292]

The prospects for an international deal are bleak. Some politicians are in denial about that and continue to insist that the push for a genuinely international successor to Kyoto is the only option. Analysts at organisations like the Carbon Trust – a body I'll look at in more detail in the next section – are more realistic, and are trying to work out what it would take to make a unilateral carbon price work without industries relocating to countries that don't impose the same burden. They released a report looking at the issue in March 2010.

They underestimate the extent of the problem. They only look at sectors deemed to be 'at significant risk of carbon leakage':[293]

Specifically, the EU Emissions Trading Directive states that 'a sector or sub-sector is deemed to be exposed to a significant risk of carbon leakage' if:

The sum of direct and indirect additional 'costs induced by the implementation of this directive' is at least 5 per cent of the Gross Value Added and the Non-EU Trade intensity is above 10 per cent; or

The sum of direct and indirect additional costs is at least 30 per cent of Gross Value Added; or

The non-EU trade intensity is above 30 per cent.

That is a very flawed approach. The cost of climate change policies will affect plenty of industries which don't meet that threshold; where the new costs aren't – as Lord Adair Turner put it at the launch event for the report – the 'defining determinant' of where to locate. It will affect decisions at the margin. In other words, even small increases in costs will swing some

---

292 Department of Energy and Climate Change, Climate Change Act 2008 Impact Assessment, March 2009, p.7

293 Grubb, M. & Counsell, T., 'Tackling carbon leakage: Sector-specific solutions for a world of unequal carbon prices', Carbon Trust, March 2010, p.24

important decisions – over where to invest and who to buy from – and lead to carbon leakage. The more energy costs are pushed up, the more carbon will leak. That effect needs to be estimated across all the firms in the economy, you can't just ask which industries and firms will be completely unable to compete.

They also only look at the EU ETS, which isn't the only climate change policy pushing up energy costs. Lots of the other policies we've looked at so far in this book, like renewable energy targets, are also increasing energy prices, and when they are combined with the ETS the burden is even greater on many manufacturers.

Figure 6.5: Carbon Trust sector-specific carbon leakage responses

Chart ES-1 Choosing an approach to tackling leakage based on the characteristics of the sector concerned

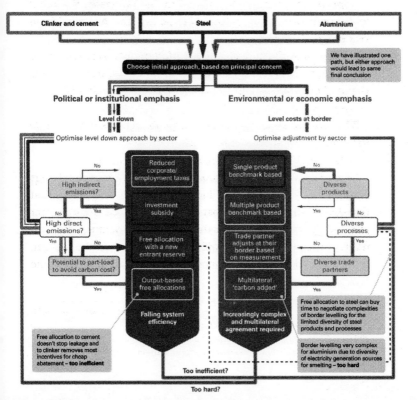

The response to carbon leakage proposed by the Carbon Trust analysts is a byzantine mess. They argue that we should adjust for the burden on manufacturers in different ways, in different sectors. The glorious graphic reproduced in Figure 6.5 is used to decide how three sectors – cement, steel and aluminium – should be treated.[294]

That flowchart sets out – based on the characteristics of the industry – whether the authors of the Carbon Trust report think the best way to help is to give them free allocations of permits to emit under the ETS or to put a tariff on imports to protect them against foreign competitors. They generally prefer the latter – as it messes up the principle of the ETS less – but think it is sometimes not possible as you can't come up with a simple, appropriate carbon price to adjust by at the border.

Leaving aside for the moment the question of which approach is better, either would leave firms and industries far more dependent for their continued survival on government support. The fortunes of different companies would be determined more by the amount of political support they enjoy and less by their ability to efficiently produce goods that people want to buy. That will mean a huge amount is wasted on lobbyists and lawyers as companies fight for protection against competitors outside the ETS. And it will mean good people and capital are diverted away from those who are best at making things and towards those with the most political muscle.

And firms won't be able to rely on that political support over the long term. Similar special deals have proved unreliable in the past. Energy intensive industries get a discounted rate under a British green tax called the Climate Change Levy in order to avoid undermining their competitiveness. At the Pre-Budget Report in 2009, the government increased the rate of the Climate Change Levy on energy-intensive industries by 75 per cent.

Businesses have to be wary of building a new factory, for

294 Ibid., p.3

example, if it only makes sense on the basis of a free allocation of emissions permits or a border adjustment that could be scrapped next year. Investment and jobs could still move to other countries that don't have these expensive climate change policies in the first place.

At the launch, I put those points to Michael Grubb – the former Chief Economist at the Carbon Trust who wrote the report – and he didn't really have an answer. He just thought that was a necessary price to pay for putting a price on emissions. In other words, there isn't a reliable solution to carbon leakage and it will continue to undermine the effectiveness of putting a price on carbon.

The cure could be worse than the disease. Border adjustments, green protectionism, could easily lead to a trade war. There is no reason to think that developing countries would respond well to developed countries putting up tariffs against their industrial goods. It would look an awful lot like an attempt to coerce them into policies they have rejected themselves, like a new eco-imperialism. They would surely have a good case at the World Trade Organization, particularly if the border tariff was often not equal to the exact carbon price at that moment. The onset of green protectionism would mean that climate change goes from being an object of cooperation between nations to a cause of confrontation.

Climate change policies like cap and trade rely far too heavily on an international agreement that was never likely to be feasible. That is one reason why they are such a bad deal, and why a more realistic approach is needed.

Bureaucracy
One area where there are green jobs to be had is in bureaucracy. Governments throughout the developed world have established departments and agencies to manage their response to climate change.

In Britain the Department of Energy and Climate Change employed 948 staff in 2009–10. That does include staff working on managing 'energy liabilities effectively and safely' (82) and ensuring 'secure energy supplies' (267). There are more of them working on objectives like reducing 'greenhouse gas emissions in the UK' (302); ensure 'the UK benefits from the business and employment opportunities of a low carbon future' (12); and promoting 'fairness through our climate and energy policies at home and abroad' (52), though.[295] The objectives are a bit fuzzy but it is pretty clear that there are more people working on reducing emissions than keeping the lights on. Many of those nominally working on ensuring a secure energy supply are likely to be focusing their attention on renewable energy as well.

Other departments also have staff working on the issue of climate change. William Hague, the Foreign Secretary, boasted in a speech on 27 September 2010 about the Foreign and Commonwealth Office's 'unique network of climate attachés throughout the world'.[296]

There are more green government jobs at agencies. For example, the Carbon Trust employed 214 staff[297] and the Sustainable Development Commission another 60 'dedicated policy staff'.[298]

There are even green jobs for bureaucrats in local, municipal authorities. The TaxPayers' Alliance found that British councils employed 350 climate change officers at a cost of over £10 ($15.7) million a year in 2009–10.[299] The London borough of Camden alone employed more than thirteen climate change officers at a cost of nearly half a million pounds ($783,000) a year.

295 Department of Energy and Climate Change, Resource Accounts 2009-10, 26 July 2010, p.75

296 BusinessGreen, 'William Hague's climate change speech – in full', 27 September 2010

297 Carbon Trust, Annual Report 2009/10, August 2010, p.65

298 Sustainable Development Commission, 'Our People', http://www.sd-commission.org.uk/pages/our-people.html

299 Daniel, C., 'Council savings: unnecessary jobs', TaxPayers' Alliance, 12 October 2010

The Carbon Trust is a good example of what poor value taxpayers get from a lot of this spending.

It doesn't address a genuine market failure. If large businesses can genuinely save money by cutting their energy use, then they have an incentive to do so; particularly with all the policies we've looked at in this book increasing energy prices. If they need external advice to achieve that result, they can pay for it. There was no need for the over £100 ($177) million a year spent subsidising the Carbon Trust.[300]

It is unaccountable and inscrutable. The Freedom of Information Act does not apply to the Carbon Trust: taxpayers cannot find out how their money is spent because it is technically a private company, even though it was set up, and is funded, by the government. We do know, from the Association of Professional Political Consultants register, that they hire the political consultancy Grayling Public Affairs, using taxpayers' money to defend their access to taxpayers' money.[301]

Remuneration for some staff is very high. Chief Executive Tom Delay received £248,492 ($389,153) in 2009–10.[302] It is difficult to tell how many people working at the organisation get high pay thanks to its complicated structure.

Three executive partners who manage investment funds for the Carbon Trust at the organisation's investment management arm CT Investment Partners LLP (Peter Linthwaite, Jonathan Bryers and Adam Workman) appear to be very generously compensated. They paid £50,000 initially for their share in CT Investment Partners LLP and – between the three of them – are now getting £380,000 ($595,000, €427,000) a year in profit on fees from the Carbon Trust.[303] They work out of the same office as the Carbon Trust itself and the National

---

300 Carbon Trust, Annual Report 2009/10, August 2010, p.41

301 Association of Professional Political Consultants, Register, June to August 2010, p.38

302 Carbon Trust, Annual Report 2009/10, August 2010, p.39

303 CT Investment Partners LLP, Financial statements for the year ended 31 March 2009 together with Partners' and Auditors' reports, p.13

Audit Office has raised concerns at potential conflicts of interest, saying that there 'is a risk that CT Investment Partners
staff could influence publicly funded research and development or incubator support for emerging businesses that they,
in time, may back by way of investment and thus from which
they may earn carried interest'.[304]

All this isn't just a concern for British taxpayers. The
Carbon Trust has been trying to expand into other countries,
as if it were a multinational company, through its Carbon Trust
International programme. In August 2009 they were advertising for a head of Carbon Trust USA position.[305] Working with
financial support from the Foreign and Commonwealth Office,
they were lobbying American politicians to spend their taxpayers' money setting up similar organisations in the States.

Thankfully, the Carbon Trust has recently had its core
grant withdrawn. They'll now have to apply for funding on a
project by project basis at least.

All these climate change bureaucrats like to try and justify
themselves by claiming that they save money by cutting
energy bills. The numbers are always dubious. When the
Department for the Environment, Food and Rural Affairs
announced its intention to cut funding to the Sustainable
Development Commission, its former chair, Jonathon Porritt,
claimed that 'the SDC's advice on reducing costs through
increased efficiency has already saved the government many,
many times that negligible amount'.[306] That claim was ultimately based on a report that looked at the amount government had saved through measures that improved energy

....

304 National Audit Office, 'The Carbon Trust: Accelerating the move to a low
     carbon economy', report by the Comptroller and Auditor General, 22
     November 2007, paragraph 3.13
305 The job advert has since been taken down, but was the subject of a joint
     press release from the TaxPayers' Alliance and the Competitive Enterprise
     Institute
306 Porritt, J., 'The greenest government ever? Don't make me laugh', *The
     Guardian*, 23 July 2010

efficiency. It estimated that had led to £70 ($110) million of savings.[307]

Companies and households are constantly using energy more efficiently. In Chapter 2 we looked at how emissions intensity, the amount of carbon dioxide emitted per dollar of GDP, tends to fall – and was falling well before we were worrying about climate change. That is the result of families and businesses finding new ways of doing things more efficiently. It is the daily work of a free-market economy and results in the huge improvements in prosperity that we have seen generation after generation since the Industrial Revolution. While there isn't the same commercial incentive to do things more efficiently in much of the public sector, staff will still spot and take opportunities to reduce costs by using energy more efficiently from time to time. Adding up the resulting savings and finding that they are worth £70 million doesn't tell us anything about the utility of the Sustainable Development Commission.

This is an extreme version of a widespread problem. Government agencies and consultancies claim credit for work that would have gone on anyway; they put their sticker on achievements they have little role in. It also affects the Clean Development Mechanism, which is covered in Chapter 8.

We don't get good value from Britain's expensive climate change bureaucracy but this is one area where the green jobs promised have materialised, and not just in Britain. All the expensive subsidies and targets that are being implemented need to be designed, managed, regulated and monitored. Unfortunately, many more jobs will be destroyed by the taxes needed to pay all those government paycheques and the regulations that the officials dream up.

....
307 Sustainable Development Commission, 'Becoming the Greenest Government Ever', 22 July 2010

Where are the green jobs?

The promise of green jobs has been seized on by politicians because they can't sell the public on the huge sacrifices that most analysts expect would be necessary to meet radical targets to cut greenhouse gas emissions. The promise that in a hundred years' time we will be somewhat better off for it, or even a lot better off, is easily discounted as scarcely credible jam tomorrow. Voters want policies that deliver more jobs and greater prosperity, not a lower temperature. In response, politicians claim that avoiding global warming is almost a side effect of climate change policy, which is really about seizing the high ground in the battle for the markets of the future.

That is a fantasy, even if it is an appealing one.

Right now, it will be formidably expensive to give up the fuels that have powered modern economies since the Industrial Revolution. Regulations that force up the price of energy will endanger huge numbers of manufacturing jobs and, in time, employment in many service industries as well.

On the other side of the ledger, green jobs are unlikely to be created in the numbers that optimistic politicians expect. There are jobs installing and operating renewable energy plants or installing energy efficiency measures, but not many. The only way the sums add up is if a country can become a major exporter of green goods. That isn't a game in which everyone can win. The winners – the exporters – won't necessarily be the ones who embrace the most radical climate change policy either. Strong domestic demand will matter less than costs and established expertise. Solar panels installed in Britain to obtain lucrative subsidy are as likely to be made in Malaysia.

One of the fatal flaws in the current approach to climate change policy that these problems expose is the potential for carbon leakage. Unilateral targets for drastic cuts in emissions can be satisfied by moving emitting industries to other countries and then importing the goods they produce. Regulations that put a high price on carbon might have that effect: redirecting investment and jobs to other countries and not cutting emissions.

Plenty of bureaucrats do have lucrative green jobs: officials in government departments and agencies employed to manage the various climate change policies, or to help the organisation do its bit. They tend to offer pretty poor value, and it is hard to see how one more old-fashioned, taxpayer-funded job creation scheme is such a great economic opportunity. The taxes that ultimately pay for those new official posts are likely to reduce employment themselves.

It isn't just officials who can do well out of climate change. Special interests in business can make big profits, as I've set out in earlier chapters. Chasing those profits creates plenty of opportunities for financiers, whether they are in Wall Street or the City of London, and for lobbyists, whether they are in K Street, Westminster or Brussels. There are also plenty of opportunities for activists. The organisational scale of the environmentalist movement is incredible. Those two groups – lobbyists and activists – and their political power and ideology are the subject of the next chapter.

Just like in the bureaucracy, the jobs are all about securing the fruits of government power, being the one who organises or finances the next big intervention in the economy. The kind of green jobs politicians want us to imagine, making and installing wind turbines or solar panels for example, are thin on the ground. None of them are enough to make up for the industries whose viability is threatened by higher energy prices.

Green jobs are a very useful myth.

CORPORATE LOBBYING AND ENVIRONMENTALISTS

Politicians don't normally invent initiatives that will pile huge costs onto their constituents on their own. And while many scientists are arguing something needs to be done about climate change, most have a fairly shaky idea of what. While the basic ideas might have been dreamed up quickly for Kyoto, for the set of policies discussed so far in this book to be adopted on such a scale took a sustained campaign.

That campaign initially came from dedicated environmentalists. They are still at work and have huge organisational clout, generous funding and political respectability. Environmentalist activism hasn't been the domain of the dreadlocked hippy for a long time, though there are definitely people like that around.

The adoption of radical climate change policies can't be explained by environmentalist pressure alone, though. If they were calling the shots entirely then you probably wouldn't have such generous subsidies going to biofuels. Some major environmentalist campaign groups like Friends of the Earth have also attacked cap and trade, talking about 'subprime carbon'.[308] James Hansen, originally known as a scientist but now more prominent as an activist, called emissions trading 'the temple of doom'.[309]

Along with the activists, corporate lobbyists who can see an opportunity for profit are also promoting radical climate change policy. There are lots of major firms working to

308 Chan, M., 'Subprime Carbon?', Friends of the Earth, March 2009
309 Hansen, J., 'Worshipping the Temple of Doom', 5 May 2009

lobby for cap and trade or more generous renewable energy subsidies. They won't do their shareholders many favours in the long run if they get too committed, but a little green wash is a good way of winning favour with the politicians and regulators.

The environmentalists and corporate lobbyists working together are the coalition that drives climate change policy.

Companies

One way of understanding just how big the climate change business has become is to look at the firms interested in pushing it forward. How many firms are chasing the subsidies and windfall profits discussed earlier in this book?

There is the 165-firm membership of the International Emissions Trading Association (IETA), working for 'an active, global greenhouse gas market'.[310] Basically, they are the international lobby for cap and trade. There are financial firms like Bank of America Merrill Lynch, Goldman Sachs, Deutsche Bank, Citigroup and JP Morgan Chase. Oil companies like BP, Shell, Chevron and ConocoPhillips. Electricity generators like the German firm E.ON, American Electric Power (AEP), EDF Trading and the Spanish firm Iberdrola Generación. Many other industries are also represented, including the industrial conglomerate General Electric, the lawyers Clifford Chance and the accountants KPMG.[311]

It is a collection of many of the biggest corporations in the world, all united by a common interest in the expansion of global cap and trade. How many other causes can bring together such a wide and powerful range of companies as cheerleaders?

In the United States the Climate Action Partnership,

---

310 International Emissions Trading Association, 'About IETA', http://www.ieta.org/ieta/www/pages/index.php?IdSiteTree=2
311 International Emissions Trading Association, 'IETA Members as of March 2010', http://www.ieta.org/ieta/www/pages/getfile.php?docID=556

which argues for 'legislation requiring significant reductions of greenhouse gas emissions', has a formidable corporate membership as well. It includes Ford and General Motors, General Electric – again – PepsiCo and DuPont, Dow Chemical and Duke Energy, even Alcoa, a maker of aluminium.[312]

Renewable energy companies can recycle some of the money they receive in subsidies into lobbying for more subsidies. In the UK a number of renewable energy generators show up in the register of the Association of Professional Political Consultants as clients of major PR firms: Citigate Dewe Rogerson work for 2020 Renewables; the PPS Group for EDF Energy Renewables and SSE Renewables Developments; Bellenden and Hanover for RenewableUK, one of the renewable energy trade associations; Four Communications for Renewable East; Green Issues Communications for RWE Npower Renewables.[313]

Of course, some companies are spending money opposing climate change policy. Two smaller oil companies gave money to support a proposition in California, Prop 23, which would have rolled back some climate change legislation. But in the end the only committee supporting the proposition was outdone in total contributions by $10 million to $30 million from the largest committee opposing the measure.[314]

Activists who claim that they would prevail if it wasn't for corporations and well-funded lobby groups are deluded. The world's largest companies are generally lobbying for more climate change regulation not less.

Some executives may sincerely believe that legislation like cap and trade is a good idea. But their job is to look out for the interests of their shareholders, and most should be and are

---

312 A list of their members can be viewed on the homepage of their website, here: http://www.us-cap.org/

313 Association of Professional Political Consultants, Register, June–August 2010

314 Walsh, B., 'California Election: Environmentalists Get Green', *Time*, 1 November 2010

hoping to extract some benefit for their company. The major corporate proponents of climate change policy fall into four main categories: those who expect to be subsidised directly by the regulation; those who want to sell to the companies getting the subsidies; those that aren't really affected either way but think signing up will bring a PR coup; and finally the poor unfortunates who know their industries could be destroyed by climate change regulation and hope that they can at least limit the damage if they are involved.

The biggest companies in the first category are electricity generators. They can make windfall profits under cap and trade if they can hold onto free allocations of allowances. They will also get special subsidies, or guaranteed prices, if they can claim to be producing 'clean energy'. Car companies also hope to profit from subsidies for electric cars.

As I mentioned in Chapter 3, EDF Energy put a lot of work into lobbying for a floor under the cap and trade price on carbon in Britain. That would guarantee a premium for power generated at the nuclear plants they own since buying British Energy, and at any new plants they built. Once the Government had signed up to implement the policy, and it became apparent it could make EDF Energy a £350 ($620, €463) million profit, the nuclear industry quickly changed its tune and announced that would not be enough to support new nuclear.[315] What they actually need is some kind of protection against other financial risks to building a nuclear plant, particularly construction risk.

Renewable energy generators don't just hire lots of the UK's biggest lobbying firms, they also have their two industry associations, the Renewable Energy Association and RenewableUK, which used to be called the British Wind Energy Association. The same thing goes on in the United States. In August 2010 OpenSecrets.org reported that

315 Mason, R., 'Carbon windfall for EDF', *Daily Telegraph*, 7 August 2010

the amount renewable energy firms spend lobbying has risen rapidly:[316]

By 2007, the alternative energy industry had begun to drastically increase its lobbying spending, almost doubling its expenditures from the previous year. In 2009, alternative energy organisations shelled out an unprecedented $30 million to protect and promote their interests on Capitol Hill, and this year, it's on pace to equal that record output.

Other firms will lobby for more money to support carbon capture and storage, biofuels or renewable heat; any form of energy they can plausibly claim is green and have a competitive advantage in.

The next category is the companies who think climate change policies will create new markets for them, even though they aren't getting the subsidies directly themselves. General Electric hope to sell a lot of wind turbines if the US adopts ambitious renewable energy mandates. Financial services firms like Goldman Sachs and JP Morgan want to be the ones arranging finance for the huge amounts of capital expenditure needed to meet the targets and trading emission allowances.

There are specialist firms just set up to organise financing for green investments and they are often ardent lobbyists. Climate Change Capital, in the United Kingdom, is one example. Along with the government agency the Equality and Human Rights Commission – in a sign of the amount of money being ploughed into these sorts of politically correct causes in the UK – the company occupies the second floor of one of the most impressive office blocks in London, 3 More London Riverside, which overlooks the river and City Hall and is otherwise home to a major City law firm. Climate Change Capital is sufficiently well connected to have pretty much written – along with a few other similar companies – a report for

....

316 LaRussa, C., 'Solar, Wind Power Groups Becoming Prominent Washington Lobbying Forces After Years of Relative Obscurity', www.OpenSecrets.org, 25 August 2010

a body called the Green Investment Bank Commission. The commission was set up by the Conservative Party in opposition in order to work out how a new institution, founded with taxpayers' money, could channel even more capital into investments to curb emissions. James Cameron, Executive Director and Vice-Chairman of Climate Change Capital, was a member of the Commission, another member of the Climate Change Capital staff was on the advisory panel and the report was published on their website.[317]

The Green Investment Bank is an attempt to mobilise the capital needed to deliver on climate change targets. The commission expect that will take a massive £550 ($975) billion in Britain by 2020.[318] With investors increasingly wary of the risks involved, and not making the investment required to meet the targets as I set out in Chapter 4, they plan to use taxpayers' cash to found the bank and then help channel retail investment into products like green bonds and green ISAs (regular ISAs are a popular tax exempt saving product in Britain). The report even talks about how, if all the capital required came from pension funds over the next five years, green investments would make up nearly 10 per cent of their total assets:[319]

If green bonds were to finance all the investment needed to support the low carbon transition over the next five years (£265 million, according to E3G), pension funds and insurance companies would have to allocate up to 5 per cent of their total bond investment (1.7 per cent overall assets) to them. In 2015, this would lead to average pension fund and insurance compa-

---

317 The report can be viewed here: http://www.climatechangecapital.com/media/108890/unlocking%20investment%20to%20deliver%20britain's%20low%20carbon%20future%20-%20green%20investment%20bank%20commission%20report%20-%20final%20-%20june%202010.pdf
318 Green Investment Bank Commission, 'Unlocking investment to deliver Britain's low carbon future', June 2010, p.xiii
319 Ibid., p.20

nies owning £265 billion of assets in this sector or almost 10 per cent of their total assets.

Our pension funds won't be mismanaged to that extent, but it does show the amount of money politicians are hoping to stake on dubious, expensive technologies like offshore wind. While ordinary people's savings will be put at risk, the Green Investment Bank could easily be a boon for an 'environmental investment manager and advisory group specialising in the opportunities generated by the global transition to a low carbon economy', like Climate Change Capital.[320] How convenient.

Then there are firms that just don't have a lot immediately at stake. Apple and Nike were among the companies that quit the US Chamber of Commerce, trying to pressure it to stop fighting climate change regulation.[321] The others were energy companies jealously watching their European peers make huge windfall profits out of cap and trade. Companies that make their money out of premium brands don't have nearly as much at stake with regulations that push up their costs: manufacturing is a relatively small part of their costs and often done abroad. As Apple outsources the production of iPods to China, they don't need to worry about cap and trade; those emissions have been exported already.

Finally, there are companies that just desperately want a seat at the table. No matter how disastrous the regulation looks for their industry, they just hope that so long as they play along they will get a relatively favourable deal.

Sometimes it works for the firms – though not for consumers. The coal industry knows that it makes sense to replace ageing coal power plants now – the Japanese Research Institute of Innovative Technology for the Earth (RITE)[322] and

320 Climate Change Capital, 'Company Overview', http://www.climatechange-capital.com/about-us/company-overview.aspx

321 Yarow, J., 'Apple Quits Chamber of Commerce Over Global Warming', Business Insider Green Sheet, 6 October 2009

322 Akimoto, K., 'Global Warming Mitigation Analyses Based on Sectoral Approach', Research Institute of Innovative Technology for the Earth,

many others have pointed to more efficient coal plants as a key means of cutting emissions that won't increase costs and heap a burden on ordinary consumers. Waiting and limping along with plants well past their sell-by date increases emissions for no good reason, but that is what is achieved insisting that no new coal plants are built without Carbon Capture and Storage (CCS). The coal industry in many countries has chosen not to focus on that obvious point. They play along and talk up CCS as relatively affordable, which it is only compared to spectacularly expensive sources of electricity like offshore wind. The companies get their subsidies for new 'demonstration' CCS plants and consumers miss out on the more affordable option of newer, better coal power plants.

In other cases, it doesn't work at all. British energy intensive industries had secured a special rate under the Climate Change Levy but, as I mentioned earlier, a large part of that discount was suddenly withdrawn in 2009.

Am I saying that the businesspeople supporting these policies get out of bed each morning with a gleam in their eye, eager to rip off unsuspecting consumers? No. But their sense that they are doing a powerful good, that they are a part of the solution to a global crisis, makes profits seem justified and the price consumers have to pay a necessary evil at worst; the sense that they are doing good gives them a moral licence to take advantage of the situation.

An experiment at the University of Toronto suggests that when people buy green goods they might become less likely to behave altruistically and more likely to cheat and steal.[323] The researchers sat 156 students down at computers. They offered half of them an online store with lots of green goods and the

....

presentation to Ministry of Economy, Trade and Industry, 22 January 2009
323 Mazar, N. & Zhong, C-B., 'Do Green Products Make Us Better People?', *Psychological Science*, 27 August 2009, http://www.rotman.utoronto.ca/NewThinking/greenproducts.pdf

other half a different store with fewer green goods. They then asked them to choose products to buy on the understanding that one in twenty-five would get the goods they notionally purchased. After that their willingness to be generous was tested in a simple game allocating a modest monetary reward. That experiment revealed that exposing people to more green products made them more altruistic, but those who actually bought those products became less altruistic. A second experiment in the same study looked at willingness to lie and steal and found a similar pattern.

The researchers explained their findings, which fit with other research on 'priming and licensing':

People do not make decisions in a vacuum; their decisions are embedded in a history of behaviours. Across three studies we consider pro-social and ethical decision-making in the context of past consumer behaviours and demonstrate that the halo associated with green consumerism has to be taken with reservations. While mere exposure to green products can have a positive societal effect by inducing pro-social and ethical acts, purchasing green products may license indulgence in self-interested and unethical behaviors.

When you think you are saving the world other moral considerations seem a bit less significant. As a result the costs to others of attempts to cut emissions aren't taken nearly seriously enough.

If you work at or invest in one of the companies I've listed, you might be glad they are lobbying for a good deal in this way. Better that than antagonising politicians and influential activists. Swimming against the tide can be hard work. That would be a mistake though, particularly if a company gets too involved. Current climate change policy isn't working and is too expensive to last. Having your livelihood or your pension fund dependent on the green rip-off continuing is a bad risk.

In many ways, the problem is that playing along with politicians pushing expensive climate change regulations is better for company executives than it is for shareholders. The executives can get subsidies in the short term, which will boost the performance their bonus depends on. It is also much more enjoyable to be praised for being a good corporate citizen instead of having your Annual General Meeting stormed by angry environmentalists. The people who are likely to lose out are those depending on the firm's long-term returns to pay their pension. The price shareholders pay will depend on how far the management go. It can just be a waste of money, but sometimes huge amounts of capital and the very future of an established business are being staked on climate change policy.

Environmentalist campaigns

Environmentalists are no longer just marginalised hippies, if they ever were. Major environmentalist campaigns have multi-million dollar budgets and huge political influence. In his book, *The Really Inconvenient Truths*, Iain Murray at the Competitive Enterprise Institute set out the scale that the biggest environmentalist campaigns in the United States have attained:[324]

CENTER FOR SCIENCE IN THE PUBLIC INTEREST, founded by three veteran allies of Ralph Nader in 1971. It has a budget of around $15 million and 900,000 supporters.

CERES   (COALITION   FOR   ENVIRONMENTALLY RESPONSIBLE ECONOMIES), founded in 1989, it has an annual budget of around $2 million.

ENVIRONMENTAL DEFENSE (formally the Environmental Defense Fund), founded in 1967 to campaign against DDT, it now says it 'brings together experts in science, law and economics to tackle complex environmental issues that affect our oceans, our air, our natural resources, the livability of our man-made environment and the species with whom we share

---

324 Murray, I., *The Really Inconvenient Truths*, Regnery Publishing, 2008, pp.190–192

the world'. It has an annual budget of around $50 million, has 300,000 members and employs 247 full-time staff.

ENVIRONMENTAL WORKING GROUP, founded in 1993, supposedly provides 'cutting edge research on health and the environment'. Much of this research appears to be aimed at promoting organic foods. (Michelle Malkin commented in 2002 that its agenda is 'to cripple agribusiness altogether in favor of organic alternatives'.) It has an annual budget of around $2 million and boasts of its 'bang for buck' in getting better results than groups twice its size.

FRIENDS OF THE EARTH, founded in 1967, has an international presence, with its headquarters in the Netherlands and groups in over seventy countries. It claims to represent more than a million people worldwide. It has a US budget of around $2 million. In the UK, it has two organisations, the Friends of the Earth Trust, with an annual income of £5,556,000 (more than $11 million) and Friends of the Earth Limited, which has a similar income.

GREENPEACE was founded in 1969 and is certainly the largest environmental organisation in the world, with 5 million members and staffed offices in twenty countries. Its total annual budget is reckoned by activistcash.com to be in the order of $360 million. Its US presence is more modest, about $10 million. Greenpeace's finances are so complicated that former Enron finance officials would find them mystifying.

NATURAL RESOURCES DEFENSE COUNCIL [...] was founded in 1967 and has an annual budget of $70 million, about 300 employees, and 1.3 million members/supporters.

PEOPLE FOR THE ETHICAL TREATMENT OF ANIMALS, was founded in 1980, claims 750,000 members and has a budget of around $25 million. It is the largest animal rights organisation in the world.

THE SIERRA CLUB is one of the oldest environmental groups, having been founded in 1960. It has over one million members, organised in sixty-five chapters and four hundred local groups across America. It funds projects to the tune of $20 *million a year, but in some years spends much more ($73 million in 2002).*

WORLD WILDLIFE FUND, otherwise known as the Worldwide Fund for Nature or WWF, was founded in 1961 and famously uses the panda as its logo. It is a massive organisation, with its US branch alone having a budget of over $100 million.

These are conservative estimates, not including some of the more innovative funding methods or a host of smaller groups. It also does not include more staid, but still leftist, environmental groups such as the Nature Conservancy ($731 million in revenues) and the Wildlife Conservative Council ($311 million) that are not as politically active.

Table 7.1 provides an updated set of figures for the total revenue of the major US environmentalist campaigns he looked at; all the data is from returns to the IRS.[325]

Table 7.1: US environmentalist organisation funding

Organisation	Revenue, 2009-10, $ million
Center for Science in the Public Interest	16;6
Coalition for Environmentally Responsible Economies (CERES)	9.6
Environmental Defense	54.9
Environmental Working Group	3.5
Friends of the Earth (2008-09)	4.9
Greenpeace (2008)	26.0
Natural Resources Defense Council	97.0
People for the Ethical Treatment of Animals	35.3
The Sierra Club (2009)	84.8
World Wildlife Fund	177.7

As Murray pointed out, many of those groups enjoy budgets significantly larger than even the best funded US conservative think tank, the Heritage Foundation, which received $69.2 million in 2009. And the Heritage Foundation is a generalist

---

325 The Guidestar service was used to find the Form 990 submissions for all the US non-profit organisations whose revenue is described in this report

think tank that covers a host of issues, not just environmental policy. In 2010 they produced 5,135 publications of all kinds, from blog posts to major reports. Searching for 'energy' in their archive returns 807 publications; 'global warming' returns 212; and 'climate change' returns 213 (there will be a lot of overlap and not all the 'energy' publications will be about this sector).[326] Groups like the Competitive Enterprise Institute that are more focused on climate change policy are much smaller; they had a budget of $4.7 million in 2008/09. Overall, Murray reports that the environmentalist organisations have a budget of over half a billion dollars in the United States.

The global budget is far larger. Greenpeace alone report that in 2009 'total gross income from fundraising for Greenpeace worldwide was €196 (£175, $273) million'.[327]

In the United Kingdom the difference in scale between environmentalist campaigns and their conservative adversaries is even starker. The funding a handful of the bigger environmentalist groups get is set out in Table 7.2.[328]

Table 7.2: UK environmentalist organisation funding

Organisation	Revenue, 2009-10, £ million
Friends of the Earth	2.4
Friends of the Earth Trust	8.1
Greenpeace	9.2
Greenpeace Environmental Trust	2.7
World Wildlife Fund	56.7

The largest organisation in Britain openly sceptical of draconian climate change regulations is probably the Institute of

---

326 The same search can be carried out at www.heritage.org
327 Greenpeace International, Annual Report 09, p.31
328 The Charity Commission website was used to find the details for all the UK charities whose income is described in this report

Economic Affairs. It has only devoted very limited attention to the issue. Its last dedicated report on climate change policy was released in September 2008. Other groups like the TaxPayers' Alliance also take the issue on as part of their broader work and there is the new Global Warming Policy Foundation founded by Nigel Lawson with a few staff.[329] Apart from a few bloggers writing in their spare time, that's it.

Generous funding means generous pay for the bosses of the major environmentalist campaigns. On Earth Day 2009, the campaign group Freedom Action released an advert – 'For some people Earth Day is Pay Day' – highlighting some of the most generous deals. The compensation they found, eight environmentalist CEOs in the United States getting over $300,000 (£190,000) a year, is listed in Table 7.3.[330]

Table 7.3: Environmentalist CEO remuneration

Organisation	Annual reevenues	President/CEO	Total compensation
Alliance for Climate Protection	$88,303,373	Cathy Zoi	$330,280
Environmental Defense Fund	$125,425,925	Frederic D. Krupp	$474,596
National Wildlife Federation	$94,573,828	Larry J. Schweiger	$345,004
Natural Resources Defense Council	$107,999,911	Frances Beinecke	$432,959
The Nature Conservancy	$856,246,824	Stephanie K. Meeks and Mark R. Tercek (each part of the year)	$592,298
Pew Center on Global Climate Change	$1,388,294	Eileen Claussen	$335,099
World Resources Institute	$21,224,697	Jonathan Lash	$385,388
World Wildlife Fund	$151,560,547	Carter Roberts	$509,699

The money for such big organisations, with such well-paid bosses, comes from a variety of sources.

Some of it will come from those who really believe in the cause: from individual donations. It is unclear how many donors to these groups understand how their money is being

---

329 Their website is here: http://www.thegwpf.org/
330 Freedom Action, 'Earth Day is Pay Day', http://freedomaction.org/earthday

spent. Many supporters and small-scale donors give expecting their money to be spent directly looking after plants and animals. They don't necessarily realise that a lot of the money will be spent on advertising campaigns and lobbying aimed at securing expensive regulations to try and reduce greenhouse gas emissions. How many people giving to Friends of the Earth know that it works to get policies put in place that will increase their electricity bills?

In Europe many environmentalist groups enjoy taxpayer funding. A TaxPayers' Alliance report in December 2010 exposed how the EU provided £8 ($13) million in 2009 to environmentalist groups, and UK public bodies a further £2 ($3) million in the 2009/10 financial year.[331] Friends of the Earth got nearly £725,000 ($1.1 million) and the World Wildlife Fund got nearly £600,000 ($940,000) from the EU. Both received tens of thousands more from various public sector bodies in the UK. The International Network for Sustainable Energy (INFORSE) got £80,100 ($125,000) in EU funding.

The Brighton Peace and Environment Centre received nearly £43,000 ($67,000) from the Department for International Development and the National Lottery. Its activities have included a naked bike ride, which it argued would allow participants to 'cast off the clutter of consumerism', as 'nudity symbolises our vulnerability as cyclists and also as a species'; it also trains and supports teachers to promote its cause in the classroom.

The radical New Economics Foundation is an almost perfect exemplar of environmentalist ideology. Its work includes running the Green New Deal Group, which launched with a call for major increases in government spending on green objectives and recently released a report by Caroline Lucas MP, leader of the Green Party, which argued for 'a bold new

---

331 Sinclair, M., 'Taxpayer funded environmentalism', TaxPayers' Alliance, 2 December 2010

programme of "green quantitative easing"'. It received funding from a range of public sector bodies in 2009/10, including Bradford council, who gave it over £45,000 ($70,000); the Department of Health gave it nearly £30,000 ($47,000); and Natural England over £30,000. I'll look at its work in more detail later, in the section on ideology.

The Women's Environmental Network runs campaigns that a principled feminist might accuse of pandering to stereotypes. It used to campaign against the use of disposable nappies, and promote the use of washable cloth ('real') nappies. That campaign received public funding but it was cancelled after a four-year report by the Environment Agency found there were no net environmental benefits to more people using washable cloth nappies. Sadly, the Government had already spent £30 ($53) million on a campaign against disposable nappies over a number of years before they got the evidence and discovered it was a complete waste of time and money. The Women's Environmental Network also organises the Three Tonne Club, using the concept of dieting clubs to urge women to 'slim down [their] carbon footprints'. Tower Hamlets council in East London, responsible for some of the most deprived urban areas in Britain, gave them over £38,000 ($60,000) in 2009/10.

The biggest example of taxpayer-funded environmentalism in the UK was the Sustainable Development Commission that I mentioned earlier.[332] It was a government agency, with a budget of over £4 ($7) million a year. It was run by the former Green Party candidate Jonathon Porritt, who describes himself as a 'hardened anti-nuclear campaigner' and 'an environmentalist with a bit of a track record', for nearly a decade after its foundation. In March 2009 the organisation released a report from one of its commissioners entitled 'Prosperity without Growth?'. The report claimed that it 'challenges the assumption of continued economic expansion in rich coun-

332 Sinclair, M., 'Taxpayer funded lobbying and political campaigning', TaxPayers' Alliance, 3 August 2009

tries and asks: is it possible to achieve prosperity without growth?' The organisation then went on to recruit a Senior Economic Policy Analyst to '[work] with the SDC's Economics Commissioner to lead and develop opportunities for engagement and advocacy of SDC's recent report: Prosperity without Growth: Transition to a sustainable economy with stakeholders including government'.

That report, pushing the environmentalist case against economic growth, was part of a pattern. Another report called for a 'sustainable new deal', which would involve spending £30 ($53) billion a year for three years on a 'green recovery package'. Yet another stated that 'natural justice tells us that individual emissions of CO_2 must, in the long run, "converge" around the same per capita entitlement' and called for 'personal carbon budgets' – cap and trade for individual people.

Environmentalist campaigns also get taxpayer funding in the US, though the payments aren't quite as shameless. The EU provides funding explicitly to help environmentalist campaigns lobby and fight for changes in policy: hundreds of thousands of euros go to radical campaigns. In the US the money at least nominally tends to be payment in return for actual services. Funding for specific projects can free up room in their budgets for spending on lobbying and campaigning, and makes them larger more powerful organisations. Mark Tapscott reported for the *Washington Examiner* on the scale of taxpayer funding for 'Big Green':[333]

An Examiner *analysis of the most recently available IRS Form 990 tax returns for major Big Green groups found six that collectively received more than $160 million in federal grants and contracts in return for providing services and as reimbursement for expenses.*

Topping the six is the Nature Conservancy's $110.6 million, followed by the Trust for Public Land ($28 million), Audubon

---

333 Tapscott, M., 'Crucial funding for Big Green comes from taxpayers', *Washington Examiner*, 27 September 2010

Society ($17.5 million), the Environmental Defense Fund (parent of the EDF Action Fund) with $3.6 million, Natural Resources Defense Council ($358,072) and Defenders of Wildlife ($205,021).

The Heritage Foundation has revealed that some US environmentalist groups get funding from the EU. Sally McNamara revealed that a number of groups had received tens of thousands of dollars. For example, the Californian non-profit Global Footprint Network, Inc. received $145,376 in 2009.[334]

Many also get corporate funding. Sometimes government and industry even unite to fund a campaign against the interests of ordinary consumers. The Campaign for Better Transport received £243,000 ($381,000) from the Department for Transport in 2009/10.[335] An investigation by the *Daily Telegraph* revealed that around a fifth of their total budget came from bus and train companies, who could do well out of the campaign's attacks on cars and calls for greater spending on public transport.[336] In *Power Grab* Chris Horner described how a major investor in renewable energy has claimed to have given a lot of money to the Sierra Club:[337]

For example, in late 2009 we learned that a David Gelbaum regretted he could no longer fork over millions to the Sierra Club's campaigns, facing tough times of his own due to being so heavily invested in struggling alternative energy projects. In the letter communicating his despair, Gelbaum claimed to have anonymously given Sierra Club $47.7 million from 2005 through 2009.

This is what the Italians call *regalo con l'elastico*, an elastic gift; giving a family member a CD you really like for Christmas, then insisting you all listen to it in the car.

---

334 McNamara, S., 'Swaying American Opinions: Congress Should Investigate EU Advocacy'
335 Sinclair, M., 'Taxpayer funded environmentalism', TaxPayers' Alliance, 2 December 2010
336 'Funding leads to another', *Daily Telegraph*, 4 February 2006
337 Horner, C., *Power Grab*, Regnery Publishing, p.280

Finally, there is funding from established foundations. In the UK one of the biggest funders of radical environmentalism is the Esmée Fairbairn Foundation. Environmentalists from Friends of the Earth to the 10:10 campaign have received significant amounts from the foundation. It was originally founded in 1961 by Ian Fairbairn as a memorial to his wife. Ian Fairbairn was a pioneer in unit trusts, and the foundation proudly reports that his work helped open up the possibility of investing in equities to more people. They report his intention for the fund:[338]

His purpose in establishing the foundation was two-fold. In the interests of wider prosperity, he aimed to promote a greater understanding of economic and financial issues through education. He also wanted to establish a memorial to his wife, Esmée, who had played a prominent role in developing the Women's Royal Voluntary Service and the Citizens Advice Bureaux. She was killed in an air raid during the Second World War.

It is hard to see how the trustees have divined that this means they should give money to radical campaigns to cut emissions. They paid towards the core costs and director's salary of the 10:10 campaign in 2009[339] and are still listed by 10:10 as supporters. The campaign released a video – directed by Richard Curtis, with music from Radiohead and starring Gillian Anderson – that graphically imagined blowing up anyone who refused to take action to cut emissions, turning them into a bloody mess. It has to be seen to be believed.[340] Would Ian Fairbairn be happy his money was spent supporting that?

Environmentalists are a very legitimate part of the political debate. There undoubtedly are a decent number of people out there who don't think that the free-market, growth-oriented

---

338 Esmeé Fairbairn Foundation, 'Our history', http://www.esmeefairbairn. org.uk/history.html

339 Esmeé Fairbairn Foundation, 'Main Fund 2009', http://www.esmeefairbairn.org.uk/grants2009/main.html

340 The video was taken down by 10:10 but can still be found on YouTube

economic model is the right one. But they aren't the only people whose money supports environmentalist campaigns advocating draconian climate change policy.

Anyone who gives to an organisation like Friends of the Earth – or even Oxfam, who spend money placing prominent adverts on this issue – expecting them to directly look after vulnerable animals, plants or people; taxpayers whose money is given to green campaigns in grants or other payments; shareholders of companies that finance green groups; philanthropists who set up foundations decades ago that are now run by trustees who make their own decisions about how to spend the money – they are all funding environmentalist groups who campaign for policies that reflect a distinctive ideological hostility to economic growth.

Lawyers

What environmentalist campaigns can't achieve by legislation, they can try and achieve through the law. In that environment there aren't pesky voters to worry about in the same way. This strategy has been by far the best developed in the United States. In *Power Grab* Chris Horner gives the example of new coal plants being increasingly blocked by environmentalist law suits and pliant bureaucrats:[341]

The Obama Administration's close ally, the Sierra Club, now boasts of having killed 100 planned coal-fired power plants since 2001. This is out of what Sierra says was 150 total plants slated for development.

[...]

The one hundredth plant blocked, per Sierra Club, was the Desert Rock Energy Company facility in the Four Corners (New Mexico) area, on Navajo land. Following an increasingly familiar script, the Environmental Protection Agency issued the air quality permit to the 1,500-megawatt plan, only to have the greens lead a lawsuit to block it. As has also become a famil-

341 Horner, C., *Power Grab*, Regnery Publishing, pp.279–281

iar scenario, once the Obama administration was ensconced, the Agency decided to rescind the permit [...] It should also be the end of the project, since the green groups have raised the projected costs to bring the plant on line to $4 billion.

[...]

According to the Arizona Republic, Sierra casualty #100, Desert Rock, would have been 'fuelled by coal from a new mine, bringing more jobs and revenue to the Navajos'. And now it won't. The greens are also pushing the Environmental Protection Agency to impose new costs on the Navajo Generating Station near Page, Arizona, which the Navajos say will lead to its closure.

The most likely result of all that litigation is probably that older fossil fuel plants will be kept in service for longer. That will mean higher emissions and higher costs unnecessarily. Over time, the US will probably move towards using more natural gas in its generation mix, now that technological advances are making huge domestic reserves economical to extract. Litigation against coal might accelerate that process, which would reduce emissions, but how long before gas becomes the next target? Litigation won't be enough to force the adoption of renewable energy, which requires huge subsidies to provide a significant share of electricity generation in Europe.

Legal assaults, one plant at a time, are just the start. More recently, the EPA decided that carbon dioxide was a pollutant after the Supreme Court agreed it could be covered by the Clean Air Act. CO_2 didn't fit with the existing Clean Air Act legislation, which is aimed at actual pollutants where small quantities can harm human health and regulates any installation emitting 100 or 250 tonnes per year, so they had to, arbitrarily and with no legislative authority, increase the threshold to tens of thousands of tonnes per year.[342]

The threat of EPA action was the basis of a bizarre kind of legislative extortion. The Obama Administration played good

---

342 Lewis, M., 'Motion to Stay Makes Strong Case Court Should Overturn EPA Global Warming Rules', www.OpenMarket.org, 22 September 2010

cop, threatening Congress with the EPA's bad cop: 'pass cap and trade or you'll get EPA, and he's crazy'. The New York Times Greenwire reported Yvo de Boer, head of the UNFCCC at the time, saying that:[343]

If I were a businessman, I would say, 'Please, please, please do a deal in Copenhagen, and please, please, please make it market-based.' Because if we fail to get a market-based deal here, and if the US Senate fails to pass cap-and-trade legislation, then the EPA will be obliged to regulate.

Congress didn't buy it, and the Senate refused to pass cap and trade. Now the question is how far the EPA can go without an increasingly sceptical Congress slapping them down. The Murkowski Resolution, which would have stopped them, was only narrowly defeated in the Senate, with some promises that similar, alternative legislation would be brought to the floor and before the 2010 midterms when a lot more sceptical lawmakers entered Congress. New attempts to stop the EPA are currently on the table.

Still, the greens have made a lot more progress through the courts in the United States than they have through legislation at the state or federal level. There is every reason to think that, particularly if it doesn't look like they will be able to pass the legislation they want, well-funded environmentalist campaigns will resort to legal action more and more. They have the money.

Environmentalist campaigns are trying to bring this kind of legal action to Europe. In the United Kingdom one obstacle to that sort of judicial review case is that, if you lose, you have to pay the costs of the other side and the court, and judges have a fair bit of discretion over what that amounts to. The organisation ClientEarth recently won a case under the Aarhus Convention arguing that wasn't good enough and

343 Samuelsohn, D., 'U.N. Summit 'Wasn't Our Impetus' for Endangerment Release on Greenhouse Gases – EPA Chief', *NY Times*' Greenwire, 9 December 2009

the government is now looking at changing the rules.[344] That might create a get-out for a major environmentalist group when they bring a case, and lose it.

We have already seen one incredible legal decision on the basis of climate change. Activists with Greenpeace were accused of £30,000 ($56,000) worth of criminal damage after they vandalised a coal power station in Kingsnorth, Kent, protesting at its potential replacement by a new, more efficient coal plant. They pleaded not guilty, not because they didn't do it, but on the grounds that trying to stop climate change was a 'lawful excuse'.[345] The lawful excuse defence is there to stop injustices like a fireman being prosecuted for damaging a house when they kick down a door to get in and save someone from a fire. A range of prominent environmentalists, including Zac Goldsmith (incredibly, now a Conservative Member of Parliament) and James Hansen, testified about the dangers of climate change and, on that basis, the activists were let off. We haven't seen radicals using the same legal defence to get away with torching Range Rovers yet, but give it time.

From speaking to a lawyer who has worked on similar cases, though not that particular one, the result in the Kingsnorth case was the result of pressing the wrong charge in a court known to be a bit of a wildcard. Still, it is another development that suggests the courts could increasingly be a forum that endorses radical environmentalism, even in the UK. It may be possible for environmentalists to achieve through litigation what they can't through new policy even here, let alone in other jurisdictions more accustomed to activist law.

Ideology

The two key planks of the environmentalist ideology are

344 ClientEarth, 'ClientEarth wins landmark case against the UK for failing citizens on access to justice', 26 August 2010

345 BBC News, 'Power station protesters cleared', 10 September 2008

criticisms of economic growth: an attack on its value and, more importantly, the possibility of sustaining it over time.

The attacks on the value of economic growth centre on happiness economics and the contention that higher growth does not lead to greater well-being. This is based on surveys asking people how happy they feel. There has been no particular trend up or down in recent decades despite considerable economic growth. The Institute of Economic Affairs published a report in 2007 which set out a number of reasons why that analysis doesn't stand up.[346]

Lots of other social trends that those arguing against economic growth might expect to promote happiness, like increased longevity, equality between the genders and public spending, have all also failed to improve reported happiness.

People answering the surveys are asked to describe their happiness using a scale with a limited number of categories, which means 'noticeable changes in average happiness can come about only through substantial numbers of people changing their categories'. This approach to measuring happiness also means there is an upper bound to happiness that there isn't for income, which creates serious statistical problems. Giving up on economic growth on the basis of those surveys and the dubious statistical conclusions greens have come to looking at them would be madness.

There is a more robust way of understanding happiness scientifically:[347]

This is based upon the analysis, not of aggregate happiness data over time, but of so-called panel, or longitudinal, data, which tracks specific individuals over time. It shows that stable family life, being married, good health, having religious faith, feelings of living in a cohesive community where people can be

---

346 Johns, H. & Ormerod, P., 'Happiness, Economics and Public Policy', Institute of Economic Affairs, 2007

347 Ibid., p.14

trusted, and good governance contribute to happiness. Chronic pain, divorce and bereavement detract from happiness.

So happiness economics isn't remotely sufficient to base a serious criticism of capitalism on. Of course, money isn't everything; the evidence backs up the common intuition that lasting, meaningful relationships are critical to happiness.

Happiness isn't everything anyway. Higher incomes allow us to live long lives, full of opportunities to see and do new things. Even if being able to see China isn't going to make me happy, it can be meaningful and important in a different way. Aldous Huxley's *Brave New World* is the classic caution against empty hedonism. We might be able to drug ourselves happy with enough soma but live empty lives.

Figure 7.1: Global death and death rates due to extreme events, 1900–2006

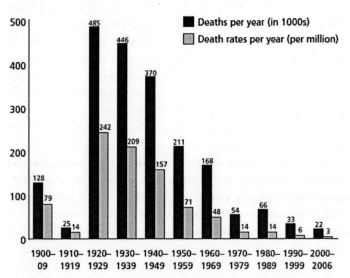

Note that in figures 1 through 4, data for the last period are averaged over seven years worth of data.
Sources; EM-DAT (2007); McEvedy and Jones (1978); WRI (2005, 2007)

Spurious opinion polls testing people's happiness are a poor justification for denying them the more comfortable life and exciting opportunities that the wealthy enjoy today, and which everyone can enjoy if the economy continues to grow strongly.

Economic growth is also critical to our ability to respond to climate change.

Richer societies are better able to adapt. Higher incomes mean that people are less vulnerable to extreme weather, for example. Indur Goklany, in a study for the November 2007 Civil Society Coalition Report, set out how globally, 'mortality and mortality rates have declined by 95 per cent or more since the 1920s'.[348] The mortality figures he provided are reproduced in Figure 7.1.[349] You can see the same phenomenon today – so many more people die when poorer countries face natural disasters.

Greater economic growth will also make us better able to innovate. Dynamic and prosperous economies are more likely to produce the new technologies that will make fossil fuels obsolete. And they will produce more options in the event that something drastic needs to be done about climate change. If we have passed, or pass, some point where cutting emissions is no longer sufficient to avoid catastrophic climate change, then a higher global income improves our odds of being able to devise and implement one of the drastic geo-engineering projects that scientists have already begun to discuss as an insurance policy in case things really go wrong.

The final problem with the greens' attack on economic growth is that they try to separate out growth in the developed and developing world. Attacks on the value of economic growth in relatively well-off countries are mistaken, but it is rare to see even the most ardent green attack the value of growth in poorer countries. In a September 2009 report

....

348 Goklany, I. M., 'Death and Death Rates Due to Extreme Weather Events', International Policy Network, November 2007, p.3

349 Ibid., Figure 1

UNICEF gave just one example of the progress we've made in recent decades. Their Executive Director, Ann M. Veneman, reported:[350]

Compared to 1990, 10,000 fewer children are dying every day.

That isn't entirely down to economic growth; other factors like improvements in governance will also make a difference. Material progress is vital though: the greater resources it affords make it possible for society to advance on a number of different fronts at the same time.

The problem for critics of growth in richer countries is that it is very hard to disentangle from growth in poorer countries. Finance organised in London can help to build factories in Laos. Entrepreneurs in California design products that are then made in China. Indians are paid to take customer service calls from customers in Indiana. If the developed world lost its taste for growth then that would make it much harder for the big developing world economies to maintain their impressive performance. They would also likely see less altruistic support from a rich world that had stopped economic growth than they would if it kept getting richer. People tend to give more when they have something to spare. The human cost of all that would be terrible.

The second part to the criticism of economic growth articulated by environmentalists is an attack on its sustainability. They argue that it is simply impossible to keep growing the economy, that we are running up against the limits of finite natural resources. This is a modern form of the argument made by Thomas Malthus in *An Essay on the Principle of Population.* Instead of arguing that population will outstrip the productive capacity of agriculture, the new Malthusians say the needs of growing economies and populations will outstrip finite natural resources. The New Economics Foundation explained the concept in January 2010 with 'The Impossible Hamster'.[351] The animation charted the life of a baby hamster that doubled in size every week. Instead of stopping growing once it had reached a certain size, it kept going and quickly grew to be bigger than the planet. The message is simple: growth can't be maintained indefinitely and will end in disaster.

Fortunately, such pessimism is invariably confounded. Malthus has the best excuse for getting it wrong: he was writing just before the Industrial Revolution. Paul Ehrlich wrote *The Population Bomb* in 1968, arguing: 'The battle to feed humanity is over. In the 1970s, the world will undergo famines. Hundreds of millions of people are going to starve to death in spite of any crash programs embarked upon now. Population control is the only answer.'[352] Needless to say, that prediction proved way off the mark. World population has risen drastically but hunger has declined and is now mostly inflicted by bad politics. Either a country is sufficiently dysfunctional that food can't be delivered, or world prices have risen as our politicians decide we have enough food so as to be able to burn some in our cars.

In order to try and settle the debate, in 1980 Paul Ehrlich made a bet with the economist Julian Simon that a basket of five commodities (chosen by Ehrlich) would increase in price and lost spectacularly. The price of every single one fell if the price was adjusted for inflation and most fell even in nominal terms.[353]

As Ben Pile, editor of the Climate Resistance blog, put it:[354]
Ehrlich predicted dire consequences, but the resource depletion, mass famine and economic collapse he saw in his

---

351 You can still view the animation they used to make the point here: http://www.impossiblehamster.org

352 Ehrlich, P. R., *The Population Bomb*, 1968

353 Moore, S., 'Julian Simon Remembered: It's A Wonderful Life', Cato Policy Report, April 1998

354 Pile, B., 'What the greens really got wrong', www.spiked-online.com, 8 November 2010

calculations failed to materialise. Undaunted, the environmental movement merely deferred the date of eco-tastrophe further into the future, and made an ethic out of life within presumed environmental limits – 'sustainability'. The result has been the tendency of the environmental movement to produce ideas which are hostile to technological development and appear to be anti-human in consequence.

In another recent bet, journalist John Tierney challenged Matthew R. Simmons, a member of the Council on Foreign Relations, head of an investment bank and author of an influential book arguing that oil is running out. They wagered $5,000 on whether the average price of oil in 2010 would be at least $200 a barrel at 2005 prices. Tierney won: the average price was about $71 in 2005 dollars.[355]

Larger populations with higher incomes don't just consume more; they also have a greater capacity to innovate. Human ingenuity continues to frustrate those that keep seeing shortages just around the corner. While the prices of some commodities will rise with new demand from China, that is just a signal to bright sparks everywhere that they should get to work finding ways of using those resources much more efficiently or devise some substitute.

In October 2010 Brendan O'Neill, editor of the website *spiked-online.com*, gave two dramatic examples of this process in a debate at a 'Battle of Ideas' event in London:[356]

Malthusians are simply wrong to say that resources are fixed, that we can measure and predict when they will run out. It seems commonsensical to say that the Earth is finite, and a bit mad to say that it isn't, but it's important to recognise how fluid and changeable resources are. It's important to recognise that the usefulness and longevity of a resource is determined

355 Tierney, J., 'Economic Optimism? Yes, I'll Take That Bet', *New York Times*, 27 December 2010

356 O'Neill, B., 'Think the Earth is finite? Think again', www.spiked-online.com, 8 November 2010

as much by us – by the level of social development we have reached – as it is by the existence of that resource in the first place.

Resources are not fixed in any meaningful sense. Resources have a history and a future, just as human beings do. The question of what we consider to be a resource changes as society changes.

So in Ancient Rome, one of the main uses of coal was to make jewellery. Women liked the look of this glinting black rock hanging around their necks. No one could have imagined that thousands of years later, coal would be used to power massive steam engines and an entire Industrial Revolution, forever changing how we produce things and transport them around the world.

Two thousand years ago, the only way people used uranium was to make glass look more yellow. It was used to decorate windows and mirrors. You would probably have been locked up, or subjected to an exorcism, if you had suggested that one day uranium might be used to light up and heat entire cities – or indeed destroy entire cities at the push of a button.

To come back to the New Economics Foundation animation, that just isn't the kind of thing hamsters do. One big fat hamster is a poor analogy for six billion brilliant humans.

It isn't as if our appetites will – like that fictional hamster – keep getting physically bigger. We only want so many cars, so much food. Peter Huber put it well in *Hard Green*, responding to the modern environmentalist's understanding of growth:[357]

He thinks of growth the way he thinks of everything, in collective terms, as a Marxist would: more total pig iron, more megawatts, more national population. His metrics are the traditional Malthusian ones: Nation States, World Models, Global Trends. He doesn't see the world through the eyes of the individual.

---

357 Huber, P., *Hard Green: saving the environment from the environmentalists, a conservative manifesto*, Basic Books, 1999, pp.149–150

[...]

Private wealth does not work that way at all. The individual's desire for more wealth has no limits, but his appetite for hamburgers does. Up to a point he will eat more, drive more, build more. Then his basic Malthusian desires are satiated. The individual does not wish to seize and eat, to seize and drink, to seize and fornicate, more and more, without limit. Happily, he just isn't built that way. The individual desire to grow within, to grow his waistline, his family, his estate: that is what eventually reaches a limit. The real limits to growth are rooted in nothing more complicated than that.

[...]

And when the rich man reaches the private limits of his own consumption, he puts his wealth into other things. That is what people always do as they get richer.

First, into better lives for his children and grandchildren. And the better he can take care of them, the fewer he has.

[...]

And with that secured, he pours his wealth into green.

That isn't just empty theory. Robert Fogel has put a lot of work into assessing what people want more of as they get richer.[358] As their incomes rise people want to spend more on health and education. They spend less, as a share of income, on food and manufactured goods. Those results aren't that surprising; these days in developed economies it is only a small, unfortunate minority who aspire to eat as much as they want. Plenty want to send their children to the best university – or enjoy a longer, healthier life with the best care modern science can afford. That shift in the balance of how people want to spend their money reduces our demands on the environment. Each dollar, pound or euro spent on education or healthcare creates fewer emissions than if it is spent on food or manufactured goods.

....

358 Fogel, R., 'Forecasting the Cost of US Healthcare', *The American*, 3 September 2009

What is ironic about some of the arguments that there are hard limits on growth is that they actually undermine the case that we should really worry about climate change. Many environmentalists believe passionately in Peak Oil, that we are approaching dramatic shortages in fossil fuels. If that was the case, we wouldn't need regulations to stop us using coal, oil and gas. Scarcity will lead to high prices much more surely than any carbon tax. The scarcer hydrocarbons are, the less we have to worry about the externalities of burning them. You don't need regulations to tell people not to use what they don't have.

The reality is that fossil fuels are still plentiful and new technologies have allowed countries like the United States to extract far more, at far lower cost. In November 2010 the *New York Times* reported:[359]

Three summers ago, the world's supertankers were racing across the oceans as fast as they could to deliver oil to markets growing increasingly thirsty for energy. Americans were grumbling about paying as much as $4 a gallon for gasoline, as the price of crude oil leapt to $147 a barrel. Natural gas prices were vaulting too, sending home electricity bills soaring.

[...]

But no sooner did the demand-and-supply equation shift out of kilter than it swung back into something more palatable and familiar. Just as it seemed that the world was running on fumes, giant oil fields were discovered off the coasts of Brazil and Africa, and Canadian oil sands projects expanded so fast they now provide North America with more oil than Saudi Arabia. In addition, the United States has increased domestic oil production for the first time in a generation.

Meanwhile, another wave of natural gas drilling has taken off in shale rock fields across the United States, and more shale gas drilling is just beginning in Europe and Asia. Add to that an increase in liquified natural gas export terminals around the

---

359 Krauss, C., 'There Will Be Fuel', *New York Times*, 16 November 2010

world that connected gas, which once had to be flared off, to the world market, and gas prices have plummeted.

Energy experts now predict decades of residential and commercial power at reasonable prices. Simply put, the world of energy has once again been turned upside down.

The US Energy Information Administration has since released an estimate of the technically recoverable reserves in forty-eight shale gas basins in thirty-two countries.[360] They found 6,622 trillion cubic feet, which is an incredible amount compared to the estimate of total global technically recoverable gas at around 16,000 trillion cubic feet. There is every sign that technological developments are delivering more than enough gas to supply the world for some time to come.

The New Economics Foundation's Happy Planet Index shows how absurd the results can get when you combine happiness economics, and its suggestion we don't gain much from greater economic growth, with an overwhelming pessimism that we are at the natural limits of economic growth. They claim 'the nations that score well show that achieving long, happy lives without over-stretching the planet's resources is possible'.[361]

Looking at the results of the second edition of the index, that claim seems a bit of a stretch. Saudi Arabia (13th), Mexico (23rd), Burma (39th) and Haiti (42nd) are way ahead of Sweden (53rd), the United Kingdom (74th) and the United States (114th).[362] Where would you rather live?

The answer is obvious. Thousands risk death each year attempting to get from 23rd-placed Mexico to the 114th-placed United States. This is just one way that people reveal their

360 Energy Information Administration, 'World Shale Gas Resources: An Initial Assessment of 14 Regions Outside the United States', 5 April 2011

361 New Economics Foundation, 'About the Happy Planet Index', http://www.happyplanetindex.org/learn/

362 Abdallah, S., Thompson, S., Michaelson, J., Marks, N. & Steuer, N., 'The Happy Planet Index 2.0: Why good lives don't have to cost the Earth', June 2009, HPI results table

preference for a higher standard of living. I'm sure the New Economics Foundation can blame this on some kind of false consciousness. The reality is that it shows the dynamic economies and resulting high living standards that they deride are what people actually want.

While it does produce the most ludicrous results, the Happy Planet Index isn't the only attempt to use green economics to understand how economies have performed. In yet another example of British taxpayer-funded environmentalism, the South West Regional Development Agency paid £6,857.12 ($12,714) as their contribution to funding the 'Measuring Regional Progress: regional index of sustainable economic well-being for all the English regions' report written by the New Economics Foundation. Other British government agencies also supported the project.[363]

That report consisted of calculating an Index of Sustainable Economic Well-being (ISEW) for each of the English regions. The idea behind the ISEW is that you correct for various things not included in a raw measure of output like GDP and produce a more reliable measure of economic progress. It is used to substantiate a claim that growth in recent decades, in particular, has been illusory. Professor Nicholas Crafts, one of the world's leading authorities on historical growth statistics – a professor until recently at the London School of Economics and now at Warwick University – found that, if the ISEW's various flaws were corrected and omitted variables included, 'the revised ISEW calculation suggests growth of real GDP per person substantially underestimates rather than overestimates growth of utility-based real national income per person'.[364]

---

363 Sinclair, M., 'Taxpayer funded lobbying and political campaigning', TaxPayers' Alliance, 3 August 2009

364 Crafts, N. F. R., 'UK real national income, 1950-1998: Some grounds for optimism', *National Institute Economic Review*, No 181, July 2002

The attack on economic growth distinguishes environmentalists from advocates of free-market capitalism or socialism. Both sides of that ideological divide argued that they could deliver greater economic growth. While the environmentalist movement is predominantly a creature of the left – probably because it offered an alternative project after outright socialism was discredited in the 1990s – it can also appeal to conservatives. Particularly among the Tory establishment and aristocracy in Britain there has been unease about industrial capitalism since the onset of the Industrial Revolution. It is a mistake to see environmentalism as exclusively a creed of left or right.

The ideology of environmentalist campaigns could simply be a curiosity, like the cornucopia of far-left factions that still struggle along in most developed economies dreaming of subtly different revolutions. Unfortunately, subscribers to the environmentalist ideology are often very influential people. When Paul Ehrlich made his bet with Julian Simon he was joined by John P. Holdren.[365] Holdren has done well since; he is now assistant to the President for Science and Technology, Director of the White House Office of Science and Technology Policy, and co-chair of the President's Council of Advisors on Science and Technology (PCAST).[366]

The environmentalist contempt for economic growth is at the heart of a lot of what has gone wrong and why the critical challenge of reconciling the targets with increasing prosperity hasn't been taken nearly seriously enough.

Population

As part of their broader Malthusian concern that we are hitting the limits of growth and are heading for disaster, many environmentalists believe passionately in population control.

---

365 Tierney, J., 'Economic Optimism? Yes, I'll Take That Bet', *New York Times*, 27 December 2010

366 White House Office of Science and Technology Policy, Leadership & Staff, Director John P. Holdren, http://www.whitehouse.gov/administration/eop/ostp/about/leadershipstaff/director

Jonathon Porritt, very much part of Britain's green establishment, has praised China's One Child Policy:[367]

I can't recall any environmental or climate change organisation ever suggesting that 'births averted' is probably the single most substantial and cost-effective intervention that governments could be using. Just to give another example, the Chinese government calculates that since the introduction of the One Child Family Policy in the early 80s, at least 400 million births have been averted.

Each Chinese citizen today emits an average of 3.5 tonnes of CO_2 every year. Multiply the one (400 million) by the other (3.5 tonnes per annum), and you get a figure of 1.4 billion tonnes of CO_2 per annum. By a million miles, that's the biggest single CO_2 abatement achievement since Kyoto came into force – a fact that George Bush conveniently forgets when he whinges on about Kyoto being useless because China doesn't have the same target as the United States.

The logic there is obviously faulty. Whether or not China has restrained its emissions with the One Child Policy from what they might have been, it is still the largest emitter and, along with other rapidly developing economies, set to render any progress in the developed world cutting emissions irrelevant. And China not participating doesn't just mean it isn't cutting emissions, it also means that a carbon price in developed countries will result in emissions being exported, not cut.

What is more striking though is the attitude to humanity. The contempt for economic growth that we looked at in the last section has become contempt for people. They are just mouths to feed, emitters of carbon. There is no consideration of the potential upside of more people. 'Births averted' are valuable enough that Porritt is willing to overlook the abuses

---

367 Porritt, J., 'Population: boom and bust', 17 May 2007, http://www.jonathonporritt.com/pages/2007/05/population_boom_and_bust.html

that have been part of the One Child Policy, like forced abortions on a huge scale.

He is a patron of the Optimum Population Trust, a sinister bunch. In July 2008 it published a report attacking the UN declaration that people have a 'basic human right to determine freely and responsibly the number and timing of their children'.[368]

They released calculations based on a WWF report in 2002 setting out the number of people that each country was allowed, if it was to be sustainable.[369] Apparently Britain needs to fall from 60 million to around 29 million, even if we limit ourselves to a 'modest' lifestyle (two fifths of present European energy use). With our present lifestyle, they argue only 15 million is acceptable. The number of Americans needs to fall to 90 million at their present lifestyle, enjoying high incomes and using a lot of energy. If they cut their energy use to the 'modest' level then they can get away with a population of 241 million.

The report argues that, at its present prevailing lifestyle, Israel's population needs to fall from 6 million to zero. Apparently the authors weren't worried about the historical parallel with that one. Only Canada, a big and empty country, is allowed some population growth, from 30 to 44 million, even at the present Canadian lifestyle.

Most of the action is in the developing countries though. With declining fertility rates, populations in the developed world control themselves. The Optimum Population Trust explicitly state that if both developed and developing countries converge on their 'modest' standard of energy use then population can rise a little in developed countries, but has to be cut dramatically in the developing world. They say that

368 Dillard, C., 'Is there a "right" to have children? Summary and key extracts', Optimum Population Trust, July 2008

369 Optimum Population Trust, 'The Living Planet Report 2002 and Sustainable Populations by Country', http://www.optimumpopulation.org/opt. sustainable.numbers.html

low income countries 'would need to reduce their populations from a present level of 2110 million to 550 million'.

They are taking practical action on the basis of that thinking. Brendan O'Neill pointed out the implications of one programme in a speech at the 'Battle of Ideas' conference in London in October 2010:[370]

The Malthusian view of humans as little more than consumers leads to some very dodgy ideas. So last year, the OPT launched a website called PopOffsets, which involved encouraging well-off Westerners to offset their carbon emissions by paying for people in the Third World to stop procreating.

The idea is that you log on, enter information about a flight you recently took or how much you have been driving your car, and then the site tells you how much carbon you have used and therefore how much you should donate to a Third World reproductive charity. That charity makes up for your carbon-use by cutting back on the pitter-patter of tiny carbon footprints in countries like Kenya. So if you took a round-trip from London to Sydney, that adds up to 10 tonnes of carbon, in which case you are asked to donate £40 to help prevent the birth of one child in Africa.

That is the value that modern-day Malthusians put on new human life: it is roughly equal to 10 tonnes of carbon, or one holiday Down Under. Apparently these lives have no intrinsic worth, no moral or cultural meaning; they're simply bargaining chips in some wealthy Westerner's desire to absolve himself of eco-guilt.

Population control tends to be the issue that drives environmentalists to the most extreme actions. The *Daily Mail* reported on a woman in Britain who had an abortion and then had herself sterilised once she found a doctor willing to go along with the procedure.[371] She told the newspaper that having 'children is selfish. It's all about maintaining your

---

370 O'Neill, B., 'Think the Earth is finite? Think again', www.spiked-online. com, 8 November 2010

371 Courtenay-Smith, N. & Turner, M., 'Meet the women who won't have babies – because they're not eco friendly', *Daily Mail*, 21 November 2007

genetic line at the expense of the planet'. Another woman, who worked for *Ethical Consumer* magazine, and her husband, a healthcare worker, decided he needed a vasectomy. He told the newspaper, 'We do everything we can to reduce our carbon footprint. But all this would be undone if we had a child. That's why I had a vasectomy. It would be morally wrong for me to add to climate change and the destruction of Earth.'

Whether it is the respectable face of population control in the Optimum Population Trust or stronger stuff, excessive concern about population isn't warranted. In reality, if you are interested in curbing emissions then population is a silly issue to focus on. It is one of the components of the Kaya Identity, but when you are talking about wanting to cut emissions drastically and rapidly then only severe reductions in population will do. After all, another variable in the Kaya Identity, emissions intensity, is already falling at several per cent a year and it still isn't outweighing rising incomes. Slight differences in the number of children people have aren't going to make a lot of difference. Over time, the population is likely to stabilise as incomes rise. Prosperity is the answer, not population control by guilt or ugly state control.

And the idea there is a certain stock of people that the world can sustain is absurd. It depends on how that land is used. Certainly pre-industrial societies wouldn't be able to sustain anything like current populations. In the last century we have simultaneously sustained a drastic increase in the population and incredible improvements in living standards. In *The Rational Optimist* Matt Ridley set out how we might go about feeding a population of nine billion, without putting more pressure on the wilderness:[372]

This is what it would take to feed nine billion people in 2050: at least a doubling of agricultural production driven by a huge increase in fertiliser use in Africa, the adoption of drip irrigation

---

[372] Ridley, M., *The Rational Optimist: How Prosperity Evolves*, Fourth Estate, 2010, p.148

in Asia and America, the spread of double cropping to many tropical countries, the use of GM crops all across the world to improve yields and reduce pollution, a further shift from feeding cattle with grain to feeding them with soybeans, a continuing relative expansion of fish, chicken and pig farming at the expense of beef and sheep (chickens and fish convert grain into meat three times as efficiently as cattle; pigs are in between) – and a great deal of trade, not just because the mouths and the plants will not be in the same place, but also because trade encourages specialisation in the best-yielding crops for any particular district. If price signals drive the world's farmers to take these measures it is quite conceivable that in 2050 there will be nine billion people feeding more comfortably than today off a smaller acreage of cropland, releasing large tracts of land for nature reserves. Imagine that: an immense expansion of wilderness throughout the world by 2050. It's a wonderful goal and one that can only be brought about by further intensification and change, not by retreat and organic subsistence.

None of that is science fiction. It basically implies that we just keep doing what we have been doing for some time now: spreading the gains from better agriculture, modifying the genes of crops and animals (directly now, rather than through selective breeding), using those resources that are growing scarcer more carefully and trading the proceeds to everyone's advantage.

It isn't just that we can sustain a higher population. More people might help us overcome all sorts of challenges, including the burdens we place on the natural environment. Sir David Attenborough is known to most Britons, and around the world, as the charming voice of BBC nature documentaries. In April 2009 he became a patron of the Optimum Population Trust and gave this quote:[373]

I've never seen a problem that wouldn't be easier to solve with fewer people, or harder, and ultimately impossible, with

373 Optimum Population Trust, 'Attenborough is new OPT patron', 13 April 2009

*more. That's why I support the OPT, and I wish the environ-
mental NGOs would follow their lead, and spell out this central
problem loud and clear.*

He is wrong. People are the solution, not the problem. Any
one of the 400 million Chinese that Jonathon Porritt is so
relieved have not been born could have been the one who
figured out nuclear fusion, or affordable, large-scale electricity storage so wind and solar are more feasible, or any one
of a myriad of other, smaller innovations that would make
tackling climate change immeasurably easier. Having one or
two more gigatonnes of carbon dioxide to cut, but 400 million
more people to figure out how, would be a great trade.

The balance of campaigning and lobbying
Lots of environmentalists like to comfort themselves, to explain
away the public's resistance to measures like cap and trade
and extravagant renewable energy subsidies, with the thought
that it is all the result of evil deniers leading people astray;
that there is just too much money being spent by irresponsible
corporations who don't want to see those regulations in place.

In a debate after the Channel 4 documentary 'What the
Green Movement Got Wrong', George Monbiot said that 'the
trouble is we are massively outspent and outgunned by these
corporate funded movements' that are 'being played through
these conservative think tanks which have received hundreds
of millions of dollars'. Greenpeace have constructed elaborate
flowcharts showing groups who – in most cases a few years
ago – received funding from ExxonMobil. Greens have this
notion that if they had a level playing field, if they could spend
on the scale their opponents do, they would swiftly triumph.
That is a myth.

The reality is that campaigns for draconian climate change
policies are vastly better funded than those campaigning against. Even the biggest conservative think tanks are
much smaller than the environmentalist campaigns, and a
think tank will only devote a small amount of its attention

to a single issue like this. Those that really focus on climate change policy, like the Competitive Enterprise Institute, are minnows compared to global environmentalist behemoths like Friends of the Earth.

You can count the number of people working in Britain full-time to make the case against draconian regulations to control emissions on one hand. Most of those working to make the case against these incredibly expensive policies do so as a small part of their wider work. On the other side, major environmentalist campaigns with huge funding have hundreds of staff working to promote ever more stringent climate change policy. While that imbalance might be less extreme in other countries, particularly the United States, the financial advantage does still firmly lie with the greens.

There is direct corporate lobbying, but most executives much prefer trying to skew policy slightly in their favour. They aren't lining up to confront politicians who they expect have made their minds up. There is also an incentive to free ride. If a company spends its money lobbying for changes to climate change policy to lower energy prices, it won't capture all the benefits. Other companies, and families, will also be better off. Unfortunately, the rational strategy is often to keep quiet and hope someone else speaks up; take the benefits while they pay the financial and political price of confronting the environmentalists.

A good example of how an industry behaves when it is under attack as a wanton polluter is aviation. Airlines have a good case that the industry has made huge strides in improving efficiency; there is ample incentive with fuel such a critical part of their costs. Fuel prices still put them out of business. The latest victim went to the wall just a few years ago. The price of airline fuel put the low-cost transatlantic carrier Zoom Airlines out of business in summer 2008.[374] Flights are only a small share of global emissions, so why intervene when

---

374 BBC News, 'Zoom Airlines suspend all flights', 28 August 2008

there is already such a strong private incentive for an airline to use fuel more efficiently and thereby cut emissions?

Lobbyists for the industry aren't going around making that kind of argument. Instead, they normally propose different regulations that give their company a particular competitive advantage. Working at the TaxPayers' Alliance, I must have heard half a dozen different proposals for the 'right' set of policies that will put a price on carbon in the aviation sector. Each one is best for a particular firm – the age of their aircraft, the distances they typically fly, or the airports they use. They try to convince you that it is the most effective, lowest cost of the different proposals, but the common effect of all of them is that flying will become more expensive and less convenient for consumers.

There is nothing wrong with environmental campaigns trying to push expensive climate change policy. Their opposition to growth is a legitimate, if mistaken, position. But it is deeply undemocratic for them to be receiving taxpayers' money. In the same way, it is fine for corporate lobbyists to be promoting their shareholders' interests. Too often, though, they don't actually secure value for shareholders but just boost the reputation of their executives among the political class.

The coalition that has secured current climate change policies has managed to get a lot of their favoured policies implemented, at least in Europe. Still they aren't exactly over the moon. Environmentalists have had to put up with some compromises and windfall profits for special interests they aren't exactly enamoured of, like energy companies. Some businesses have got their subsidies, but they and others have paid a price in terms of new political risks.

And all their successes are hollow so long as the biggest emitters, and the expected source of most new emissions in the decades to come, aren't playing ball. The environmentalists have been influential but they haven't provided a recipe for low emissions economic growth, so their programme holds little appeal for developing countries in particular.

DEVELOPING COUNTRIES

Without the cooperation of developing countries, the current set of climate change policies is utterly hopeless. You just can't cut enough emissions in the developed world to make up for the huge rises expected with rapid growth in poorer countries. At the same time, if increasing energy prices with cap and trade in Europe or the United States sends factories to China, it doesn't even cut emissions in the first place.

In many years recently, China has increased its annual CO_2 emissions in a single year by more than the UK's total. The figures are shown in Table 8.1.[375]

Table 8.1: CO_2 emissions, China and UK, Mt

	2003	2004	2005	2006	2007
China	3,829.7	4,546.1	5,058.3	5,603.5	6,027.9
Change on previous year	*520.9*	*716.5*	*512.2*	*545.2*	*424.3*
United Kingdom	535.9	535.6	534.3	535.8	523.0

In July 2007 the US Climate Change Science Program released estimates of how emissions are likely to rise in the coming decades.[376] In their reference scenario, where there is no climate change policy intervention beyond the Kyoto protocol,

375 International Energy Agency, 'CO_2 Emissions from Fuel Combustion', (2009 Edition), http://www.iea.org/co2highlights/co2highlights.xls
376 US Climate Change Science Program, 'Scenarios of Greenhouse Gas Emissions and Atmospheric Concentrations; and Review of Integrated Scenario Development and Application', 10 July 2007

emissions from the rapidly growing, developing Non-Annex 1 countries come to dwarf those from the developed Annex 1. The more aggressive attempts to cut emissions that we have had from Europe in recent years are likely to strengthen that trend. Their estimates are shown in Figure 8.1.

Figure 8.1: MiniCAM reference scenario, Annex 1 and Non-Annex 1 countries, 2000–2050, GtC

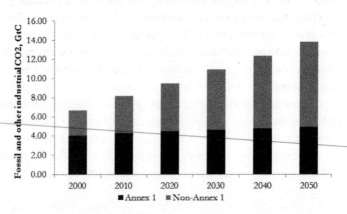

Suppose we modified the current international target very slightly to fit that set of predictions, and look at what it would take to achieve a 50 per cent cut by 2050 from 2000 emissions. That would mean bringing global emissions down to 3.35 Gt CO_2. Then imagine the Annex 1 countries decarbonised entirely: they cut their emissions 100 per cent and stopped using fossil fuels altogether. If that happened, but the Non-Annex 1 economies didn't cut their emissions from the expected level, global emissions would still be 8.84 Gt CO_2, or over two and a half times the target.

At the moment, the international negotiating process is being undone primarily by the inability of Annex 1 countries, particularly in the European Union, to persuade Non-Annex 1 countries to limit their greenhouse gas emissions.

Der Spiegel managed to get hold of a recording of the meeting at Copenhagen where the talks collapsed.[377] It is a stunning insight into how a 'too big to fail' negotiating process failed. German Chancellor Angela Merkel tries to push China and India towards putting figures on the targets for cutting world emissions by 2020 and 2050; they adamantly refuse, despite the urgings of British Prime Minister Gordon Brown and US President Barack Obama. Nicolas Sarkozy gets upset and accuses the Chinese of being hypocritical. They reject that charge and then quickly move the meeting to a break.

The talks never restarted and the final Copenhagen Accord was drawn up without the EU leaders even in the room and didn't involve any binding commitments to cut emissions. At Cancun the negotiating ministers avoided the humiliation of Copenhagen by fudging every important issue.

While attempts have been made to buy the support of countries like India and China, they are never likely to succeed. Many of the attempts to buy support mean a chronic, often counterproductive, waste of consumers' money. That is what has happened with the Clean Development Mechanism set up under Kyoto.

When people like me point out that climate change policies being implemented in Europe and elsewhere are a waste of time because the Chinese won't join in, that is often misconstrued as China-bashing. Nothing could be further from the truth. The problem is Western politicians who have signed their countries up to impractical targets that could lead to an economic disaster. It is actually the environmentalists who, by failing to properly understand the motivations of rapidly developing economies, often traduce them.

There is a reason why they are wary of signing up to targets for emissions cuts. It could mean curbing indispensable economic growth.

---

377 Rapp, T., Schwagerl, C. & Traufetter, G., 'How China and India Sabotaged the UN Climate Summit', *Der Spiegel*, 5 May 2010

Controlling emissions and economic development

The Chinese leadership feel that the country needs to maintain economic growth at a rate of 7 per cent or higher in order
to avoid threats to its social and political stability. That is
non-negotiable. As Susan Shirk points out in *China: Fragile
Superpower*, anything else would mean trouble as the Chinese
industrial economy couldn't absorb the huge numbers of new
workers entering the labour force:[378]

*The Communist Party considers rapid economic growth
a political imperative because it is the only way to prevent
massive unemployment and labour unrest. For more than a
decade, the government has based its economic policies on an
algorithm derived from its priority on stability. The economy
must grow at an annual rate of 7 per cent or more in order
to create a certain number of jobs (nine million each in 2004
and 2005), and keep unemployment rates at levels that will
prevent widespread labour unrest (set at 4.7 per cent in 2004
and 4.6 per cent in 2005). These explicit growth and employment targets remain in the minds of all Chinese officials as
they create foreign as well as domestic policies.*

Maintaining that kind of growth indefinitely may not be
possible. There are plenty of threats to China's ability to maintain headlong economic growth. The boom they have enjoyed
in recent years could yet turn to bust. Protectionism could
take over in the United States and block Chinese access to
that lucrative export market, for example, or their banking
system could get in real trouble. If China's growth does stall,
though, it will be extremely bad news for hundreds of millions
of Chinese people hoping for a better life – for the prosperity
of ordinary families in the West who are better off with cheap
goods and for our security if the regime there feels they need
to make up for a lack of growth with nationalist sabre rattling.
Eventually growth will peter out to a certain extent but hope-

378 Shirk, S. L., *China: Fragile Superpower*, Oxford University Press, 2008,
     pp.54–55

fully it will happen once ordinary Chinese people are a lot better off.

If we come back to the Kaya Identity, which we looked at in Chapter 2, it is clear why that sets them against aggressive targets to curb emissions. Even with dramatic improvements in efficiency it just isn't likely to be possible to combine growth at 7 per cent with restraining emissions.

In recent years China's economy has grown even faster than 7 per cent a year. Reductions in emissions intensity have not just failed to keep up with that headlong growth; intensity has actually risen in some years. That is why emissions have grown so rapidly, why China's emissions growth has sometimes been enough that it could have offset Britain decarbonising completely, stopping burning fossil fuels altogether. The pattern in recent decades, and the incredible spike in the last decade, is shown in Figure 8.2.[379]

Figure 8.2: China emissions and emissions intensity, 1971–2007, Mt CO_2 and kg CO_2/US dollars (2000 prices)

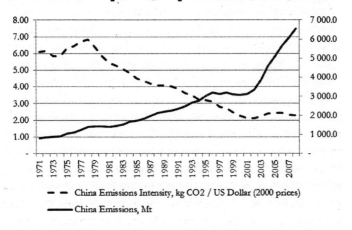

- - - China Emissions Intensity, kg CO2 / US Dollar (2000 prices)

——— China Emissions, Mt

379 International Energy Agency, 'CO_2 Emissions from Fuel Combustion, (2010 Edition)', http://www.iea.org/co2highlights/co2highlights.xls

We can't feel too smug about our performance relative to China. That's where a lot of the developed world's emissions have gone. Factories and manufacturing jobs have relocated, driving rapid increases in emissions in China and flattering the figures in Europe.

Look out to 2050 and, on current trends, emissions are set to rise massively. Suppose their economy kept growing at 9.1 per cent a year – the long-term average, though the economy has grown at 9.6 per cent a year in the last decade of the data – and emissions intensity kept falling by 2.9 per cent a year – again the long-term average, but more than the 2.4 per cent a year it has managed on average in the last decade. That would take China's emissions to over 70 Gt CO_2 a year, far more than the roughly 10.5 Gt CO_2 a year target for the entire world's emissions that we discussed in Chapter 2.

It is unlikely that China's economy will keep growing at that pace. Suppose instead that growth falls and averages around 5 per cent a year over the period – and remember that is less than the Chinese leadership think is essential to maintain social stability. And also let's assume more rapid emissions intensity improvements, significantly above the developed world norm at 4 per cent a year. China is still heading for far higher emissions than could possibly be accommodated within a goal of halving emissions by 2050; their total would be 8.5 Gt CO_2 a year.

That is why the Chinese, and other high-growth, industrialising economies, are going to reject binding limits on their emissions. No one has a remotely credible vision for how they can get there. They will invest in manufacturing facilities to sell us wind turbines and solar panels; they might even install a few themselves as part of a potentially dangerous asset bubble, though not on a significant scale compared to the amount of coal capacity being developed; and they will certainly adopt emissions intensity targets, and likely meet them. None of those policies involves limiting emissions and therefore likely limiting economic growth. What they won't do, and this is the critical test, is stop using coal as the mainstay of their energy sector unless a cheaper option is available.

Environmentalist Mark Lynas was appalled by China's intransigence at the Copenhagen negotiations:[380]

Copenhagen was a disaster. That much is agreed. But the truth about what actually happened is in danger of being lost amid the spin and inevitable mutual recriminations. The truth is this: China wrecked the talks, intentionally humiliated Barack Obama and insisted on an awful 'deal' so Western leaders would walk away carrying the blame. How do I know this? Because I was in the room and saw it happen.

He shouldn't have been so surprised. Campaigners may prefer to see rich Americans as the problem for advocates of draconian limits on emissions, but actually it is billions of people in the developing world, not ExxonMobil, who will frustrate attempts to limit growth. Their aspirations to an improved standard of living aren't up for negotiation and current climate change policies aren't able to reconcile those aspirations with the targets thrown around at international conferences. Attempts to win developing countries over with cheques written on behalf of taxpayers in the developed world will fail.

Clean Development Mechanism

The idea behind the Clean Development Mechanism (CDM) is quite a simple one. It will sometimes be cheaper for rich countries to pay poor countries to cut their emissions instead of making cuts at home. It is irrelevant to global warming where greenhouse gases are emitted, so why not let rich countries with tough targets pay poor countries to help achieve them?

The CDM was set up under the auspices of the United Nations to encourage that kind of trade. So long as they can establish it is genuine, and wouldn't have taken place without the mechanism in place, those running projects that cut

380 Lynas, M., 'How do I know China wrecked the Copenhagen deal? I was in the room', *The Guardian*, 22 December 2009

emissions in the developed world can get Certified Emissions Reductions (CERs).

In Europe, to a certain extent, operators can meet their obligations under the ETS by surrendering CERs from the CDM. CERs have a similar value to ETS allowances. Emissions Reduction Units (ERUs) under another programme called Joint Implementation can also be used, but have only been employed on a very limited scale so far.

Table 8.2: The use of CERs and ERUs in the ETS in 2008

Country	Total surrendered 2008 compliance	Surrendered CERs 2008 compliance	Surrendered ERUs 2008 compliance	% CERs-ERUs surrendered 2008
Austria	32,021,392	1,067,616	0	3.33%
Belgium	55,535,565	1,545,367	0	2.78%
Bulgaria	0	0	0	
Cyprus	0	0	0	
Czech Republic	80,392,791	1,845,344	0	2.30%
Denmark	26,545,884	375,230	0	1.41%
Estonia	13,552,575	0	0	0.00%
Finland	36,005,403	1,146,106	0	3.18%
France	120,995,743	5,716,589	0	4.72%
Germany	475,022,826	23,721,741	0	4.99%
Greece	69,854,442	193,945	0	0.28%
Hungary	27,243,806	1,743,420	0	6.40%
Ireland	20,381,707	713,192	0	3.50%
Italy	220,590,710	7,411,755	0	3.36%
Latvia	2,736,517	103,271	0	3.77%
Lithuania	6,103,720	466,169	0	7.64%
Luxembourg	2,098,895	87,000	0	4.15%
Malta	0	0	0	
Netherlands	83,490,797	1,988,560	0	2.38%
Poland	204,181,420	4,887,256	0	2.39%
Portugal	29,908,003	1,985,373	0	6.64%
Romania	63,721,253	890,591	0	1.40%
Slovak Republic	25,287,867	2,115,087	0	8.36%
Slovenia	8,860,105	797,115	0	9.00%
Spain	164,601,119	18,277,327	0	11.10%
Sweden	20,052,515	592,297	0	2.95%
United Kingdom	265,453,656	4,605,119	48,338	1.75%
Total	2,054,638,711	82,275,470	48,338	4.01%

CERs are a significant part of the total allocations surrendered, particularly in some countries like Spain where they made up 11 per cent of the total allowances surrendered in 2008. The data is shown in Table 8.2. [381]

Unfortunately, the CDM appears to be offering extremely poor value.

Michael Wara, at the Program on Energy and Sustainable Development at Stanford University, has described the programme as having three aspects:[382]

A subsidy that pays developing countries to pollute less than they otherwise would.

A market where subsidy through CERs can be used to comply with developed country obligations under the Kyoto Protocol.

A political mechanism to encourage developing countries to participate in the Kyoto Protocol.

He argues:

The CDM fails as a market because it has animated accounting tricks that allow participants to manufacture CERs at little or no cost. It fails as a subsidy because the developed world has had to purchase these emissions reductions at an extremely high premium that bears no relation to their cost. The CDM, even as it is supplying CERs to developed world parties to the Kyoto Protocol at prices that are less than they would otherwise have to pay, is an excessive subsidy that represents a massive waste of developed world resources.

In other words, the scheme isn't working to deliver a proper market or as an efficient subsidy of emissions cuts. All it has achieved is to persuade countries who might otherwise have sat out to take part in the Kyoto process, but it isn't much of an achievement to persuade people to take free money.

....

381 Data taken from www.carbonmarketdata.com

382 Wara, M., 'Measuring the Clean Development Mechanism's Performance and Potential', Stanford University Program on Energy and Sustainable Development, Working Paper 56, July 2006

Some projects appear to have received credits for emissions reductions that would have taken place without the CDM. For example, the Xiaogushan Hydropower Project in China is expected to have received nearly 2.2 million CERs by 2012,[383] but NGOs have argued that the large dam would have been completed regardless of the existence of the CDM.[384] So we may have just paid a handsome subsidy that lined the pockets of investors in the project and did nothing to actually reduce emissions.

There are bigger problems. Seventy-four per cent of the CERs that have been issued so far have gone to projects for destroying gases like N_2O and HFC-23. The figures are shown in Figure 8.3.[385] They are incredibly powerful greenhouse gases – HFC-23 is 11,700 times as powerful as carbon dioxide – so it is worth destroying them where possible.

Figure 8.3: Total CERs issued by type, at 1 November 2010

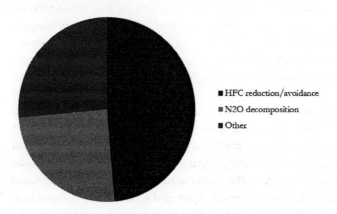

■ HFC reduction/avoidance
■ N2O decomposition
■ Other

383 Institute for Global Environmental Strategies, 'CDM/JI Project Data', http://www.iges.or.jp/en/cdm/report_cdm.html
384 International Rivers, 'Xiaoxi and Xiaogushan CDM Hydropower Projects: Report from a Field Trip', 27 November 2008
385 Institute for Global Environmental Strategies, 'CDM/JI Project Data', http://www.iges.or.jp/en/cdm/report_cdm.html

The subsidies to destroy those gases are spectacularly generous. HFC-23 is a by-product in the production of HCFC-22.
HCFC-22 was used a lot as a propellant and in air conditioning but is being phased out now as a contributor to depletion of the ozone layer. But Michael Wara describes how the
subsidies to destroy HFC-23 are incredibly high relative to
the value of the actual HCFC-22 produced. The 'net from
subsidy minus abatement costs to an HCFC-22 producer is
approximately €3.08/kg HCFC-22. This subsidy compares
quite favorably with the wholesale price for HCFC-22, which
as of fourth quarter, 2005, was approximately €1.60/kg.'

As a result, despite measures like keeping new facilities
out of the scheme, production of HFC-23 appears to have
actually increased in order to take advantage of the CDM:

*Even with these highly restrictive rules on eligibility, there is
relatively strong evidence that HCFC-22 producers participating in the CDM have behaved strategically to direct a greater
share of the subsidy to themselves by artificially inflating their
base year production in two ways. First, the fraction of HFC-23
produced by the production of HCFC-22 can be reduced by
modification of the conditions under which chemical synthesis occurs. Dupont has been able to consistently produce, in
its United States-based HCFC-22 plant, HFC-23 by-product
percentages as low as 1.3 per cent. The economics of HCFC-22
production in the absence of a CDM subsidy dictate that HFC-23
production be minimised because it is in effect a waste product
costing both energy and materials. For this reason, almost all
plants have historically monitored the HFC-23/HCFC-22 ratio
in their production. The CDM methodology eventually approved
for HFC-23 abatement set 3 per cent as the maximum percentage of HFC-23 by-product allowable in the baseline data of a
participating plant. The average of all reported baseline data
at the eleven participating plants is 2.99 per cent – very close
to the maximum allowable value. This suggests that even if the
project participants were not actually aiming for the 3 per cent
sweet spot that would minimise their production costs (due to*

wasted feedstocks) but maximise their CDM subsidy (due to more CERs for a given production rate of HCFC-22) they were certainly not as concerned with minimising this percentage as developed world producers, not eligible for the CDM subsidy, seem to be.

In addition, at least some of the HCFC-22 plants participating in the CDM appear to have ramped up production during the baseline period (2000–2004) far beyond the expected growth in the sector (15 per cent). Figure 5 (not shown here) shows the baseline data supplied by plants participating in the program compared with the predicted growth rate for the industry over the 2002–2004 period. Most plants exceeded the growth rates predicted for the developing world industry as a whole. These increases in HCFC-22 production among the 75 per cent of developing world producers participating in the CDM led to a CDM participant production growth rate of 50 per cent rather than 33 per cent, as had been predicted ex-ante by market analysts. Whether or not these plants increased production due to demand for HCFC-22 or in anticipation of higher CER revenue is impossible to say given publicly available information. Nevertheless, a circumstantial case exists that at the least, rather than building new plants, HCFC-22 producers elected to add capacity at existing plants during the CDM baseline period in order to take advantage of the CDM subsidy.

In other words, there is a distinct possibility that the CDM has increased the amount of the incredibly powerful greenhouse gas HFC-23 being produced. That is a dismal failure and means consumers in Europe are getting a very bad deal.

There is also a significant risk that the combination of cap and trade and the CDM encourages emissions exports rather than cuts. Firms will be rewarded for improving the emissions intensity of their activities in the developing world, while they have to pay to hold allowances in order to emit at all in countries with schemes like the EU ETS. They may find that the most profitable strategy is to move capacity to developing countries, which will not cut emissions but will mean a substantial reward under both the ETS and CDM.

This should be particularly concerning for countries implementing cap and trade as the developing countries that produce the most CERs are not the very poorest, but mostly significant industrial economies whose manufacturing industries compete with those in ETS countries. Figure 8.4 shows the biggest recipients under the CDM.[386]

Figure 8.4: Total CERs issued by host party, at 1 November 2010

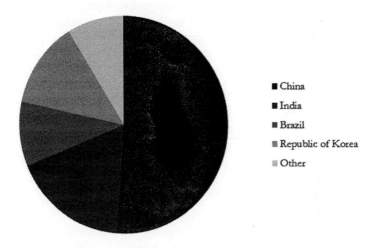

- China
- India
- Brazil
- Republic of Korea
- Other

It gets worse though. Mark Schapiro – the senior correspondent at the Center for Investigative Reporting in Berkeley, California – reported on the problems for *Harper's Magazine* in February 2010.[387] The problem is that not emitting isn't a tangible commodity and genuine savings are hard to verify:

386 Institute for Global Environmental Strategies, 'CDM/JI Project Data', http://www.iges.or.jp/en/cdm/report_cdm.html

387 Schapiro, M., 'Conning the Climate: Inside the Carbon-Trading Shell Game', *Harper's Magazine,* February 2010

[U]nlike traditional commodities, which sometimes during the course of their market exchange must be delivered to someone in physical form, the carbon market is based on the lack of delivery of an invisible substance to no one. In an attempt to compensate for this intangibility, the United Nations has certified twenty-six firms worldwide – in UN lingo, Designated Operational Entities (DOEs) – to 'validate' the promises of emissions reducers and then to 'verify', often years later, that those reductions actually occurred.

SGS is one of two companies that dominate the carbon-validation business. The other is Det Norske Veritas (DNV), a Norwegian firm whose primary business is shipping inspection.

The integrity of the scheme hangs on the credibility of the validations. If they don't stand up to scrutiny, then the entire scheme is compromised and consumers in the developed world might be subsidising projects that would have gone ahead anyway, or emissions savings that might not have been made. Unfortunately, it looks like the validation process is full of holes.

Lambert Schneider, a German environmental engineer who serves on a UN panel on methodologies, reviewed nearly a hundred offset projects for the peer-reviewed journal Climate Policy. *He found that just 60 per cent of projects actually provided evidence that the CDM funding made a difference, and that 40 per cent of companies would likely have reduced emissions anyway. 'You're a project developer, and you're telling a story about how your project is "additional",' Schneider told me. 'The DOEs check the story. They are relied on for their judgement, and it's often a very selective judgement.'*

It turns out that overestimating reductions is the trapdoor in the offset system. Study after study has demonstrated that CDMs have not delivered the promised amount of emissions reductions. According to a report by the UN's Intergovernmental Panel on Climate Change, the margin of error in measuring emissions from the cement and fertiliser industries can be as high as 10 per cent. For the oil, gas and coal industries, the margin of error is 60 per cent; and for some agricultural processes, the margin of error can actually reach 100 per cent. A Berlin think tank, the Öko-Institut, conducted a review of the validation process on behalf of the World Wildlife Fund International and concluded, last May, that none of the top five validators scored higher than a D in an A-to-F grading schedule based on challenges and questions about their projects.

But it isn't just that there is a big potential for error. There are serious conflicts of interest, which could bias the validators in favour of a generous interpretation of credits claimed by developers. Not only are they paid by the people who develop the projects they are validating, they often then go on to work for them.

In this highly specialised new industry, perhaps a thousand people really understand how onsite measurement of CDM projects works, and there is a serious potential for conflicts of interest. It is not uncommon for validators and verifiers to cross over to the far more lucrative business of developing carbon projects themselves and then requesting audits from their former colleagues. Schneider points out that young university graduates entering the field commonly spend several years learning the ropes at DOEs and then 'go to work for a carbon project developer, where they make three times the salary doing more interesting work'.

These problems aren't just a hypothetical concern. Two of the biggest validators – DNV and SGS – have received temporary suspensions. As Schapiro reported, they 'have been responsible for nearly two thirds of the emissions reductions now being utilised by industries in the developed world'. Despite the firms that validated them being temporarily suspended when they couldn't establish that the quality of the procedures and the qualifications of their staff were up to scratch, the credits are still valid and can't be revoked.

The problem is that this scandal is happening quietly. European consumers don't know that their money is being wasted. Everyone else has an interest in not tightening up the rules. This anecdote from Schapiro's article summarises the problem neatly:

We sat down over coffee, and I raised my concerns about the validation system. Trexler claimed that any problem was not with the validators – 'We only enforce the rules of the UN,' he averred – but instead with the 'interests' that devised the priorities of the system and prized volume over accuracy. He offered home pregnancy tests as an analogy. Such tests deliver news that can be good or bad, he said, but there will always be a percentage of false readings in either direction; and if one tries to design the test to reduce false positives, 'you will increase the number of false negatives, and the reverse'. A similar equation held, he believed, for measuring offsets. 'If the United Nations only permits projects with airtight additionality, you'll have a huge increase in the pool of false negatives. Some legitimate projects will be kept out.' But, he went on, the reality is that everyone – emitting businesses, carbon-project developers, entrepreneurs in the developing world, and governments – has a vested interest in validating as many projects as possible.

The CDM has been a goldmine for developers, including major firms in London and on Wall Street, who have spotted the profits to be had. They are a highly articulate and self-righteous lobby for the scheme. It is a chronic waste of consumers' money though. New attempts to bribe developing countries on board, like the billions that our politicians have pledged at Copenhagen and Cancun, are likely to prove just as wasteful.

International negotiation

It is hard for anyone to sustain the idea that it is really worth developed countries acting alone, without those countries that emit the most now and are likely to continue to in the future. Emissions from the United States are significant, but even its best efforts will have a limited effect on future temperature if the major developed economies keep putting out much greater quantities of greenhouse gases every year. That is why draconian regulations tend not to be sold on their own merits, but as a means for us to enable a global deal – to 'lead'.

At the moment the Europeans clearly have the best claim to be leading in this area. They have accepted the toughest targets for emissions cuts; they have introduced cap and trade and eye wateringly expensive renewable energy targets; and they have tried out a whole range of other policies as well. But the final Copenhagen accord was negotiated without the European representatives even in the room. Why is no one following the leaders?

It's pretty obvious really. The Europeans have started doing everything unilaterally, before other countries take up similar policies. They have given away the store without getting anything in return. While they might, in theory, have signed up to a 30 per cent by 2020 emissions cut target if a deal had been reached at Copenhagen, they have tried to take that tougher target up since then anyway.

There is no need to negotiate with European leaders because they are so keen on taking action in this area that they will go ahead regardless. It is much better to avoid their sanctimonious lectures and talk with those countries that you need to make a compromise work. The Europeans won't say no to any deal. Why would they when they will be going ahead anyway?

In the end, one country acting unilaterally doesn't necessarily encourage the others to follow suit. Countries aren't embarrassed or inspired by each other's actions like that. It can just encourage other countries to slack off, to leave the hard work of cutting emissions to the Europeans, who seem keen to take up the challenge. The Scientific Advisory Board to the German Federal Ministry of Finance points to that problem with unilateral climate change policy:[388]

....

388 A translation is available here: http://pgosselin.wordpress.com/2010 /06/30/summary-and-conclusions-of-the-scientific-advisory-board- report-buried-by-germanys-ministry-of-finance-english-translation/

Efforts by single countries to act as a leader in climate protection and to influence climate policy by imposing emissions reductions on itself can cause other countries to slack off in their own climate-policy efforts rather than intensifying them. As a result, taking a leadership role in climate policy leads to, as a rule, higher costs in that country without assuring any decisive improvement in the global climate.

It is worse than that. Acting unilaterally doesn't just encourage other countries to slack off. It can actually make it more difficult for them to take action to cut emissions.

Imagine a world in which there are just two countries: A and B. They each engage in two kinds of productive activity: manufacturing and services. Manufacturing uses a lot of fossil fuel energy and creates a lot of greenhouse gas. Services use less fossil fuel energy and produce less greenhouse gas.

If country A puts a price on carbon unilaterally, it will increase the cost of manufacturing there relative to the cost in country B. Some industries, particularly those already making a marginal decision about where to locate, will move a part or all of their capacity to country B.

It is then politically harder for country B to put a price on carbon and cut its emissions. It has more manufacturers and more people working in manufacturing; they all oppose a policy that might make their jobs move back to country A and put them out of work.

That is roughly what has happened in recent years with Europe in the place of country A and China playing country B. Unilateral policy distorts the location of economic activity, by exporting emitting industries, in such a way that it is then harder to get a multilateral deal. Every time artificially high energy prices drive a manufacturing job from Europe to China there is one more worker who a Chinese government terrified of being unseated by industrial unrest has to keep on side. That worker stands to lose if the Chinese adopt policies that push up energy prices themselves.

That isn't all; suppose we actually succeeded and significantly reduced our demand for fossil fuels. Those fossil fuels would still be there and countries like Saudi Arabia would still be desperate to sell them. After all, as Bernard Lewis puts it, 'the total exports of the Arab world other than fossil fuels amount to less than those of Finland, a country of five million inhabitants'.[389] All we would achieve by cutting out our demand would be to make it easier for the most rapidly developing economies to get hold of cheap fossil fuels. It would further tilt the balance in those countries' decision making towards continuing to burn coal, oil and gas.

It will be particularly difficult to secure a practical deal now after the disaster in Japan. If Japan and Germany, two of the world's largest economies, are retreating from nuclear power and the huge amounts of low carbon energy it provides, it will be much harder for them to credibly pledge to reduce their emissions significantly. They can bluster that renewable energy will fill that gap, but Germany in particular already spends a huge amount subsidising renewables and heaping further costs on industrial energy consumers would threaten vital manufacturing industries.

Does that mean there is nothing that countries can do in the absence of a global deal that may not be forthcoming?

No. The only reliable way of persuading other countries to take action is to convince them it is in their interests to do so. Threats aren't likely to work; there isn't the political will in the developed world to sustain a trade war over climate change policy and the economic consequences of doing so would be awful. Instead the focus has to be either showing or making it so that cutting emissions isn't expensive. In other words, the very last thing you would want to do is start putting in place renewable energy, for example, when it is ruinously expensive. Demonstrating to the world that offshore wind and solar panels cost a fortune by experimenting on your own

389 Lewis, B., *What Went Wrong? Western Impact and Middle Eastern Response*, Oxford University Press, 2001

people doesn't help anyone. If we try to lead other countries into an expensive disaster, we shouldn't be surprised if they won't follow.

What environmental activists and politicians will try to do in the absence of a global deal is just decide that it isn't necessary and press ahead regardless. That is why those of us trying to stop the green rip-off can't take the deadlock in the international treaties as a victory and move on. Even if they can't agree any kind of continuation of the Kyoto process before 2012, they can just point to some illusory signs that countries like China are acting to cut emissions, like the wind turbines they are installing alongside huge amounts of coal power, and use that as an excuse to keep imposing ever more draconian policies at home. We can't rely on China to do our job for us.

Selling low growth to the tiger economies

Good climate change policy has to work outside the developed world. Poorer countries just emit too much to be ignored and their emissions are growing too rapidly. Even complete decarbonisation by richer countries won't be nearly enough if that continues.

For all the affinity they claim for the world's poor, environmentalists have never really been able to offer a programme that can be reconciled with their aspiration to a better standard of living. Attacking consumption and economic growth might appeal to some well-off elites in richer countries, but ordinary people in countries that don't enjoy the relative comfort we do are never going to accept that poverty is good for them. In the face of that failure, all the activists can do is step up the rhetoric attacking Western excess. That rhetoric sometimes clashes violently with the evidence. For example, with NGOs blaming the United States for the collapse at Copenhagen when it was China that wasn't willing to sign up to binding limits on its emissions.

The extent of the developing economies' involvement

in the Kyoto process is dodgy programmes like the Clean Development Mechanism. Politicians feel proud they have convinced them to take our money. As a means of buying their notional support it has worked well; as a robust way of cutting emissions it has been a dismal failure.

The whole international process is heavy on posturing, light on serious thinking about how to deliver the global deal that is necessary to make current policies work. Unilateral policy is sold as 'leadership' when there is no sign that anyone is following, when that unilateral policy is actually cementing the differences that make it harder for some countries to restrain their emissions without serious economic disruption.

Current climate change policy just can't be reconciled with the developing world's immediate need for affordable and reliable energy. Driving up prices in developed countries while developing countries pursue cheaper energy as a means of improving their standard of living is not a good idea. It will mean emissions are exported on an incredible scale, instead of being cut. It will mean that the huge sacrifices being imposed by policies like cap and trade and renewable energy subsidies are wasted. Instead of strengthening international efforts to cut emissions, cuts in the developed world will be undermined by more and more emissions from developing countries.

Along with all the other problems looked at so far in this book, that is why climate change policy is rightly unpopular and why a new approach is needed.

THE POLITICS

Climate change policy is an expensive failure. Scheme after scheme is costing ordinary families a fortune but not delivering the results it is supposed to. Continuing to heap such a burden on families would be irresponsible and a dreadful waste. Too many elderly people are shivering in their beds and too many manufacturing jobs are being driven abroad.

Two questions are left. How do we stop this rip-off? And, is there a better option?

Electoral results

So long as people are made aware of the price that they are going to be made to pay and there is a real opposition, climate change policy is a political disaster for the parties pushing it. It isn't that no one wants to do anything about climate change, even when most do not think it is the result of human emissions people will still endorse taking action in theory, without a bill attached. And why wouldn't you? If it was free to cut human greenhouse gas emissions in half then it would be a pretty good deal.

When the huge cost of many of these policies becomes apparent, the billions that we looked at in the earlier chapters on policies like cap and trade and renewable energy subsidies, public opinion rightly turns against them. That is why, when climate change policy is politically contentious, it tends to be rejected. The clearest examples so far have come from Canada, Australia and the United States.

In Canada the Liberals went to the polls against the minority Conservative government pledging a new carbon tax. The Conservatives attacked it as a permanent 'tax on everything' and asked Canadians, 'Will you be tricked?' One of the graphics for that campaign is shown in Figure 9.1.

Figure 9.1: Canadian Conservative election poster attacking 'Dion's tax on everything'

Patrick Muttart, a political strategist now a Managing Director at Mercury LCC who played a key role in forming the Conservative strategy to oppose the carbon tax, told me:

Our objective was clear: frame the Liberals' so-called 'Green Shift' as an economic policy rather than an environmental initiative.

The strategy was two-fold: attack the Liberals' motives and drive the economic consequences.

Attacking their motives meant leveraging the public's tremendous scepticism about 'good cause' taxes (e.g. road taxes never seem to improve roads, income tax was a temporary measure to pay for WWI, the GST was supposed to be revenue-neutral etc...).

Driving consequences meant focusing like a laser on real world expenses: petrol, electricity, home heating fuel, groceries etc...

The Green Shift was initially very popular but it didn't take long to move public opinion. Quite simply nobody believed in the capacity of Government to actually deliver. But they did believe they would pay more.

The Conservatives won 143 seats, up from 14, while the Liberals slumped from 103 to 77 seats. The carbon tax was the defining issue of that election and it was clearly rejected by Canadian voters, who handed the normally dominant Liberal party an incredible defeat.

In Australia Labor's Kevin Rudd was elected as Prime Minister to replace the sceptical John Howard, who had kept Australia out of Kyoto. Rudd signed the treaty and then moved to implement an emissions trading scheme called the Carbon Pollution Reduction Scheme (CPRS). The conventional wisdom was that the Liberals (in Australia, they are the relatively conservative party in coalition with the Nationals) would be mad to oppose that cap and trade legislation.

The Liberal leader, Malcolm Turnbull, instructed his party to support cap and trade but they rejected it. Senator Cori Bernardi, who played a critical part in stopping the ETS in Australia, wrote in his book, *As I See It*, that within

moments of our official support of the ETS becoming public, a torrent of emails and phone calls started to hit our offices. Our supporters were outraged about supporting Labor's ETS and demanded we change our position. Tens of thousands of communications were received with most expressing a similar view: 'I have voted Liberal all my life and if you do this I will never support you again.' Turnbull tried to stick to his guns but Bernardi records that 'the emails, letters and phone calls from the grassroots contin-ued without respite. My office alone received an estimated 10,000 contacts with 99 per cent telling me to vote against the ETS.[390]

---

390 Benardi, C., *As I See It*, Dallancorp Ltd, 2010

The Liberals deposed their leader and elected a new one, Tony Abbott, who rejected the CPRS, which he called a 'giant new tax on everything'.[391] Instead of proceeding quickly to either pass the legislation or win a mandate for it at an election, as he surely would have if cap and trade were really that popular, Prime Minister Kevin Rudd responded by putting cap and trade plans on ice. After stumbling over an attempt to implement a mining tax Rudd was deposed by his party, who then went to an election. At that election the Labor government, which many had expected to rule for a long time after Rudd's initial win just a few years earlier, fell to a tie with the Liberal/National coalition at seventy-two seats each. They clung on to power by their fingernails by making a deal with a handful of independents. Abbott had defied expectations and restored his party's fortunes.

In the United States the Democrats moved to implement cap and trade after President Obama was elected in 2008. In the House, they managed to pass the Waxman-Markey bill, which I looked at in Chapter 3. That bill would have cost consumers $137.2 (£77.4) billion a year by 2020.[392] In the face of its unpopularity the Senate wouldn't pass cap and trade. Despite repeated pledges to bring it to the floor, and the release of bills like Senator John Kerry's American Power Act, which would have cost a similar amount to Waxman-Markey, the push for cap and trade in the Senate went nowhere. It didn't look to the senators like the representatives who voted for Waxman-Markey were being thanked for it. In fact, it looked distinctly like the American public were pretty angry at such a huge new tax.

At the midterms in 2010 the American electorate expressed their distaste for cap and trade along with other major government interventions in the economy like the healthcare bill.

---

391 Taylor, L., 'Tony Abbott's next policy vow: anything but a "great big new tax"', *The Australian*, 2 December 2009

392 Congressional Budget Office, Letter to Honorable Henry A. Waxman, 26 June 2009

The Republicans, who had opposed the measure, gained sixty-three seats in the House of Representatives and six seats in the Senate.

Of course, at that election there was one case where the greens won a victory. The Californian electorate rejected Prop 23, which would have stopped state legislation controlling emissions. That legislation is part of the Western Climate Initiative that encompasses a number of US states and Canadian provinces hoping to be a precursor to a comprehensive North American cap and trade system. That initiative has struggled as few of the states and provinces involved have actually passed the legislation for it to take effect in 2012.

The campaign supporting the proposition was outgunned by the far better funded 'no' campaign, which ran against in Texas more than it ran in support of the law. At the same election, Prop 26, which could also cripple Californian emissions regulations by requiring all new levies and charges to gain a two-thirds majority, passed. And there were setbacks for the Western Climate Initiative elsewhere as Republican Susana Martinez was elected in New Mexico opposing cap and trade.[393] California is just about the best case for climate legislation in the United States: it has already lost a lot of the energy intensive industries that would be put at risk by higher energy prices elsewhere, and even there the environmentalists could only win a partial victory.

Overall the evidence is very clear. Voters don't like expensive climate change policies. They dislike them so much that there are two simple rules that aren't perfect, but I have generally found to be pretty reliable in predicting how things will turn out.

The First Law of Climate Change Politics: National climate change legislation will not pass in countries where a mainstream political party opposes it.

---

393 Canadian Energy Law, 'US elections provide divided result for western climate initiative', 5 November 2010

The Second Law of Climate Change Politics: Climate change regulation will tend to proceed by the least democratic route.

The first law speaks for itself. In Europe, where aggressive climate change policy is in place, it has passed by political consensus. There is nowhere for voters to go if they oppose it. Britain is one example. The Climate Change Act 2008 passed – in the snow – with 463 votes in favour and 3 opposed. There were two more on each side acting as tellers. That means heavy majorities in all three major parties endorsed the bill. Who exactly are people supposed to vote for if they don't want radical, unilateral attempts to cut emissions and the associated rises in energy bills?

That doesn't mean political parties aren't losing out for sticking with the current agenda. They are neglecting the opportunity to be the party of low energy prices. No party in Britain is receiving the political dividend that the Canadian Conservatives, the Australian Liberals and the US Republicans have by opposing these measures.

The second law is a bit more complicated. Essentially though, draconian regulations to control emissions are a lot more popular with the politicians, bureaucrats and judges than the public. For that reason it tends to go through channels where the political elite can get their way relatively easily and democratic checks are weak. That explains why, in the United States, regulation is being pushed through the Environmental Protection Agency, acting at the behest of the courts. It also explains why European climate change policy has been implemented through the European Union, where there is no functional democracy. Individual countries can still row back on many policies, and some have on renewable energy subsidies. It is very hard for them to alter the direction of policy by giving up on biofuels or renewable energy targets altogether, though, as they are locked in by EU targets. To change that they need to be prepared to confront the EU bureaucracy.

Those two laws put together also explain why different countries have embraced these policies to differing degrees.

The difference isn't down to public opinion. Comparative polling by YouGov for *The Economist* and the Hoover Institution in March 2008 looked at opinion on these issues in Britain and the United States.[394] Britain has taken up these policies as aggressively as any country in the developed world, while the United States has been reviled by environmentalists as a laggard. Public opinion is remarkably similar though, as you can see in Table 9.1. There are some differences of degree, but the basic direction of the polling is the same in both countries on every issue, and on most the degree of public hostility is similar. Higher taxes on petrol get a big thumbs-down on both sides of the Atlantic.

Table 9.1: Would you support or oppose the following measures to reduce global warming? YouGov, Fieldwork, 7–11 March, 2008

United Kingdom		United States	
Increase taxes on petrol		Increase taxes on gasoline	
Support	15	Support	14
Oppose	76	Oppose	79
Not sure	9	Not sure	8
Increase airline fares		Increase airline fares	
Support	40	Support	20
Oppose	50	Oppose	67
Not sure	10	Not sure	14
Build more nuclear power stations		Build more nuclear power stations	
Support	44	Support	48
Oppose	34	Oppose	33
Not sure	23	Not sure	18
Increase taxes generally in order to subsidise 'clean energy' such as solar power and wind farms		Increase taxes generally in order to subsidize clean energy such as solar power and wind farms	
Support	33	Support	36
Oppose	51	Oppose	50
Not sure	17	Not sure	14

It is about political institutions and choices by the parties in the different countries. In Britain there is a lack of institutions

394 YouGov, 'Survey for The Economist and the Hoover Institution: Results', Fieldwork 7–11 March 2007

like primaries where incumbents can be challenged freely and the resulting strength of party leaderships make it easier for the parties to lock out public scepticism of climate change policy; in the United States, Republicans who wavered on cap and trade risked being kicked out of office in a primary challenge, particularly with the tea party spirit in the air.

At the same time, the US doesn't have an equivalent of the EU, where decisions can be stitched up and then presented as a fait accompli. I'm currently engaged in a dispute with the Department of Energy and Climate Change that shows just how undemocratic that supranational process has become.

At the Copenhagen Summit the EU had said it would adopt a target to cut emissions 30 per cent by 2020 if an international deal could be reached. If that happened, Britain's share of the burden would be to cut its emissions 42 per cent by 2020. As I mentioned in Chapter 2, an analysis based on the Kaya Identity suggests that could require drastic cuts in national income.

I put in a Freedom of Information request asking for what the government thought the cost would be or, to be specific, 'any and all documents concerning the potential financial and/or economic cost of Britain meeting a pledge to cut emissions by 42 per cent from 1990 levels by 2020. Or, any such analysis provided to the delegation by e-mail.'

They admitted that they had that information and acknowledged that there was a clear public interest in disclosure. But they rejected the request on the grounds that disclosure would affect 'international relations', more specifically that it would make a mess of the negotiations.

The idea that revealing the government's estimate of the cost would really affect Britain's negotiating position vis-à-vis other countries and result in us taking a greater share of the European emissions cuts is far-fetched. Any great insight that suggests the cost of cutting emissions to meet the target is likely to be much higher or lower than we think is almost certain to affect other European countries in a similar way. Even if we accept the spurious case that making the cost public will affect the negotiations over a new deal, it is a necessary price to pay. There is no way that parliamentarians, the media and the public should be expected to just trust the government's judgement on such a major commitment. There are public estimates of the cost debated before we enter a war; there is no reason the same can't be done before climate negotiations. There is no way for a proper democratic debate to take place if they aren't open about the costs they expect the country to have to bear to meet the proposed target. And that has to happen before we are signed up to a new target in an international treaty.

It might be that the government estimate of the cost is high and they are worried the public will reject the new target. Or, it might be that the analysis suggests a low cost on the basis of some very suspect assumptions about the economy or the task of rapidly cutting emissions. Maybe the department have bought their own hype that Britain can capture the markets of the future by making people pay a fortune for expensive renewable energy in higher electricity bills; maybe they really believe that if someone buys enough copies of Microsoft Office they'll become as rich as Bill Gates. In that case, we should be able to challenge their thinking. Regardless, it is completely unacceptable for the decision to be stitched up behind closed doors. No matter how important climate change policy is, it can't be above democratic scrutiny.

Climate change policy is enough of a political disaster that those promoting it are going to extravagant lengths to avoid the issue being settled democratically. Whether they are using the courts, the European Union or just good old-fashioned secrecy they are doing what they can to circumvent the public's unwillingness to pay a heavy price to cut greenhouse gas emissions. Over time, that strategy may not even be tenable in Europe.

How it ends

In the developing world they will keep seeing what they can get out of our taste for expensive climate change policies. There is an opportunity for canny entrepreneurs here. Their politicians will keep up the mix of hysteria and opportunism at international conferences that they displayed at Copenhagen. Companies there will improve their efficiency over time, bringing down their carbon intensity, and governments will encourage them. They are unlikely to go a lot further than that.

In countries like the United States, Australia and Canada the drive to ever more radical climate change policy has mostly been halted, but some regulations need to be reversed. In Europe the green agenda is still very firmly entrenched. Renewable energy subsidies are being cut back where they are unaffordable, as I mentioned in Chapter 4, but mostly the regulations are getting more draconian, not being rolled back.

It was really vital to stop cap and trade in the United States. That was far more important than the failure to secure a deal at Copenhagen in setting back draconian climate change regulations. After all, the American executive signed the deal at Kyoto – domestic ratification was the critical step that couldn't be taken then and wasn't in 2009 with the failure of the Senate to pass its equivalents of Waxman-Markey. Now it looks like federal cap and trade is dead everything else can fall into place. The EPA needs to be put on a shorter leash, we need to hold off the perennial threat of a federal renewable portfolio standard, and state cap and trade needs to be rolled back. We can't let the proponents of draconian climate change regulations regain the initiative.

We also need to start fighting back in other countries. This can't be another issue where the United States has to stand alone in the Western world. That would be a disaster for Europe and dangerous to the United States. There would always be a threat of environmentalists there reviving the project at a future date. While they might have to take a more incremental approach than Waxman-Markey, which would have given the United States a whole range of the policy mechanisms in place in Europe in one go, the greens will be able to get back on the offensive soon.

Canada and Australia, meanwhile, would be insane to adopt draconian climate change regulations when the United States and the major Asian economies haven't.

It is time to start trying to unwind climate change policy in Europe. How do we convince politicians here that they need to reassess the current suite of climate change policies? I think the key is to point out that it will make already painful, but widely accepted as vital, attempts to restore their nations' public finances to health much harder.

Hopefully politicians will realise that their other objectives are going to be put at risk if they try to maintain expensive climate change targets. People working on the climate change issue tend to forget that there are other things going on in domestic and global politics, other priorities also making a claim on our collective resources. And the Treasury types who have to get fiscal policy right aren't paying enough attention to the huge costs of the programmes environmentalists are putting in place.

To avoid a sovereign debt crisis, or just limit the amount spent in the future on interest on government debt, politicians need to cut public spending. I edited a book about how to do that effectively – *How to Cut Public Spending (and Still Win an Election)*[395] – and one of the things that becomes very apparent studying the issue is that the critical challenge for policymakers is limiting the overall pressure on family budgets. Every penny you can save by scrapping agencies that the public won't miss is vital as it means a bit less austerity for the ordinary households who necessarily bear the brunt of any fiscal adjustment. The same goes for regulations that create significant costs for families and put pressure on their finances, making it harder to absorb a cut in benefit payments, for example.

Politicians in Europe are hoping to push through painful spending cuts and massive investment to meet renewable energy targets at the same time. If you look at the numbers

395 Published by Biteback Publishing, March 2010

in Britain's case the problem becomes obvious, you can see it in Table 9.2.[396] Add up the cumulative spending cuts and tax hikes in the government's fiscal plan and you come to about £438 ($776) billion, but investment in the energy sector alone to meet environmental targets is expected to add hundreds of billions to that.

Table 9.2: UK fiscal crunch to 2020

Item	Amount, £ billion	Timescale
Fiscal adjustment	435.4	2010-11 to 2015-16
Water network investment	22	2010-11 to 2015-16
Energy sector: replacement and renewal	80	By 2020
Energy sector: environmental targets	202	By 2020
Total	739.4	By 2020

That is as much as £28,000 ($50,000) for every family in Britain to find out of their household budget over this decade. It is why politicians plotting a fiscal adjustment need to do all they can to target the cuts in areas where they will have the least impact on people's standard of living. But it is also why we particularly can't afford expensive climate change policies now. Most other developed economies are facing similar pressures.

If you look further out, the picture becomes even more desperate. Researchers at the Bank for International Settlements have looked at the likely path of public sector debt across the major developed economies. Ageing populations and a poor start with the fiscal crisis now mean that by 2040 a number could be facing economic ruin:[397]

396 TaxPayers' Alliance, 'Budget 2011 Briefing', 24 March 2011
397 Cecchetti, S. G., Mohanty, M. S. & Zampolli, F., 'The future of public debt: prospeccts and implications', BIS Working Papers, No 300, March 2010

[In] the baseline scenario, debt/GDP ratios rise rapidly in the next decade, exceeding 300 per cent of GDP in Japan; 200 per cent in the United Kingdom; and 150 per cent in Belgium, France, Ireland, Greece, Italy and the United States. And, as is clear from the slope of the line, without a change in policy, the path is unstable. This is confirmed by the projected interest rate paths, again in our baseline scenario. Graph 5 (not shown) shows the fraction absorbed by interest payments in each of these countries. From around 5 per cent today, these numbers rise to over 10 per cent in all cases, and as high as 27 per cent in the United Kingdom.

There isn't just a short-term problem now but a need for a sustained fiscal adjustment. In that environment, any major commitments that aren't getting results need to be reassessed, including climate change policy. While most of the costs of climate change policy don't directly affect a country's public finances, as the cost isn't paid out of general taxation but directly by consumers, they put pressure on household budgets just the same and thereby make it harder for them to tolerate a fiscal adjustment.

That kind of trade-off has to force European politicians to think again about their response to the threat of climate change. Hundreds of billions of pounds, euros and, if the activists get their way, dollars and yen are being put into subsidising prohibitively expensive and unreliable sources of energy. There is no way that is tenable right now.

To really be persuasive, though, we need an alternative.

An alternative

What climate change policy really needs is a dose of reality. A realist approach to climate change would mean not trying to drive people into using much more expensive sources of energy; accepting that cars and planes are the only practical way of making many journeys; and expecting countries to act in their immediate economic interests rather than trying to unite them in a grand global pact to cut emissions at the price of reduced economic growth.

The policy should also leave us with as few regrets as possible if the mainstream, IPCC understanding of the science of climate change is too optimistic or too pessimistic. We have to be realistic that we only know so much

There are three elements to that more realistic climate change policy: adapting to limit the social and economic harms of rises in temperature; developing the technologies we are likely to need; and building wealthier, more democratic societies that are more resilient to whatever the world throws at them.

Adaptation has been a particular theme of Nigel Lawson's work. As I mentioned in Chapter 2 he has pointed out in *An Appeal to Reason* that human societies have flourished in climates as diverse as Helsinki, Finland and Singapore, at average annual temperatures of 5°C and 27°C. Our ability to adapt is huge, and there are a couple of advantages to adapting to climate change instead of stopping emissions.

First, while it might be worth preparing for some changes, most of the work of adaptation can be left until climate change is actually happening. That means there is more flexibility to respond to the actual extent of the change rather than projections. It is why we should be sceptical of aid programmes designed to bribe developing countries into signing new treaties, which provide lots of aid on the pretext of supporting adaptation now. And it is less likely we'll plough our money into one way of adapting to climate change only to discover a better option further down the line, the way that under current policies we could easily waste huge amounts of money on expensive technologies like offshore wind only to discover a better option in the coming decades.

Secondly, adaptation will mostly just happen as a result of individual decisions. Farmers will plant different crops; people will move away from areas with flood risks if their insurance premiums aren't subsidised; if it gets too hot and they have the money people will air condition their office. Government might be able to help make that process easier in some ways,

but adaptation doesn't rely upon huge and unfeasible interventions in the economy.

Another component of a realist climate change policy
would be supporting the development of new technologies.
There are two obvious objectives: low carbon energy that is
cheap and some kind of option if things really go wrong.

Technology can sound like a bit of a gamble, like you're
saying 'let's just hope something turns up'. Even speculative,
high-cost research like nuclear fusion actually looks like a
reliable deal compared to renewable energy. In Britain alone
the cost of investment in the energy sector to meet environmental targets is estimated at €229 billion, as shown in Table
4.8. The total cost of the ITER project that aims to show fusion
can work is currently expected to be about €15 billion.[398]
And that is spread across a number of countries. Britain's
investment in offshore wind can't offer a sustainable global
alternative to burning fossil fuels; it isn't reliable or affordable
enough. If we actually want to cut emissions, particularly to
avoid consequences for other species that can't adapt as well
as we can, new technologies are the key.

Even if we are willing to pay £100 per MWh extra in subsidy
for our energy, other countries that are bigger emitters won't
be. By contrast, for the €15 billion we've put into ITER there
is a real chance we could come up with an actual alternative.

I'm not saying that ITER is necessarily the right project.
It looks uncomfortably like a French job creation scheme at
times. But if you want to encourage the replacement of fossil
fuels for policy reasons it makes more sense to go looking for
a replacement than spending a fortune to deploy technologies
that aren't practical alternatives to coal, oil and gas.

Geo-engineering is an ugly idea. Doing something like
seeding the oceans with iron or spraying sulphur dioxide
into the air to mimic the cooling effect of a volcano sounds to

....

398 BBC News, 'EU member states agree on Iter funding shortfall', 13 July
2010

most people like dangerous hubris. The unintended consequences could clearly be huge with such a grand intervention. Unfortunately, it is the only real, practical way forward if some of the most pessimistic accounts of the science of global warming are right. We aren't going to radically decarbonise the world economy within the next few years, so a strategy that relies on that happening is bound to fail. If we are approaching an imminent tipping point then we need a drastic option.

The key to getting this research right is not to use research and development as a code word for funding deployment. The 'demonstration' CCS projects are a bit of a farce. If it was really about demonstrating that CCS could work then you would just fund one or two plants, not the dozens that are in planning around Europe alone.[399]

At the same time, we want to minimise the extent to which the government is picking winners. Obviously we already have the patent system to reward all kinds of innovations. In order to focus innovations in a particular area, there is an approach that has been shown to work in the past: prizes.

Tom Nicholas, an association professor of Business Administration at Harvard Business School, has looked at the effects of prizes on innovation. A paper he wrote with Josh Lerner and Liam Brunt found that they were effective in encouraging agricultural innovation in nineteenth and twentieth century England:[400]

We examine prizes as an inducement for innovation using a novel dataset of awards for inventiveness offered by the Royal Agricultural Society of England from 1839 to 1939. At annual shows the RASE held competitive trials and awarded medals and monetary prizes (exceeding one million pounds in current prices) to spur technological development. We find

399 Brown, M., 'Carbon Capture and Storage in Europe', Citigroup Global Markets, 19 June 2009, Figure 4. CCS projects in Europe over 700,000t CO_2 by status

400 Brunt, L., Lerner, J. & Nicholas, T., 'Inducement prizes and innovation', Centre for Economic Policy Research, Discussion Paper No 6917, July 2008

large effects of the prizes on contest entries, especially for the society's gold medal. Matching award and patent data, we also detect large effects of the prizes on the quality of contemporaneous inventions. These results hold even during the period when prize categories were determined by a strict rotation scheme, thus overcoming the potential confounding effect that awards may have targeted 'hot' technology sectors. Our evidence suggests that prize awards can be a powerful mechanism for encouraging competition and that prestigious non-pecuniary prizes can be a particularly effective inducement for innovation.

Nicholas has written another paper looking at how in Meiji Japan they combined patents and prizes to encourage innovation. Again, it worked, though the cost might have been significant despite the prizes not coming with cash attached:[401]

Japan's hybrid system during the Meiji era of technological modernisation provides a useful laboratory for examining whether complementary mechanisms to patents induce innovation. Patents were introduced in 1885 and by 1911 1.2 million mostly non-pecuniary prizes were awarded at 8,503 competitions. Prizes increased patent outcomes by 35 per cent, a conservative causal estimate based on the timing of patents and prizes and the boost to patents observed in prefectures adjacent to those with prizes, relative to control prefectures without prizes. However, linking competition expenditures with the market value of patents to determine cost-benefit reveals the financial cost of the inducement was high.

There have been a long line of prizes that have successfully rewarded incredible achievements. The X Prize Foundation list some of them, from accurate measurements of longitude to the first non-stop flight from London to Paris; from the production of soda from sea water to the first private sector

---

401 Nicholas, T., 'Hybrid Innovation in Meiji Japan', Harvard Business School, 16 August 2010

space flight.[402] Many of the prizes are so successful as an incentive that far more is invested chasing them than the actual amount of cash on offer; the prestige and attention that comes with winning is worth a lot.

There are already prizes being created in this area. Richard Branson has offered $25 (£14) million for whoever creates a device to take carbon out of the atmosphere.[403] If similar prizes are set up to address the real stumbling blocks to replacing fossil fuels, or to find options in the event things are worse than we expect, then they could be very valuable. It doesn't need to be prizes. In the absence of any better ideas, just throw some money at the universities and maybe some businesses, the way we have done to encourage innovation in the defence sector. It doesn't need to be much in the grand scheme of things. The great thing about investing in technology is that it doesn't involve the government making crazy attempts to do new things, like ration energy use, and so we have a whole load of policy tools available that have achieved reasonable results in the past, not just hare-brained optimism. And instead of endlessly ramping up costs we should control spending to avoid the programmes becoming a lucrative plaything for special interests.

Other researchers looking at alternatives to the failed combination of cap and trade and renewable energy subsidies have also hit on directly supporting technological innovation. A number of senior academics in the field worked together to produce 'The Hartwell Paper', released in May 2010. They summed up their policy proposals in the executive summary:[404]

It explains the political prerequisite of energy efficiency strategies as a first step and documents how this can achieve

---

402 X Prize Foundation, 'The X PRIZE Heritage', http://www.xprize.org/about/the-x-prize-heritage

403 BBC News, 'Branson launches $25m climate bid', 9 February 2007

404 Prins, G. et al., 'The Hartwell Paper: A new direction for climate policy after the crash of 2009', May 2009

real emissions reductions. But, above all, it emphasises the primacy of accelerating decarbonisation of energy supply. This calls for very substantially increased investment in innovation in noncarbon energy sources in order to diversify energy supply technologies. The ultimate goal of doing this is to develop non-carbon energy supplies at unsubsidised costs less than those using fossil fuels. The Hartwell Paper advocates funding this work by low hypothecated (dedicated) carbon taxes. It opens discussion on how to channel such money productively.

The insistence on a special funding mechanism seems like a mistake. I don't know why you would want a hypothecated carbon tax when the rate isn't supposed to be high enough to change behaviour. That seems like a policy tool politicians would misuse. If there are the revenues from a new tax to play for, it won't be long before the special interests get involved, the range of uses it is put to starts to grow and the rate goes up.

They do make the critical point though: it is far more productive to try and make low carbon energy cheaper instead of trying to make fossil fuel energy more expensive, that way the effort doesn't rely on impractical global coordination. Two major US think tanks, from different sides of the ideological divide, have also got together and produced similar recommendations, the *New York Times* reported in October 2010:[405]

On Wednesday, the reliably conservative American Enterprise Institute and the left-of-center Brookings Institution will release a joint proposal to increase federal spending on clean energy innovation to as much as $25 billion a year, from the currently planned $4 billion a year. The proposal would also toughen rules for such money, so that recipients could continue getting it only if they were reducing the cost of clean

---

405 Leonhardt, D., 'A Climate Proposal Beyond Cap and Trade', *New York Times*, 12 October 2010

energy. Today, many subsidies for wind, solar power and ethanol are more lenient.

The final, simplest, but most important component of good climate change policy is to go for growth, democracy and freedom – build a resilient society.

The decline in mortality from natural disasters that we saw over the twentieth century, shown earlier in Figure 7.1, was the result of people getting richer. Richer people aren't living as close to the breadline, they can't be pushed over the edge into starvation by natural disasters as easily, and richer societies are better able to help when there is trouble. Amartya Sen famously said that no 'famine has ever taken place in the history of the world in a functioning democracy'.[406] Democratic governments are much more likely to respond effectively when things go wrong. Otherwise a free press will sound the alarm and opposition parties will stand to gain from any discontent with the government's response.

Whatever climate change amounts to, or even if some new crisis surfaces in the decades to come, higher incomes will mean we have the resources to respond to crises and take real opportunities to forestall them. Jim Manzi got it right in his front-page article for the *National Review*, 'Game Plan: Wealth and technology are raw materials for options.'[407] We have a much better chance of coming through climate change okay if we have higher incomes than if we try to control emissions by limiting growth. We should go for growth.

At the same time as building a more realistic climate change policy, it is also worth thinking more about the other things people want out of environmental policy. After all, a study of the polling for the American Enterprise Institute suggests that global warming is not the environmental

---

406 Massing, M., 'Does Democracy Avert Famine?', *New York Times*, 1 March 2003

407 Manzi, J., 'Game Plan - What conservatives should do about global warming', *National Review*, 25 June 2007

issue the public worry about most.[408] On many issues, like air and water pollution, things have got a lot better over the years. In the American Enterprise Institute 'Index of Leading Environmental Indicators 2009' they give one example:[409]

Air pollution levels are falling in the ten most polluted cities in the US, by as much as 27 per cent over the last decade in the case of fine particulates in Los Angeles.

As people get richer they don't just want to spend more money on things like health and education. They also want a more pleasant environment once their immediate need for food, shelter and television are met. That will happen in a number of ways: government might be involved by setting up a national park; people might buy land as an estate for their own enjoyment or because Tropicana are giving away the protection of 100 square feet of rainforest with a carton of orange juice. So long as we don't do something foolish like turn over huge areas of fertile croplands to making biofuels, there will be space.

Government attempts to protect forests, in particular, can go wrong. Iain Murray gave one example in *The Really Inconvenient Truths* when he looked at how environmentalist dogma combined with bureaucratic incompetence led to the near destruction of the Yellowstone National Park.[410]

If we avoid old mistakes the environment will improve over time, though. Green space is a luxury that people want more of once they have got the food, shelter and consumer goods they need to live comfortably. We should be thinking about ways to help them get it. After all, more trees means less carbon dioxide in the air. Peter Huber points to the huge

408 Bowman, K., 'How Hot Is Global Warming? A Review of the Polls', American Enterprise Institute, *Outlook Series*, No 3, July 2007

409 Hayward, S. F., 'Index of Leading Environmental Indicators 2009', American Enterprise Institute & Pacific Research Institute, April 2009

410 Murray, I., *The Really Inconvenient Truths*, Regnery Publishing, 2008, Chapter Four: 'Yellowstone in Flames: The Dangers of Liberal Dogma'

amount of CO_2 that could potentially be sunk into the ground that way:[411]

If we're truly worried about carbon, we must instead approach it as if the emissions originated in an annual erup-tion of Mount Krakatoa. Don't try to persuade the volcano to sign a treaty promising to stop. Focus instead on what might be done to protect and promote the planet's carbon sinks – the systems that suck carbon back out of the air and bury it. Green plants currently pump fifteen to twenty times as much carbon out of the atmosphere as humanity releases into it – that's the pump that put all that carbon underground in the first place, millions of years ago. At present, almost all of that plant-captured carbon is released back into the atmosphere within a year or so by animal consumers. North America, however, is currently sinking almost two-thirds of its carbon emissions back into prairies and forests that were originally leveled in the 1800s but are now recovering. For the next fifty years or so, we should focus on promoting better land use and reforestation worldwide. Beyond that, weather and the oceans naturally sink about one-fifth of total fossil-fuel emissions. We should also investigate large-scale options for accelerating the process of ocean sequestration.

It will also help to alleviate pressure on vulnerable species and thereby limit the impact of climate change on biodiversity.

If there is a common thread to all of these ideas for a better environmental policy, it is that we are better off trust-ing to people's ingenuity and enterprise. The new possibilities that come with economic growth offer a better prospect than attempting to limit and ration prosperity and humanity itself.

Time to stop the rip-off

I've sketched out what I think a remodelled climate change and environment policy could look like. The key thing is that we need to start getting rid of the existing, ineffective policies.

....

411 Huber, P., 'Bound to Burn', *City Journal*, Vol. 19, No 2, Spring 2009

There is a danger with some advocates of a greater focus on technology that they succeed in getting greater research funding on top of cap and trade, renewable energy subsidies, green taxes and all the other components of the green rip-off. That would mean we still waste unimaginable amounts of money; we still drive jobs abroad; there is still huge and unnecessary pressure on family budgets; special interests keep getting their absurd subsidies; and we keep getting a bad deal.

While I do think that expensive climate change policies are deeply unpopular and the 'laws' I set out earlier are helpful to understanding the strengths and weaknesses of the greens' political project, I don't think there is anything inevitable about draconian regulations being defeated. There are too many people who should be fighting bad climate change policy tooth and nail who just assume they must be headed for victory; that somehow the politicians will have to wake up to the dismal failure of these policies; that with another fiasco at a major summit the environmentalists will see the light. They won't, and there will still be huge campaigning budgets and political talent devoted to trying to convince us to adopt draconian climate change regulations. There is no iron law that says governments can't do stupid things that wreck economic growth.

What we need to do is get out there and tell people how they're being ripped off. Not get into an obscure argument about the science, which might be interesting enough but has little relevance to most people's lives. Unnecessarily high energy bills and a massive threat to their jobs are the reason people will reject these policies.

There is a political fight out there to be won. We will need to keep telling people about what is going on until long after we are bored of saying it, convincing people that stopping this agenda is right and important, is the only way things will change in a democracy. Here in Europe either the EU institutions will have to show a new flexibility or the member states will need to shrug off unaffordable and ineffective policies. In the United States, Canada and Australia existing policies like renewable mandates and involvement in the Clean Development Mechanism need to be rolled back, and further encroachments on economic liberty in the name of curbing emissions, whether through new legislation or the actions of courts and bureaucrats, need to be rejected. In Japan there is a vital debate going on over emissions trading; they would be mad to handicap themselves in industrial competition with China.

The greens have built an enormous political edifice on the complexities of climate change targets, mandates, taxes and subsidies. Now is the time to start tearing it down.

CONCLUSIONS

With the public debate so focused on the science, there hasn't been nearly enough scrutiny of some of the disastrous policies that have been instituted to try and reduce greenhouse gas emissions. That lack of scrutiny has led to some awful mistakes becoming entrenched.

Cap and trade is supposed to be a market solution to climate change, but the artificial market has been so unreliable that British politicians are already trying to fix the price. All sorts of people – from traders to carousel fraudsters, energy companies and manufacturers cutting capacity and jobs – have made profits on the scheme, adding up to many billions of euros. Families have paid the price in higher energy bills. Even a failing emissions trading scheme has a price tag attached. Over time, cap and trade is likely to get steadily more expensive. If those in charge of the European scheme and writing new cap and trade laws for the United States get their way, international cap and trade could become the first big global tax.

Wind, solar and other sources of renewable energy aren't remotely competitive with fossil fuels and they require big subsidies. Sometimes that comes through mandates – requirements for electricity generators to source a certain amount from expensive renewable sources – and in other cases they get special tariffs setting out rates of payment per kilowatt hour of energy generated, particularly for small-scale renewables. Renewable sources also aren't reliable enough, and therefore conventional plants need to be kept on hand to back them up. Governments make things worse and pick losers so the least affordable sources of energy get the most support. It's almost as if they're trying to maximise the burden on families.

Biofuels take us even further through the looking glass. They may not even cut emissions, or do so only at an incredible cost. When we burn food in our cars, an even heavier price is paid, by poorer people – who spend more of their income on food in the first place – and fragile ecosystems.

Pigovian green taxes have been mangled on their way through the political process, like so many other ideas that look so promising when drawn up on economists' blackboards. The final result, particularly in Europe, is motorists arbitrarily and excessively singled out for fiscal punishment. Environmentalists are lining up the same treatment for airline passengers. The alternatives presented to cars and planes are electric cars and high speed trains, and they just can't do the job.

All these policies aren't just presented as a necessary sacrifice. Around the world, people are being told that green growth is the answer to their economic woes.

The case for green jobs has a strange echo of Luddites smashing machinery so that there would be more jobs, as it takes more workers to make cloth without a mechanised loom. That is an economic mistake that we should have left behind a long time ago. It is incredible that the idea that the key to prosperity is investing in much more expensive sources of energy has remained credible this long. We are even told that it is sensible to rush out and buy more expensive sources of energy today because the price might fall tomorrow. Or because we need to win the markets of the future, as if buying enough copies of Microsoft Office can make you Bill Gates.

Some people will get green jobs as activists, financiers or bureaucrats agitating for or organising new interventions in the economy. Many more jobs will be lost. Manufacturing industries will leave in search of jurisdictions that still prioritise affordable energy.

Underlying all these mistakes are the targets. Politicians have signed up to targets that can only be met with a technological miracle or a 'planned recession'. They are ambitious enough that anything can be justified, not on the grounds that it is a good idea, but because it is necessary to meet the targets.

Energy from burning fossil fuels has been critical to economic growth since the Industrial Revolution. While we can, do and will use oil, coal and gas more efficiently and thereby reduce emissions without hurting economic growth, it just isn't enough to satisfy the ambitious pledges that have been made. The best case for the targets is that no one really takes them seriously, that despite all the rhetoric they are aspirations more than concrete commitments. But with targets that could easily prove possible to meet only with an economic disaster, we shouldn't be surprised when we get economically disastrous policies.

That tension between economic growth and emissions reduction isn't taken nearly seriously enough. Unfortunately, the environmentalists who promote climate change policy see growth as fundamentally impossible to sustain. They did before we were worrying about climate change, and they don't think it contributes to human well-being much anyway. They are wrong. Limits to growth are invariably illusory and overcome by the ingenuity of the billions of humans that the greens understand as nothing but passive contributors to climate change. Rising incomes drive a huge expansion in the possibilities open to ordinary people; make us more resilient in the face of natural disasters of all kinds – whether related to climate change or not; give us the means to develop genuine alternatives to fossil fuels; and are vital to improving the living standards of billions now catching up, enabling them to enjoy the comforts we have had for some time in developed countries.

All the well-funded – often at taxpayers' expense – environmentalist campaigns like to think they are facing up to even more lavishly resourced corporate lobbying. That is why they haven't convinced the public to endorse their agenda. The reality is that big business doesn't think as some kind of monolith, interested in a growing, prosperous economy. Companies look to their own specific interests and they tend to think those interests are best served by playing along and negotiating a special deal. Why spend financial and political capital lobbying for lower energy costs, where the benefits will be shared with everyone else, when you can take on a much more manageable task and fight for an exemption or compensation that will specifically look out for your industry, or ideally your firm?

Sometimes that strategy works, sometimes it fails. But in the long term businesses that have invested heavily on the basis of climate change policies that impose a prohibitive burden on voters can never really be secure.

So draconian regulations designed to curb emissions have been implemented in many developed economies. They can't work even on their own terms without the developing world signing up too. If the regulations lead to higher energy prices and just drive a factory from Georgia to Guangdong, then they don't cut emissions. And even if the developed world could stop emitting entirely, that wouldn't be enough if developing countries increase their emissions at expected rates. All we're doing at the moment is buying their notional support; they'll sign a treaty if all it requires of them is to take our money in payment for dubious emissions reductions under the Clean Development Mechanism. Selling free money is easy.

There is an alternative. Instead of trying to control emissions by rationing energy and thereby limiting economic growth, we should bet on more growth and human ingenuity. Be prepared to adapt to rising temperatures, as we have to an incredible range of conditions throughout history and around the world. Invest in technological research so that we have more options in the event of a disaster and can find practical, affordable alternatives to fossil fuels. Most importantly, go for growth to produce more resilient societies better able to respond to whatever the world throws at them.

That would be a better route and it would also be a popular one. It is no accident that ambitious attempts to restrict emissions are invariably passed by a consensus that squeezes out the public, and rejected when a mainstream party opposes them. Or that the least democratic means are always used to advance these policies, whether it is the courts and bureaucracy in the United States or the European Union in Europe. Over time, that strategy can't be tenable though. The opportunity to be the party of low energy prices, by scrapping these regulations, is too great to neglect indefinitely. If climate change policy stalls in most of the developed world and has little attraction for rapidly growing developing economies, then eventually even the most committed environmentalists have to start thinking about doing things differently. There will be huge electoral rewards for the political parties who see that first.

The current attempt to cut emissions is proving intolerably expensive, too ineffective to be passed off as good value. Huge, unthinkable amounts of money are being staked on current attempts to cut greenhouse gas emissions. And it isn't like that money is exactly going spare. Most countries are facing huge pressure on their public finances and addressing that with spending cuts or tax hikes will put pressure on household budgets. Requiring hundreds of billions or trillions of dollars, euros, pounds and yen in investment to meet climate change targets will make that much harder, as families will ultimately have to pay for that as well. Too often climate change policy is considered in isolation, but other priorities have to be kept in mind.

It is vital that the current approach is reconsidered – before we cover our waters with rusting and expensive wind turbines; before more vulnerable people are forced to scrimp and save and give up other comforts to pay unnecessarily high energy prices; and before more manufacturing industries are rendered hopelessly uncompetitive by a rise in the price they pay for energy. We don't exactly need to storm the Bastille, just challenge wasteful subsidies and regulations we can ill afford. A little realism in climate change policy would be truly revolutionary.

APPENDIX

Currency conversion

These are the exchange rates used in this book. For dates in the future or not specified, the average over 2005–2010 is used.

Year	GBP, £	USD, $	EUR, €	AUS, $
2005	1	1.82	1.46	2.39
2006	1	1.84	1.47	2.45
2007	1	2.00	1.46	2.39
2008	1	1.85	1.26	2.19
2009	1	1.57	1.12	1.99
2010	1	1.55	1.17	1.68
Future or unspecified	1	1.77	1.32	2.18

Estimating the cost of the EU Emissions Trading System to consumers

In theory, the cost of the ETS to consumers is shown in Equation 11.1.

Equation 11.1: Theoretical ETS cost to consumers

$$\sum_{e=1}^{n} E(p_e)\beta_e$$

Where,
p = Price;
β = Pass-through rate;
e = Tonne of carbon dioxide emitted, and
n = Total number of tonnes of carbon dioxide emitted.

I.e. each tonne of carbon emitted will cost consumers the price the allowance might have expected to raise, multiplied by the rate at which the carbon cost is passed through to consumers in that particular instance.

But in practice that formula isn't very helpful. We don't know what price firms expect in each instance and it still begs the vital question of how much of the carbon price firms pass on to consumers. There are two ways of getting a decent estimate of the cost of the ETS to consumers.

Model the pattern of prices, based on variables such as fuel prices, before the implementation of the ETS, then work out the difference between the modelled and actual prices, attributing the difference to the effects of the ETS.

Use annual data on average allowance prices and total ETS emissions combined with existing estimates of pass-through rates to produce a direct approximation of the cost to consumers.

There are drawbacks to both approaches. The first approach will go badly wrong if the model isn't specified correctly, if the right variables aren't included. If there were any other changes that occurred around the time of the introduction of the ETS that are not accounted for then you will produce extremely unreliable results. The second approach relies upon using existing estimates of the extent to which carbon costs are passed through that may not generalise well to other situations. For example, pass-through rates may increase or decrease over time and they are likely to vary significantly between countries and industries.

For the purposes of this book, we want to get a reasonable idea of the scale of the cost of the ETS, and the second approach fits that objective best. It will also allow us to understand how the cost might change over time and how much cap and trade could cost the United States.

So, instead of the formula earlier, we can work out the cost of scheme to consumers as the amount emitted in each country, multiplied by the average market price and the pass-through rate in that country. Using that simple approach and data from the Community Independent Transaction Log (CITL), the database used to administer the scheme, we can produce a reasonable estimate of the cost the scheme imposes on consumers.

The basic 'carbon price' is the value of the allowances that the scheme requires emitters to hold. At the time of writing, the price in the EU ETS has been fluctuating between about €13 and €17 for a number of months.[412] Big emitting companies have to hold one of these allowances for every tonne of carbon dioxide that they emit. That doesn't cover all emissions – cars in particular are too small to be included – but it does include roughly everything from a hospital boiler up to major coal power plants. In 2010 the amount emitted by installations covered by the EU ETS was 1,864 Mt CO_2.[413] At the average closing emissions price recorded by the major exchange BlueNext in 2010 of €14.34,[414] the total carbon cost was therefore €26.7 billion.

But generally not all of the carbon cost will be passed on to consumers. There are a few reasons why only a portion of the carbon cost might be passed on:

Prices may be regulated; companies might not be allowed to increase their prices in response to the new price on carbon. That will create other problems though, as regulating prices to below the market rate can lead to shortages as firms find they can make more money shutting down production.

Companies may decide to restrain price rises in order to promote their political interests. In particular, electricity companies may be aware that perceived windfall profits will

----

412 Prices are available from a number of sources, including: https://www.theice. com/productguide/ProductGroupHierarchy.shtml?groupDetail=&group. groupId=19 and http://www.bluenext.fr/statistics/downloads.html

413 European Commission, 'Community Independent Transaction Log Verified Emissions for 2008–2009 and allocations 2008–2009'

414 Closing prices, BlueNext Spot EUA 08-12 Since 26/02/2008, http://bluen-ext.squarevale.com/bluenext/downloads/20101201_BNS_STATS.xls

hasten moves to auction allowances and thereby significantly increase their costs.

Uncertainty over the price of emissions and the actions of other companies may cause firms to restrain price increases, in order to avoid any risk of losing their market share.

In some markets, there may be competition from outside the ETS, which will make it impossible for companies to pass costs on without losing market share to rivals not subject to an ETS. That can create bigger problems though, which are covered in Chapter 6.

Still, there is little doubt that prices have increased and a substantial part of that carbon cost has been passed on to consumers. Academic research suggests that 60–100 per cent of the carbon cost has been passed on in the critical electricity market in Germany and the Netherlands, for example.[415]

Using the mid-point of the range found in that study we could assume an average pass-through rate of 80 per cent. Another approach is to assume that the roughly 73 per cent of emissions produced by combustion installations with a rated thermal input exceeding 20 MW (Main Activity Type Code 1 in the CITL)[416] – which will mostly mean power plants – pass on 80 per cent of their costs, but other installations like those producing ceramics, cement, iron and steel can't pass on any costs, as they compete in a more global market. That produces an average pass-through rate of just over 58 per cent. The results under both those approaches are shown in Chapter 3.

Estimates of additional energy sector revenue produced by analysts Point Carbon in March 2008 for the WWF are similar to those results.[417] They assume a higher carbon price than the actual average used here ($€21/t$ CO_2) and find that

---

415 Sijm, J., Neuhoff, K. & Chen, Y., 'CO_2 cost pass-through and windfall profits in the power sector', *Climate Policy*, No 6, 49–72, 2006

416 European Commission, 'Community Independent Transaction Log Verified Emissions for 2008–2009 and allocations 2008–2009'

417 Point Carbon Advisory Services, 'EU ETS Phase II – The potential and scale of windfall profits in the power sector', Report for WWF, March 2008, p.22

there is additional revenue to the energy sector (which will necessarily be paid for by consumers) of €16–€22 billion in the United Kingdom between 2008 and 2012. The mid-point of that value, spread over five years, is around €3.8 billion a year. Their estimate for Germany is also somewhat higher, with most of the difference again explained by their expectation of a higher carbon price than has actually prevailed so far. But to the extent that Point Carbon obtained different results to mine, theirs are higher.

LIST OF TABLES AND FIGURES